Autism and Worship

Autism and Worship
A Liturgical Theology

Armand Léon van Ommen

BAYLOR UNIVERSITY PRESS

© 2023 by Baylor University Press
Waco, Texas 76798

All Rights Reserved. No part of this publication may be reproduced, stored in a retrieval system, or transmitted, in any form or by any means, electronic, mechanical, photocopying, recording, or otherwise, without the prior permission in writing of Baylor University Press.

Cover design by *the*BookDesigners
Cover art: Amelie Wierenga, *Buy and Acknowledge*, 14/03/2023, digital painting with ibispaint, 3171 x 3893 pixels
Book design by Baylor University Press
Book typeset by Scribe Inc.

Paperback ISBN: 978-1-4813-1990-4

The Library of Congress has cataloged the hardcover as follows:

Names: Ommen, Armand Léon van, author.
Title: Autism and worship : a liturgical theology / Armand Léon van Ommen.
Description: Waco : Baylor University Press, 2023. | Includes bibliographical references and index. | Summary: "Considers the experiences of autistic people in contemporary churches to propose how their full inclusion in corporate worship can impact congregations and theology"-- Provided by publisher.
Identifiers: LCCN 2023018336 (print) | LCCN 2023018337 (ebook) | ISBN 9781481319898 (hardcover) | ISBN 9781481319928 (adobe pdf) | ISBN 9781481319911 (epub)
Subjects: LCSH: Public worship. | Worship programs. | Autism--Religious aspects--Christianity. | Church work with people with disabilities.
Classification: LCC BV15 .O47 2023 (print) | LCC BV15 (ebook) | DDC 264--dc23/eng/20230731
LC record available at https://lccn.loc.gov/2023018336
LC ebook record available at https://lccn.loc.gov/2023018337

To James Scannell
In friendship and with gratitude

Contents

Foreword		ix
Acknowledgments		xiii
Introduction		1
	Starting the Conversation on Autism and Worship	
1	Setting the Scene	21
	Language, Autism Theology, and Autistic Experiences of Worship	
2	How Autism Came to Be	43
	The Problem of "Autism Is . . ."	
3	The Tyranny of the Normal	71
	Exposing the Cause of Absence and Ignoring	
4	Presence and Participation	99
	Toward a Theology of Availability	
5	A Temple Community	127
	A Liturgical-Theological Redrawing of "Normal"	
6	Availability in Practice	161
	Autistic Worship in Singapore	
Conclusion		189
	A Church That "Gets You"	
Notes		199
Bibliography		231
Index		241

Foreword

> "Normalcy excludes."
> —from the Conclusion

Both research literature and public discourse have, for the most part, represented autism as a condition of deficit or disorder. Autistic people (and, yes, that is the construction that lots of us prefer) are described as *lacking* something—empathy, perhaps, or theory of mind—or as not functioning correctly. If we are celebrated, it is often for our brave efforts to overcome these perceived problems, to succeed *in spite of* autism. Occasionally, it is because our dysfunction makes us weirdly good at some things that other people find impressive, though representations of such perceived savantism[1] will usually be quick to balance such celebrations with reminders that we are pitiably bad at other things. This way of thinking about autism is reinforced by media representations and even by much well-intentioned advocacy activity, usually undertaken by people who are not themselves autistic. Its essential features reflect a *medical model* of autism, by which the "condition" is measured against a standard of "normal" function, with deviations from this mapped onto graded scales that run from high to low, or mild to profound. In some cases, the degree of deficit or deviation is such that the very personhood of the autistic is called into question.

There has been a welcome turn toward a discourse that represents autism as *difference* rather than *deficit, deviation,* or *disorder*. The term "neurodiversity" (which also embraces a number of other conditions) has become the primary label for this alternative way of thinking and speaking about autism, and it is often used critically in conjunction with a *social model* of autism. This understands the problems associated with autism to emerge largely from the imposition of certain expectations of "normality" onto the population as a whole; approaches to the treatment of autism will sometimes reflect this imposition, seeking to train autistic people to conform to social expectations. But while positive affirmations of neurodiversity are now visible, both in research literature and advocacy, the field is still largely dominated by the language of deficit and disorder, based upon the frameworks of the medical model. There are pockets of autism affirmation, but the environment is still largely characterized by negative representations.

For the Christian churches, in common with other religious and faith communities, this is a particular problem. Christians, individually and collectively, will often assume the essential validity of negative accounts of autism; while there are some churches that affirm and celebrate neurodiversity, most will still see it as an undesirable condition. They may approach autism as something to be treated with special love and care, because autistic people are seen as distinctly needy; they may create separate ministries or programs for autistic people. Autism is not affirmed or even accommodated, but is simply compartmentalized. More disturbingly, Christians may pray for autistic people to be healed or even delivered. The "tyranny of normalcy" manifests in a particular way in communities of faith, with perceived divergence from normality often mapped onto the language and thought of sin and salvation.

This is not just a popular problem: some academic theologians have used autism as a metaphor for the essential problem of sin itself. If autism is understood as a particular kind of relational abnormality, with autistic people characterized by a deficit of empathy or theory of mind, then the universal human lack of connection with God can be described as a "spiritual autism." The state of perfection toward which salvation leads us is, in such accounts, the precise opposite of autism. As an autistic person, I find myself to be an embodied metaphor of the inward curve that constitutes sin. If you don't see why that is a problem, take any feature of your own constitution and imagine that it is considered *essentially* representative of evil itself.

Christian approaches to autism do not have to be like this. Even when taking seriously the challenges that can come with autism—the difficulties that many of us are happy to call disability—it is possible to affirm autism as contributing to the diversity of Christ's body. It is possible to say that the church would be weaker, would be disabled in its own way, if some of its members were not autistic. It is possible to speak of an autistic gain that enriches the church, through its different insights and different sensorium. The sensory differences of autistic people are, in fact, particularly important to this gain and how it is to be actualized.

Sensory differences alter the perception of church and liturgy dramatically; they can be painful, when they are not taken into account, but they can also be blessed. Sensory difference can open a new world of perception that is shared with the rest of the community.

Armand Léon van Ommen's work represents this alternative approach to autism and the church. It does so, not just by imagining a utopian alternative to the awful experiences that many of us have had in churches, but by describing actual instantiations of this different approach to autism. It describes the practices of communities that have intentionally approached autism as a good, as a divine gift intended to bring blessing. These attempts to refigure the function of autism in the church may not be perfect, and may still bear the traces of the negative approaches they try to escape, but they are real.

Léon is not himself autistic, but his involvement with the Centre for Autism and Theology at the University of Aberdeen—which was created precisely in order to pursue this affirmational approach to autism and theology—means that his work is always grounded in the experience of the actually autistic. The Centre is intentionally led by autistic people (I am co-director, along with Léon, and we have an advisory board that is made up almost entirely of autistic people) and prioritizes autistic participation and leadership in the design and development of research projects. Consequently, there is a particular sensitivity that characterizes his work, a deference to the authentic autistic voice and a care to represent that voice appropriately.

Unlike so much of the research on autism, this is a work of qualitative research. It does not simply consider statistics, but considers self-representations and narratives. To do this properly requires one to ask the correct question in the correct way to begin with; questions can too easily be worded in ways that reflect our initial prejudices. Léon seeks to ask the question properly to begin with, often "piloting" it with his autistic colleagues, and then to reflect carefully on the responses to it.

Theology has a special value to the study of autism in general because it has a long history of reflecting on the effects of modern reductionism and the way that these are woven through the whole world of value and language. One of the reasons that many efforts at "inclusion" fail is because they are undertaken by people who continue to operate with an unexamined neoliberalism, isolating the "individual" from the web of relationships by which they are constituted, judging that individual according to their perceived usefulness, and treating them as a self-subsistent entity that (*sic*) can participate in an economy of material value and trade. Theology and theological ethics urge a thicker account of reality, recognizing that things are saturated by truths beyond themselves, and acknowledge that to participate in an economy of love and grace demands more than mere inclusion ever can. It demands a recognition that the things which are different to ourselves *belong*, and we would be poorer without them.

For churches, and for other communities of faith and religion, this book shows what such belonging can look like. It may not be perfect, and those involved may make plenty of mistakes, but it is real nonetheless. At the heart of the gospel is a message of repentance, forgiveness, and hope. Repentance involves a willingness to embrace a better way of being, turning from the "downright bad" but also the "not good enough." This is particularly relevant to approaches to autism; even those of us seeking to make a difference may need to repent of what we have not done well, our less than perfect efforts. The expectation of forgiveness entails a generosity toward those who have made such flawed efforts. Hope trusts in a future when God will be all in all. Liturgy performatively evokes that hope. The involvement of autism in liturgy embodies it.

Grant Macaskill
Kirby Laing Chair of New Testament Exegesis
Co-Director, Centre for Autism and Theology
University of Aberdeen
June 2023

Acknowledgments

In Dutch, the acknowledgments section of a book is called a *Dankwoord*—a "word of thanks." Indeed, wandering back in my mind to all the people who have given input or provided feedback along the way of writing this book fills me with gratitude. The journey started in 2016 when I started working in the divinity department at the University of Aberdeen. Not only am I grateful to all colleagues, who make this a wonderful department to work in, but especially teaching and researching alongside John Swinton and Brian Brock made me aware of disability theology as a field of its own. When another colleague, Grant Macaskill, asked John, Brian, and me to be part of a new research center on autism and theology, in 2018, my own research became focused on this emerging area of research that I will call autism theology in this book. Becoming codirector of the Centre for Autism and Theology in 2020 gave me the opportunity to build a network of autistic and non-autistic academics from various disciplines, professionals, caregivers, and other people who were interested in the intersection of autism, theology, and church. The many conversations I have had with these various people have shaped, and continues to shape, my thinking and therefore also this book. I am grateful for all those people and to John, Brian, and Grant for drawing me into the intriguing world of disability theology and autism theology.

The fieldwork that underpins this book was conducted in Singapore and the United Kingdom and with one interviewee from the United States. I am deeply grateful for all those interviewees who were willing to share their experiences and thoughts with me. Their stories are, implicitly and at points explicitly, the backbone of this book. I am grateful for the community of the Chapel of Christ Our Hope in Singapore, the story of which I tell in chapter 6, which has been very welcoming. I want to thank Topher Endress for analyzing worship services and interviews from Singapore and the United Kingdom with me. Thanks also to Katy Unwin who analyzed the latter sets of interviews with me, particularly with regard to the sensory aspect of worship. Funding from the John Templeton Foundation, through the New Visions in Theological Anthropology based at the University of St Andrews, made the collaboration with Katy possible, for which I am grateful. Here, I should also gratefully acknowledge the funding from the Carnegie Trust for the Universities in Scotland that allowed me to do the fieldwork. The views in this book do not necessarily represent those of both funding bodies.

The Centre for Autism and Theology has a group of researchers, many of whom identify as autistic, that gathers weekly. As part of the program, we discussed draft chapters of this book. Thank you, Ian Lasch, Chris Barber, Stewart Rapley, Joanna Leidenhag, Henna Cundill, Zoe Strong, Sarah Douglas, Bryan Fowler, Denise Maud, Harry Gibbins, Catherine Tryfona, Krysia Waldock, Claire Williams, and Jesse Radcliffe, for your helpful feedback. Some of the thinking in this book I presented in a course I taught in the PgDip in theology and disability, and I am grateful for the students in that class for engaging with the arguments and for their feedback.

I am very grateful to Phillip Tovey, Sarah Johnston, and Kimberly Belcher, who read various chapters of this book and, as liturgical theologians, gave feedback especially on chapter 5. The feedback from the two anonymous reviewers at the early stages of the book proposal was very helpful too. I am grateful to the staff of Baylor University Press and especially to Cade Jarrell for believing in this project. A special thanks should go to Henna Cundill. Henna was my research assistant for part of my fieldwork, but she also proofread the chapters, often before I sent them to anyone else. Her feedback, both linguistically and in terms of content, was very helpful. For most people, writing in another language than one's mother tongue is challenging—for me, it certainly is. To work with a proofreader who understands the project and is willing to give so much time to improve the writing is a true blessing for which I am deeply grateful. I also want to express my sincere gratitude to Amelie Wierenga, who designed the piece of art on the front cover of this book.

I am looking back at this journey of becoming interested in autism theology and the many wonderful people who traveled this journey with me—sometimes briefly, sometimes for long stretches. One companion has traveled with me from the very beginning: my wife, Nele Beutels. When it was time to rest, she often allowed me to take some more steps because I needed to finish another leg of the journey. I call these extra times "grace time"—the time during evenings and weekends when she could have asked me to be with her and our children, but instead, she let me finish another section or chapter. Nele's love, support, encouragement, and critical questions are sheer grace. Without her, this book would not be what it is. Thank you, Nele.

The final word of thanks goes to James Scannell to whom I dedicate this book. As someone who identifies as autistic, James has shared his story, experiences, views, and his own interviews with disabled people with me over the course of numerous conversations. These conversations are different from most that I have because James cannot rely on speech. Instead, James uses a spelling board to communicate. His words and sentences are formed letter by letter. This does not only take time but also requires a huge amount of concentration and energy and the support from his parents. I am grateful to all of them, and James in particular, for giving their time and energy because they believe in the work I do and the work of the Centre for Autism and Theology. There are few people who have challenged me in my thinking and my views about autism, church, ministry, and theology as much as James. For that, I am deeply grateful.

Introduction

Starting the Conversation on Autism and Worship

"IT'S NEVER THAT SIMPLE FOR ME"

> Normal people just go to church and don't think any more about it. They just get in their car or walk, they go through the door, they do the service, and they go home. And it's never that simple for me. (Rachel)[1]

The words are spoken by Rachel, sixteen years old at the time, identifying as autistic. In our interview, she explained that for her, the worship service is such an overwhelming experience that she often needs to sit outside or even go home halfway through the service. The music is often way too loud, notices on the screen and those repeated by the ministers sometimes do not match, and finding her way through the moving bodies at the entrance hall and during coffee time after the service requires a disconcerting amount of effort. Some Sundays, the result is that Rachel feels nauseous for hours after the service or has headaches for the whole day. Church is never that simple for Rachel.

Rachel is not the only one on the autism spectrum who struggles with worship services. Many autistic people have similar experiences, and many feel that their communities and church leaders do not understand them. Some people give up and leave church altogether. Church can inflict, unknowingly, a lot of pain, leaving people battered, sometimes for life. Others react in the opposite way, and instead of leaving, they advocate for understanding and change. In my interviews, I heard stories of such advocacy and the greatly varying results—for the most part, not positive. Yet others try to find ways of coping with church, to find ways of attending (sometimes not every Sunday) and of recovering afterward. In whatever way autistic people respond to overwhelming worship services and the underwhelming response and misunderstanding of the community or church leaders, church is never that simple for those who identify as autistic.

It would be wrong, however, to think of autism only in terms of the struggles it brings when trying to connect with a community. Autistic people have a lot to offer to the church. When the church puts up barriers to participation (wittingly or unwittingly), as it does so for Rachel, it misses out on the gifts and blessing that autistic people are to the church. Note that I do not say "the gifts autistic people bring"—in the body of Christ, people *are* first of all, blessings and gifts to the community, even without bringing a certain talent or skill to the task. To speak about spiritual gifts in terms of specific talents can be a conflation of two different things. Brian Brock explains that the spiritual gifts that the apostle Paul speaks about "are a 'message' of service passing between two believers," a manifestation of the Holy Spirit.[2] Such a manifestation, in the form of service toward each other, might well have to do more with who we are than what skills we bring. That said, many autistic people do have certain talents that can be gifts for the spiritual upbuilding of Christ's body. As an example, Olivia Bustion analyzed discussions by autistic people on several online platforms on which the platform's members suggested that they see the world in ways less filtered through social expectations and therefore more truthfully, that they were less prone to lie, and that they believed they experienced special intimacy with God.[3] Therefore, when autistic people are prevented to join a church because of the barriers they face, the church misses out on the spiritual gifts and talents these (potential) members of community might bring. To raise the stakes, we might say that the church misses out on the self-revelation of God, as God chooses to be revealed in the manifestation of the Holy Spirit through the spiritual gifts in the community.[4]

In this book, I try to listen to the stories of autistic people. This book is an effort to understand autistic experiences of church, in particular of corporate worship or liturgy, and to search for a theological response. The church needs to respond better to their autistic members if it wants to be faithful to the God it claims to follow. Not only do church communities need to respond better, but also academic theology has only just begun to take into account the experiences and theological understandings of autistic people.[5] This book is also intended, therefore, as a contribution to the field of liturgical studies. At the same time, I hope this book will be a worthwhile contribution to the emerging field of autism theology. In this endeavor, three questions are central:

1. What causes the absence and ignoring of autistic people in faith communities, and what might a liturgical and/or theological response look like?
2. Relatedly, what does liturgy and corporate worship look like through the lens of autism, and in what ways might that reframe liturgical theologies?
3. How can churches be communities where everybody belongs, autistic and non-autistic alike? In answering this question, the focus is on a theological response, but I hope that the examples in this book, not least that of the Chapel of Christ Our Hope in chapter 6, offers some practical suggestions.

The stories of autistic people, and also of their families and those around them, will be central to this discussion, although in some chapters, this will be more explicit than in others. The aim is to listen to the stories and experiences of autistic people and offer a response to these central questions, one that is theological, faithful, and that helps Christian faith communities to become places where every person is valued and loved as a child of God.

The picture on the front cover of this book expresses the need for seeing and listening to autistic people. The lady is selling eyes and ears for anyone who wants to see and listen—in other words, to acknowledge the presence of autistic people in the worshipping community. This book joins the lady in that invitation. The primary audience at which this book targets that invitation to see and listen is the theological academy. However, given the focus on a core practice of faith communities and the practical consequences that our (liturgical) theologies and views of autism have in practice, I hope this book will be of interest to church leaders and others in faith communities who are interested to think through the questions raised in this book. By describing the experiences of worship by autistic people, I hope not only to ground the liturgical-theological discussions in this book in lived experience but also to pique the interest of readers outside of the academic discussion.

KEY TERMS

This is a book about autism, liturgy, and worship, so first, it may be helpful to define how I will use each of those terms, although each will gain a more complex and richer meaning as the book progresses. In particular, the definition of "autism" is a highly contested area. In chapter 2, I will discuss "autism" more extensively, but here, I will establish a working definition, as well as for "worship" and "liturgy," ahead of more detailed discussion in chapter 5.

Let us first define liturgy. The term comes from the Greek word *leitourgia*, which originally meant "service for the people,"[6] such as providing a bridge, constructing a sewer, or erecting an image of the patron deity.[7] Affluent citizens were required to pay for work that served the common good or sometimes did so voluntarily. However, in the Septuagint, the word is mostly used for the service of priests in the temple. In the New Testament, the word is not often used, but when it is, it is mostly in a "cultic-sacred sense."[8] For example, Hebrews depicts Jesus as the high priest (*leitourgikos*) in the heavenly sanctuary. The apostle Paul speaks of his own ministry in terms of leitourgia, as "priest, to the Gentiles" (Rom 15:16) and "as the messenger of Christ preforming the service (*leitourgia*) of offering up the obedient faith of the Philippians to God" (Phil 2:17). In contemporary language, the notion of "service" has been retained in terms like "church service" or the German *Gottesdienst*.

Over time, "liturgy" has acquired several meanings, and liturgical theologian Don Saliers highlights three of these.[9] The first is closely related to the original Greek term: liturgy is the work of the people.[10] The emphasis here is on the activity of the entire congregation. Liturgy is not the prerogative of the liturgical ministers while the congregation is just left to watch, but all are involved. A second meaning of liturgy is "the glorification of God and the sanctification of what is human"—this is according to a classic definition.[11] Saliers unpacks the meaning of this as follows: "Worship does not make things holy by magic, but reveals and discloses what has already been rendered holy, what is already intrinsically holy by the grace of God in creation and redemption."[12] In liturgy, we worship God and by doing so discover who we are and the sacredness of creation. The third meaning that Saliers notes is liturgy defined as "the ongoing embodied word, work, and prayer of Jesus Christ in and through his body in the world."[13] This is a Christological definition that places the worship of the community in the context of Jesus Christ's ongoing leitourgia. Saliers contends that all three definitions are necessary to speak of liturgy in a rounded way. All three are informative, but it is especially the last one that will prove constructive for the liturgical theology that I will propose in this book. An extensive discussion and expansion of this last definition will take place in chapter 5.

It is somewhat remarkable that Saliers does not distinguish between "liturgy" and "worship." However, as the three definitions show, liturgy is worship, and as such, the terms overlap. Nevertheless, Frank Senn points to the fact that both have meanings that cannot be fully captured by the other term. "Liturgy is more but also less than worship."[14] Whereas worship is solely directed at God, in liturgy (as the corporate worship service, see Saliers' first definition) the believers address each other as well. At the same time, whereas liturgy is a public act of worship, worship can also be done in private. In this book, to designate the gathering of believers for public worship, typically on Sundays, I use the term "public worship" or "corporate worship." I use "liturgy" in the ways discussed above but also to denote the underlying structure of corporate worship.[15]

The question of how to define autism is a complicated one. The way autism has been diagnosed and thought of has changed significantly over time and is likely to change again in the future, as I will demonstrate in chapter 2.[16] Therefore, the phrase "Autism is . . ." should be dealt with carefully. Of course, it is possible to start with the medical diagnostic labels, especially the influential ones from the *Diagnostic and Statistical Manual of Mental Disorders*, 5th edition (*DSM-5*) and *International Classification of Diseases*, 11th revision (*ICD-11*), but (as we have just discussed) the pathologizing inherent in medical definitions is fiercely questioned and refuted by many in the autism communities.[17]

Another difficulty with definitions of autism is that no one autistic person looks exactly like another. This is often captured with the well-known phrase, "If you have met one person with autism, you have met *one* person with autism." Nevertheless, even that acknowledgment is not entirely unproblematic. Sometimes people have been unaware that they were autistic until later in life, and when they finally get a diagnosis, things fall into place and they start to make sense of their way of being. To say that everyone on the autism spectrum is different potentially takes away the meaningfulness—and in a sense, safety—of identifying with that diagnosis.

Despite these problems with definitions of autism, we will need to say somehow what we understand by autism. While any discussion of autism needs a starting point, that starting point does not need to determine the (theological) outcome of the discussion. The work of John Swinton is helpful to further explain this point. In an article on mental health, Swinton writes,

> One of the mistakes that the church tends to make when it begins to think about mental health and ill-health is to begin with the definitions

laid down by psychiatry. We then formulate our strategy in light of this and act in ways that we consider to be "therapeutic." When this happens, the road to recovery becomes defined by a clinical form of categorization that can quite easily surpass—or perhaps better, *bypass*—vital aspects of a person's own story.[18]

While not arguing that psychiatric labels are necessarily wrong, his point is that "diagnoses and clinical categories may be totally appropriate for the mental health professions, but may not be the best place for the church to begin its journey towards mental health."[19] In other words, labels, concepts, and terminology have their use in the context for which they were invented, but they may be of less use in other contexts. The problem arises when the labels are used in other contexts and dominate those other discourses, because the presuppositions of one discourse (that may or may not be right in that context) are transported into another, where they may not be right.[20] The first discourse may be meaningful and can be learned from but should not determine the other discourse. Thus, there is much to learn from medical, psychological, and other disciplines when we consider autism theologically, but the theological discourse should not be determined by those discourses.[21]

The intuition and realization that medical descriptions are shaping the discourse in a particular way, especially by their use of terms like "disability," "disorder," and "deficit," which may need to be countered by other ways of perceiving autism—indeed, by other ways of knowing[22]—is evident in the literature, especially that written by autistic authors.[23] In need of a starting point, some would still begin with a definition from *DSM-5* or *ICD-11* or along those lines and then criticize that definition. It seems that most would agree, broadly, on certain characteristics of autism, as described in medical manuals, but not with the way they are framed. For example, "repetitive interests" feature in both *DSM-5* and *ICD-11* as one of the diagnostic criteria and are clearly framed in the language of deficit. However, in and of themselves, there is not necessarily anything wrong or deserving of the descriptor "deficit" about repetitive interests; one could turn it around and say that repetitive interests enable autistic people to focus on something and become an expert in it. The observed behavior is the same, but the interpretation and the framing is different.

With this in mind and to provide a starting point for our discussion, I will briefly summarize how Macaskill describes autism.[24] I choose to start with Macaskill instead of with a medical definition for three reasons. First, it is unhelpful to start a theological discussion of a particular way of being in the world with terms like "disorder" and "deficit" as defined by the medical discipline, as explained above. Second, and this is related, I side with those in the autism communities who are critical of the medical diagnostic criteria, especially the negative framing of the autism within those manuals. Third, if choosing an alternative starting point to the medical manuals, then to me it seems right to start with an autistic writer. It would be easy to look for other literature in the field of autism studies, often written by non-autistic people; these may be excellent resources, but as a *starting* point, it is better to listen to autistic writers.[25]

Macaskill starts his discussion with the definition as can be found on the website of the National Autistic Society, the biggest autism organization in the United Kingdom. "Autism is a lifelong, developmental disability that affects how a person communicates with and relates to other people, and how they experience the world around them."[26] Macaskill considers this a helpful definition and notes that it "would be endorsed by healthcare practitioners around the world." He does immediately acknowledge that some would have an issue with the term "disability," a point to which I return shortly. A helpful aspect of the definition is that it clearly states that autism is a lifelong condition. That means that autism is not the consequence of taking certain vaccines or bad parenting, as has been thought at certain times in recent history (and still is by some). It also means that autism is not a childhood condition, which is an even more pervasive misunderstanding of autism.[27]

Macaskill discusses autism in four clusters of characteristics. The first is social interaction and communication. Some aspects of nonverbal communication are often perceived differently by autistic people compared to others, which can result in mutual misunderstanding.[28] The second cluster is around language, which entails both the acquisition and use of language. Autistic people often use language in a highly precise way (which is why metaphor may not be difficult, as is often thought, but irony and sarcasm may be more difficult, as these latter two violate the rules of language, while metaphor does not). With the use of language also comes the "use [of] language with a degree of honesty that others find difficult."[29] This may have to do with less concern for social conventions. The third cluster Macaskill describes with the word "systems." This is associated with the fact that autistic people, in general, tend to be good in seeing patterns. That translates also into the desire for routine, including routines in everyday tasks, as well as preferences that are difficult to deviate from.[30] Macaskill aptly notes that "much of this seems to be linked to an underlying need to achieve some kind of control over one's life and environment. Systems are predictable, and one can take comfort in that predictability; seeing the world in systemic terms allows at least a semblance of control over its unpredictable qualities."[31] Finally, the fourth cluster is increasingly seen as a key to understanding autism—namely, that of sensory processing. This comes in two ways: hyposensitivity (less sensitive and therefore often actively seeking sensory input) and hypersensitivity (more sensitive and therefore often experiencing a sensory overload). To give two examples: many autistic people dislike touch, so they cringe when someone greets them by shaking their hand; others are sensitive to smell, so an autistic person may be put off by the perfume of the person in the pew in front of them. It is key that non-autistic people do not brush these things under the carpet by saying that you do not need to be autistic to dislike touch or certain perfumes but to realize that for an autistic person, this may in fact be very painful and may cause the need to recover from the worship service for the remainder of the day.[32]

Thus, these four clusters of characteristics of autism are a helpful way of describing what autism is. Moreover, the way Macaskill talks about these characteristics points to both the advantages and challenges of autistic ways of engaging the world. This nuanced approach, which moves away from pathologizing autism, raises the question of whether autism should be seen as a disability. It is beyond the scope of this introductory chapter to discuss this question at length, but it should still be noted because much of the literature on autism is published in disability journals, and when a medical definition is the starting point of the discussion, the language of disability is immediately present or at least assumed. However, as said above, many autistic people push back at this language and at the pathologizing of autistic characteristics. To refer back to the example of repetitive interests, if those are enabling a person to specialize in a given topic, why would they need to be seen as a disability?

This leads me to a couple of points that need to be kept in mind when we talk about autism. First, the tension between different ways of constructing autism (e.g., as disability or not) shows, at the very least, that autism cannot straightforwardly be equated with disability. However, some autistic people say that some aspects of being autistic can be disabling indeed. For example, in his discussion about whether autism is a disability, Macaskill speaks about "our capacity to recognize nonverbal cues or to deal appropriately with sensory experience" as potentially "compromising limitations."³³ This keeps the language of disability in the discussion, but one would need to see how autism is disabling for an individual, without presuming that autism itself is universally disabling. Additionally, a brief reference to the social model of disability is relevant here. For example, when the lighting in the worship space is too bright for an autistic person, this is disabling, forcing them to leave the space. A change of lighting may solve the problem, in which case, the (hyper)sensitivity to light is not disabling anymore. This means that hypersensitivity to light may be disabling, but it is not intrinsically so. Therefore, in this example, it may be appropriate to speak about autism as a disability but only if understood within a social model of disability. That being said, these points are not meant to deny that some autistic people are affected by disabling impairments and not only in a social model of disability. For example, if one wants to speak but cannot and therefore cannot tell the doctor where it hurts, this may cause significant suffering which is not merely due to the setup of society (although that may exacerbate the presenting problem). The main point to make here is that autism and disability cannot be simply equated, but even so, it can be appropriate to speak about disability in relation to autism. The discussions in this book will often refer to literature where the distinction between autism and disability is not being made, including theological literature. It would be distracting to point to the distinction every time I refer to such literature. Therefore, this discussion serves to assure the reader that I am aware of the complicated relationship between autism and disability and to alert the reader to the same.

PROBLEMS, QUESTIONS, AND AIMS

Autistic people are attending church less than the general population. Li-Ching Lee et al., in a study that included statistics on attendance of religious services, school, and other activities, demonstrated that in the United States, autistic children were 50–70 percent less likely to attend religious services than others in their age groups.³⁴ Collecting data from the 2003, 2007, and 2011–2012 National Survey of Children's Health conducted by the Centers for Disease Control and Prevention in the United States, Andrew Whitehead shows likewise that children on the autism spectrum attend church less than their peers. In 2011–2012, the figures for never attending religious services were 32.1 percent for those on the spectrum compared to 24.4 percent for those who are not. In his study, Whitehead also compares the figures for a range of what he calls "chronic health conditions"—for example, attention deficit disorder/attention deficit hyperactivity disorder (ADD/ADHD), learning disability, anxiety, depression, brain injury, hearing or vision problems, and cerebral palsy. He demonstrates statistical proof for his hypothesis that "compared to children with no reported health conditions, children with any reported chronic health condition will be more likely to never attend religious worship services."[35] One may take issue with his terminology (see section on "The Language We Use" in the next chapter), but for now, the point to note is that remarkably, the autistic children consistently record a lower frequency of church attendance than those with other conditions.[36] Melinda Jones Ault, Belva Collins, and Erik Carter make a very similar observation. In their study of the perceptions of 416 parents and caregivers of people with, in their terminology, intellectual and developmental disabilities, parents of autistic children felt significantly less supported by their church than parents of children with (other) intellectual disabilities. This paralleled the researchers' finding that parents and their autistic children attended church less frequently than parents of children with (other) intellectual disabilities.[37]

These figures are in telling contrast with the perception of Protestant pastors and churchgoers about how welcoming their churches are. Conducting phone interviews with one thousand Protestant pastors in the United States, a study by LifeWay Research found that 99 percent of Protestant pastors believed people with disabilities ("including physical, sensory, cognitive, and intellectual impairments") would feel welcome in their church. Phone interviews with one thousand Protestant churchgoers gave almost the same percentage, namely, 96 percent.[38] Although this is only one study, the difference between the views of pastors and churchgoers on the one hand and the results of the other studies cited above on the other hand is a cause for concern. Apparently, there is a lack of awareness in Protestant churches about the hindrances that people with disabilities (which, in these studies include autism) face.[39]

The statistics seem to suggest that church services are problematic for autistic people. Erik Carter, a prolific researcher who studies participation of autistic people and people with disabilities, illustrates this further. After an extensive review of the literature on "ways in which churches support faith and flourishing of individuals with disabilities and their families," he concludes that many people with disabilities attend worship services frequently, even if less than people without disabilities, and that worship is their primary way of connecting with a church.[40] Indeed, even though the statistics point to the fact that attending church is apparently more difficult for (at least some) autistic people than non-autistic people, still many people on the spectrum join churches. However, if this is more difficult for many autistic people, then the church and its theologians will need to think hard and critically about why this is the case.

For both church and academy to do such hard and critical thinking, examining the way faith communities include or exclude autistic people, it is necessary to look behind the statistics and listen to the stories that autistic people have to tell. This can help us to understand why church can be a difficult place and to identify what should be changed. This is not simply an academic, methodological necessity but also an ethical and pastoral imperative. In Saint Paul's famous image of the body of Christ, the head cannot say to the feet, "I don't need you" (1 Cor 12:21). In the same way, all members in the church need each other, so it follows that if the church is a problematic space for some, then all members of the body need to work together to find faithful ways forward.

There are various reasons *why* autistic people find church communities problematic, and they differ from person to person. Rachel, whose words opened this introduction, struggles with sensory overload, especially loud music, and with larger groups of people when they stand and walk around, so it is hard for her to navigate the space. She also struggles with logical inconsistencies in worship services. The latter occur, for example, when certain notices are projected on the screen but not mentioned by the person giving the notices verbally or when that person adds other notices. Other interviewees, for example Alex and Tim, said that they find it problematic when sermons contain logical inconsistencies too, something that they are quick to spot.[41] Many parents of autistic children told me about the lack of acceptance they had felt as a family. Their child would be shushed and the whole family would be subjected to judgmental gazes. Frequently, people are asked to sit at the back of the church or in a different room—which is metaphorically, if not literally, close to the exit. These are all examples from my own research; the literature confirms some of these stories and adds others.[42] Central in all of this is the lack of acceptance of those who do not conform to the standards of the community.[43] In chapter 3, I will explore this in depth.

The interviewees in my study did not ask for the church to be centered around them. Many expressed the desire to find a way of being church that takes into account the needs and gifts of autistic and nonautistic people alike. But perhaps Alex spoke for all my interviewees when, while acknowledging that it would not be possible to cater for everyone's needs, he said that "[if church members were] reaching out a little bit to people on the autistic spectrum and saying, you know, we get you. Would be nice." Churches need to ask autistic people whether and why it is difficult to participate in worship and in the wider life of the church but also to inquire as to how autistic people can flourish in the congregational life and contribute to it. In that way, churches will hopefully become able to say, "We get you."

TOWARD RECONCILIATION: HOW I JOIN THE CONVERSATION

All theology is contextual.[44] Our context is hugely influential in the way we view the world, the way we live, and the way we think. I write as someone who was raised in the Netherlands, in a Christian family, attending a Reformed Church. I spent the next eighteen years or so in Belgium, which is culturally and even linguistically very different from the Netherlands. Marrying a Belgian woman, I (and she) had to work through many cultural differences. It has attuned me to ways in which cultures—even those within the Global North—can be very different from each other and to the way people and society are deeply shaped by their culture. After having spent most of my adult life in Belgium, in 2016, we moved to Aberdeen, in the northeast of Scotland. When people say that Aberdeen is quite remote, they usually do not mean that positively. For me, it is positive, as it reconnects me to the places I grew up in, which were in the very northern part of the Netherlands and therefore remote. I do not know exactly how these biographical details have shaped my theology, but I do know that all theology is contextual and, to a large extent, autobiographical. Perhaps living in remote places, attending churches in Belgium and Scotland that were rather marginal (Evangelical and Anglican in Belgium, Scottish Episcopal Church in Scotland), and an awareness of (cultural) differences, have together instilled a passion to see (faith) communities be or become places where everyone belongs, as they are, and with the stories they bring. Perhaps the biographical note that impacts my theology, in that regard, is that I know what it is to be in communities where I am valued and invited to participate, and I know the opposite.

Working in a Western country also colors my perception of church, autism, theology, and academy. Autism cuts across cultures, but it has been researched mostly in Western academic institutions. That means that voices from other cultures are largely missing. My work in Singapore counters this somewhat, although I am not in a position to compare Singaporean culture with European conceptions of autism, nor does the research that I have done allow for such a comparison.[45]

The most important question in terms of positionality when writing on autism (or disability), however, seems to be an author's relationship to autism (or disability). Deborah Creamer, as well as many others, has noted that it is commonplace in books about disability to reveal one's relationship to it: is the writer disabled themselves, or an "outsider," or related as parent or caregiver? As Stacy Simplican aptly notes, "The pull of defining our relationship to disability is so strong that to keep one's position occluded transgresses the expectations of our audience."[46] The assumption that underlies the expectation to "come out" (or not) as disabled is that those who identify as disabled have the most credibility to speak on the topic.[47] One may add that those on the outside have the least credibility, and those who are related as parent, child, caregiver, or in some other intimate way are ambiguous—they can be allies, but they can also get it quite wrong, according to disability advocates.[48] While we should be careful not to equate autism with disability, at least not in any straightforward way, the assumption that those who identify as autistic have the most credibility to speak about autism seems to underly both academic and nonacademic autism discourses. The slogan of the disability advocacy movement, "Nothing about us, without us," is also heard frequently in the autism conversation.[49] Being autistic gives one the right to speak and much more credibility than someone who is not autistic. This logic seems irrefutable, and to some extent it is, but it is not the whole story.

Creamer continues by pointing to the complexities of giving more credibility to those identifying as disabled than to other writers. She asks the question whether being disabled gives one "an epistemic privilege."[50] The answer is yes: disabled people do have a particular vantage point that others may lack. However, the answer is also yes to the question of whether "we all know these things, even though we sometimes forget."[51] Without saying that "we are all a little bit disabled" (which she says is wrong and potentially harmful), Creamer points to the fact that we are all embodied creatures and experience pain and limitations from time to time, and with aging, most of us will experience some form of disability. Creamer concludes that "this double yes to particularity and universality" is a first layer of complexifying the question whether someone writing on disability needs to have a disability him-/herself.

At this point, I would add to this that even though disability (or autism for that matter) gives a vantage point, everyone's view is always perspectival. That means regardless of our viewpoint, we are enabled to see certain things but unable to see other things. We simply do not have 360-degree vision. Moreover, our perspectival vantage point also means that we are conditioned by our social, cultural, and theological contexts to notice certain things and not others. Imagine a father and a son camping in the woods. They both sit in front of their tent, basically looking at exactly the same view. The son might notice little creatures crawling around that the father did not notice, and the father may be able to name certain flowers or birds that the son does not. They have the same vantage point, but their visual, auditory, tactile, olfactory, and other perceptions are likely to be different. Likewise, the way we name things or attribute meaning to them may differ again. The father may delight in listening to the sounds of animals in the night while they may frighten the son (or the other way around). Being autistic or disabled does give a particular vantage point, and it is not unlikely that someone else who identifies as such resonates with that point of view, but one point of view on its own cannot tell the full picture or speak in universal terms.

Creamer continues to note, citing Tanya Titchkosky, that "any experience of disability includes others' understandings of it."[52] As many authors on disability and autism have pointed out, disability and autism (and a host of other labels) are social and political constructions.[53] That is not to deny that impairments and the struggles that come with carrying the label "disabled" are very real; but the way meaning is given to them and how one lives with them in daily life is influenced, to a large extent, by one's sociocultural environment.[54] Moreover, Creamer states that even those external labels and categories do not explain the full picture. Some days, she says, she is able to go through life as if she has no mobility impairment, not using her cane, whereas other days it limits her severely in all she does or had planned to do. Is she disabled one day and not the next? This, in my view, is the crux of the argument. Noting, with reference to Lennard Davis, that the concept of disability depends on constructs of "normalcy," Creamer writes,

> As with other categories, the concept of disability is integrally related to structures of power and is dependent on sociopolitical categories constructed by an ableist culture. *Thus the object of disability studies is most accurately not the person using the wheelchair but rather the sets of social, historical, economic, and cultural processes that regulate and control the way we think about and through the body.* . . . We must recognize that even these elements of disability are not solely "individual" experiences but rather are rich with communal and societal input and implication.[55]

Clearly, Creamer does not say that it is unimportant to keep the person in the wheelchair in view in our discussions. However, that person is not necessarily the object of the study; the objects of study are the processes that inform our constructs (or "cult," to use Thomas Reynolds' term) of normalcy. It is from such processes and resulting constructs that disabilities (and autism for that matter) receive their meaning, their stigmas, and their taboos, and these processes also underly political advocacy, governmental policies, educational support, social inclusion, and social exclusion. As such, the discussion *must* involve nondisabled and non-autistic writers as well. Those writers, however, must listen, first of all, to the experiences of autistic (and disabled) people. The normalcy perspective is so dominant that most non-autistic people are caught up in it—churches are caught up in it. The autistic vantage point is well placed to show how normalcy perpetuates the processes that Creamer talks about.

To approach this latter point from a more explicitly theological angle, it is worth turning to Macaskill's work. He points out that the church is called to love, which means caring for each other.

> [4] Love is patient; love is kind; love is not envious or boastful or arrogant [5] or rude. It does not insist on its own way; it is not irritable or resentful; [6] it does not rejoice in wrongdoing, but rejoices in the truth. [7] It bears all things, believes all things, hopes all things, endures all things. (1 Cor 13:4–7, NRSV)

Being caught up, often unknowingly, in the constructs of normalcy, the community can look quite the opposite from Saint Paul's instruction. Macaskill notes, "Many autistic individuals, or their families, will testify that fellow Christians have failed to bear all things or endure all things, and have not been kind. This is something of which we must repent."[56] To use the language of repentance is to use bold language, but coming from the vantage point of an autistic author, the church needs to listen before it discards this terminology. In this regard, it should be noted that Macaskill is not playing a blame game, only going after non-autistic people; he is more nuanced than that in his writing. The very next point that he makes is an acknowledgment that non-autistic people might have been inadvertent in causing sensory and social harm to autistic people. However, Macaskill argues that "we can expect them [non-autistic people] to do something about it once they know that it has a destructive effect."[57] Moreover, Macaskill is not saying autistic people themselves are perfect in every way; elsewhere in his book, he points to the theological truth that all are sinners, and all need to work together to build up the body of Christ.[58] Such language might be provoking, but it offers rich possibilities to think through the question of normalcy and the role of theological concepts like repentance therein.

It is worth staying with the language of repentance a bit longer because the concept of repentance gets its full meaning within the concept of reconciliation. Being reconciled to God, God has given the ministry of reconciliation to the church (2 Cor 5:16–21). The believers in Corinth are instructed to regard each not from a worldly point of view (which we can read as including the processes at work in the constructions of worldly normalcy) but as new creations through Christ's reconciling work. Reconciliation is at the heart of the Christian story. Repentance is one step in the process of reconciliation, and Leah Robinson argues that other steps, or key concepts, in models of reconciliation are truth telling, justice, and forgiveness.[59] If we want to draw out the full weight of Macaskill's suggestion that churches need to repent of their harmful ways of being community, where they have not been loving and caring and bearing each other's burdens as instructed by Scripture, it is worthwhile to bring into view these key concepts in the process of reconciliation.

To start with truth telling, the conversation on autism, church, and theology needs to start with listening to the stories of autistic people. The church needs to hear the truth from autistic people about how they might feel excluded, listening for where aspects of its theology and worship might need to be rethought. If autistic people feel excluded from church, this may well be a matter of injustice—is it just, theologically, for the church to exclude fellow Christians from worshipping with them? Where there is theological and pastoral injustice, the church will need to repent. The word "repentance" comes from the Greek *metanoia*, which means "change of mind." Thus, repentance refers to turning around ways of thinking and acting. When the church's theology and practices have been caught up in constructs of normalcy, it needs to deconstruct its ways, to turn around, and to rethink its theology and change its practices. A new discourse is needed—one that starts with listening to those who have been wronged. If the church has excluded people, wronged people, it needs to repent.

In addition to truth telling, justice, forgiveness, and repentance, I would like to add a fifth keyword in the process of reconciliation—that is, reparation. Without reparation, the situation at hand can continue as it was before, even if one would hope that repentance has made a difference. Reparation goes further because it means making up for that which has been lost through the wrong actions of the perpetrator.[60] In this way, people are restored to their God-given dignity and place in the community. Applied to the context of autism in church, although listening to the voices of autistic people and asking for forgiveness for injustice is good, this is still not enough. If the church wants to repent, it needs to make reparations by ensuring that autistic members fully belong to their communities, have the same opportunities to participate, and occupy places in the leadership teams.[61]

It may seem that this discussion on reconciliation has led us away from the question about the positionality of the author and his or her credibility to speak on the issue of autism. In fact, it has not. When autistic or disabled people argue that the conversation of autism and disability needs to be led by autistic and disabled people, they often come from a place of hurt—a history of being talked about rather than talked with and listened to. Researchers, policymakers, educational professionals, occupational therapists, and even parents have often presumed to know better than the autistic and disabled people themselves what was best for them, sometimes robbing people of their dignity.[62] This calls for repentance indeed. However, if the aims are of reconciliation and of being worshipping communities together, the conversation cannot be complete without non-autistic people. Conversations are a two-way matter. Non-autistic people need to hear the stories of autistic people and therefore have a place in the discussion—perhaps not as leaders of the conversation but nevertheless as part of it. Furthermore, the conversation can be strengthened, and autistic people can be sustained in their cause when non-autistic allies join forces, in all humbleness, with autistic people. This book is an attempt to listen to the truth telling of autistic people. In a way, this book is my act of repentance and a contribution to a better church (reparation)—better, that is, in forming communities in which autistic and non-autistic people alike can belong.

I do not identify as autistic. I know quite a few autistic people in my close social environment and even more in my broader social circle. Their lives and my relationships with them have shaped me in part and certainly informed my thinking. Their stories are in the background of this book, but I will not always make these explicit because their stories are not mine to tell. Other stories are those that I have heard in the context of my research, and I have consent from my research participants to tell their stories. My self-disclosure, in Simplican's terms, as quoted above, reveals as much as it conceals, and I am very aware of that. Keeping my position (partly) "occluded transgresses the expectations of [my] audience" perhaps.[63] I am not willing, though, to tell stories that are not mine to tell. Moreover, the discussion on the complexity of revealing one's relationship to disability and autism, and the subsequent discussion on reconciliation leads us to different ways of perceiving positionality. Here is how I need and want to position myself: I have tried to listen carefully, and I hope to respectfully join the conversation, taking my lead from the stories of autistic people and their concerns. I join the conversation as a non-autistic fellow member of the body of Christ, who is keen to understand his autistic fellow Christians, and to join his fellow Christians in helping the church to understand the richness of the autistic experience of worship and liturgy. I join with a deep desire to see the church as a place where everyone belongs, autistic, non-autistic, or carrying any other label—as a place where all people are reconciled. Furthermore, I join as a theologian, with a concern for the church to engage in faithful practices, and as a researcher in the field of practical and liturgical theology. This is my position, and this is how I hope to make a contribution to the conversation on autism, theology, and church.

This book is the result of several years of listening to autistic people, their families and caregivers, people in churches, and church leaders. I was privileged to receive funding from the Carnegie Trust to do research in Singapore and the United Kingdom. In the United Kingdom, I interviewed thirteen people who identified as autistic, ages ranging from sixteen years to over sixty-five. In Singapore, I visited the Chapel of Christ Our Hope twice for over nine days, a church that has twenty-five to thirty autistic members, all of whom need significant support to get through daily life. This church tries to take autism into account in every decision it makes. In chapter 6, I will give a detailed picture of this church and especially of their worship service. Apart from this research project, I am cofounder and codirector of the Centre for Autism and Theology, based at the University of Aberdeen, where I am a lecturer in practical theology. Through the work of the center, I am privileged to be connected to many autistic people, both academics and nonacademics. My many conversations and email correspondences with these people have further helped me to listen and to sharpen my understanding of and thinking about autism, church, and theology. All this is not to say that I pretend to get everything right—which would be quite impossible anyway regarding autism as there are many different views, opinions, theories, and theologies around (see more in chapter 2).

This chapter started with a quotation from Rachel: "Normal people just go to church and don't think any more about it. They just get in their car or walk, they go through the door, they do the service, and they go home. And it's never that simple for me." During the past few years, I have tried to listen to Rachel and many others. This book is my attempt, as a fellow member in the body of Christ, to acknowledge that church is often not that simple for autistic people and to think through the complexity of worship and liturgy in relation to autism. As such, I hope that what I say in this book will resonate with many, that it furthers the emerging field of autism theology, and that it will help churches to become more faithful in following the One they claim to worship.

OVERVIEW OF CHAPTERS

The first chapter discusses three elements that are important for framing the discussions in this book. The chapter first looks into language and terminology that is used in discussions and studies of autism because the language we use reveals a lot of our underlying assumptions. The second part of that chapter reviews key literature and events in the emerging discourse that we might call autism theology. As a book in practical theology, with the desire to listen to autistic people, the chapter furthermore presents the stories of autistic people and how they experience worship. The chapter is based on stories from the literature and from my own fieldwork and conversations with autistic people. A liturgical theology that takes the autistic experience of worship seriously—which any liturgical theology should do—should be able to be read through the lens of these stories.

The disproportionate absence of autistic people and the lack of autistic people in leadership roles, as discussed above, presents the church and liturgical theology with a problem. This book addresses that problem, but before going to the root cause of the problem in chapter 3, the second chapter discusses at length the difficulty of the phrase "Autism is . . . ," a discussion that has already started in this introduction. The concept of "autism" has been in flux since its inception in the early twentieth century and as diagnostic label since 1944. This chapter is not only informative for understanding what autism is but also suggests that theological criticism of the (medical) label is necessary for faithfully worshipping with autistic people.

The third chapter continues the discussion by further analyzing the way in which we construct reality, in dialogue with Lennard Davis, Thomas Reynolds, and others who have elaborated on the concept of "normalcy." This discussion shows the dynamics of exclusion of which churches often are unaware. In my view, "normalcy" is the root cause, or is at least one of the root causes, of the ignoring and/or exclusion of autistic people in church.

After the deconstruction work in chapters 2 and 3, chapter 4 starts the constructive work by proposing that a theology of presence and availability can counter the exclusion of autistic (and other) people. As such, the chapter is the contrasting image of chapter 3. It starts by outlining the philosopher Gabriel Marcel's theory of availability, which helps us to think through the concept of "presence" as an answer to the absence of autistic people in church. The chapter discusses how availability might be thought of in theological terms as *kenosis*, which in turn leads to a theology of participation. In this way, chapter 4 starts to occupy the space for theological reflection on autism that will be created in chapter 2.

Chapter 5 continues the discussion of chapter 4 but now from a liturgical-theological stance. The theology of participation in chapter 4 introduces the temple image—chapter 5 will explore that image and its concomitant concept of purity as well as the ideas of liturgical and sacramental participation. Thus, I offer a liturgical-theological response to the absence of, or the ignoring of, autistic people in corporate worship. The result is a proposal for a kenotic liturgical theology of availability.

The last chapter asks the question how the kenotic (liturgical) theology of availability, developed in chapters 4 and 5, helps us to envision a worshipping community in which everyone belongs. This chapter tells the story of a church in Singapore, the Chapel of Christ Our Hope, which is centered on autism. I will describe in detail how they live their vision to be inclusive of all people, in particular those who identify as autistic. The chapter describes how the church came into being, how it worships, and then offers a theological interpretation of their worship. As such, the chapter shows how the liturgical theology of availability that I develop in this book might look like in practice—not as a blueprint for all churches to follow but as an inspiring example.

The conclusion, finally, answers the three main questions that are central to this book by summarizing the main arguments of this book. Furthermore, the conclusion illustrates what a liturgical theology of availability might look like by returning to the story of the Singaporean church and other stories told throughout the book. It is my hope that this inspires liturgical theologians and churches to think what it means to be a place of worship where everyone belongs—autistic and non-autistic alike.

1

Setting the Scene
Language, Autism Theology, and Autistic Experiences of Worship

Three elements that frame the study of autism and worship in important ways are the focus of this opening chapter. The first is with regard to the language we use. Those readers who are familiar with autism or disability studies will recognize the debate between person-first (person with autism) or identity-first (autistic person) language. In most journal articles, this discussion is referred to briefly, but in a book-length treatment of autism and worship, it is worth discussing this issue at length. This is not just an academic debate (in fact, it is also part of the discourse in autistic communities and autistic self-advocacy); as we will see, the choice of a few simple words has profound implications for, or reveals, one's view of what it means to be human and therefore what it means to be an autistic human. Because language matters, at the end of this first section on language, I will also discuss a few other terms that surface in the discourse time and again (e.g., low- and high-functioning autism). Then I will turn to the second element that provides the context for this study—the fact that autism theology is a field that is very young. I will offer a brief sketch of how the discussion is emerging by reviewing some key publications and events in this field. Finally, the study of autism and worship needs to resonate with autistic people themselves in the first place, and it needs to be grounded in their experience of worship. Therefore, in the third section of this chapter, I will present stories that are drawn from the literature and my interviews.

Thus, this book is an academic discussion set in the reality of the lived autistic experiences of worship.

THE LANGUAGE WE USE

The language we use to speak about autism reveals a lot about how we view autism. The way we name ways of living, conditions, behavior, people, and everything else reveals what we think of these elements, which in turn determines how we deal with them. John Swinton puts it succinctly:

> The ways in which we describe the world determine what we think we see. What we think we see determines how we respond to what we think we see. How we respond to what we think we see is a measure of our faithfulness. Language and description matter.[1]

Ultimately, the question about the language we use—and therefore how we relate to people—is a theological question, "a measure of our faithfulness." Writing about disabilities, Brett Webb-Mitchell makes a similar point to that of Swinton. He argues that churches often use the language of the health-care professionals and social sciences, thereby adopting not only their language (instead of language of the kingdom of God) but also their philosophies.[2] For example, if we see autism primarily as a disability, what we see is that which an autistic person is unable to do, which may in turn lead to questionable intervention methods, trying to "cure" the autistic person or to "treat" them so that they fit into what is considered acceptable by society.[3] Seeing the autistic person as someone created and loved by God leads more easily to seeing that person as valuable as they are and as a gift to the community. Moreover, language shapes our ideologies and reveals the power structures: who gets to narrate the social phenomena around us? The language we use reveals the dominant narratives that shape our thinking.[4] It is clear, then, that we need to think carefully about the language we use.

One issue that is debated in the world of autism is whether we should use person-first ("person with autism") or identity-first language ("autistic person"). At the beginning of a book on church and autism, we need to look deeper into the reasons why people prefer one usage over the other, especially as identity-first language, which I will mostly use, runs counter to common parlance in much of the academic discourse and perhaps also to the language commonly used in society at large.[5] Identity-first language can even come across as offensive to some, so it is necessary to consider what the language we use reveals about our views of autism and to examine what is at stake. As Swinton highlights, this is not a language game for academics; it is a matter of faithfulness.

The core issue in the person-first or identity-first language debate is human dignity—and both sides of the debate argue for the same in that sense. Person-first language came into use in the disability movement from the 1970s, during what Michael Wehmeyer et al. call the "third wave" in the disability movement.[6] Wehmeyer et al., writing about intellectual disabilities, identify the first wave as taking place around the end of the nineteenth century and until the middle of the twentieth century. This first wave was dominated by the professionals. People with disabilities were not thought of as being able to advocate for themselves and were not taken seriously. Quite the contrary, the "feebleminded" were mentioned on a par with, and "feeblemindedness" even as cause of, "paupers, criminals, prostitutes, drunkards, and examples of all forms of social pest with which modern society is burdened."[7] Parents were not taken seriously, and while some parents of disabled children supported the professionals (as in the case of the parents of Donald Triplett, who was one of the first children that formed the cohort of Leo Kanner's initial work on autism[8]), the professional was always the "expert," and the parents were certainly not. From the 1950s, this started to change; a second wave emerged. Parents started to meet in groups, forming networks primarily to support one another but increasingly also to advocate for their children. This led to organizations that exist to this day such as the National Autistic Society.[9]

The third wave of the disability movement began in the 1970s. This was the wave of self-advocacy. In this context, person-first language emerged. Giacomo Vivanti traces the terminology back to a discussion during a disability rights convention in Oregon in 1974, when a self-advocate said, "I am tired of being called retarded. We are people first."[10] The tagline of People First of Washington is equally clear: "We are people first. Our disabilities are secondary."[11] Vivanti explains the stakes:

> By literally placing the person before the disability, person-first language conveys an emphasis on the person's unique combination of strengths, needs, and experiences (both related and unrelated to their disability), and the acknowledgement that these might be different from those of others who happen to have the same diagnosis. Additionally, it serves to recognize that the person with disability, being "a person first," should be given the same human rights standards, protections and opportunities expected for any other person.[12]

The good intentions of using person-first language are obvious to see. The advocates of this terminology ask us to look beyond the disability of a person in order to see the person holistically instead of reducing the person to his or her disability.

These good intentions notwithstanding, this is where the difference between person-first and identity-first advocates can be seen most clearly. The case for identity-first language hinges primarily on two related arguments. I will use autism here as an example. First, identity-first advocates argue that autism is an inherent part of who they are and not an "add-on" as "person with autism" might suggest. Botha et al. explain that person-first language "literally serves to drive a wedge between the person (good), and the autism (bad)."[13] They explain further the linguistic side of the formulation. Person with autism is a noun + noun structure: person + noun (autism). The latter noun can be replaced by other nouns, such as cancer, COVID-19, or the like. These are nouns that suggest a pathology or an illness. It would be possible to replace the latter noun with words that have a more positive connotation (e.g., "person with integrity"). Nevertheless, the point made by Botha et al. remains that linguistically, there is a risk of bringing in pathological connotations to person-first language. Instead of seeing autism as a pathology, many proponents of identity-first language see autism as part of the neurodiverse makeup of humanity (hence the designation of "neurotypical" for non-autistic and "neurodivergent" for autistic people).[14] The second argument for identity-first language follows logically: there is nothing wrong with autism, so why not identify with it by calling oneself "autistic" instead of "a person with autism"? Rather than seeing autism as a disability that people need to live with as best they can (which often means, adapt to the "normal" society as much as possible by acting as "normal" as you can), identity-first advocates wear their autistic identity as a proud badge. Whereas "autistic" may have been used pejoratively in earlier years, now the term is reclaimed by those identifying as autistic; it is a way of being that is to be embraced.

The debate around person-first versus identity-first language is not easily resolved. Even though the roots of person-first language might be traced back to a comment by a disabled person, as we just saw, person-first language is advocated by professionals who can be seen to be working in a medical model. Deborah Creamer describes the medical model of disability as focusing its attention "around what one can or cannot physically or functionally do."[15] The assumption is that disability is "primarily a medical or biological condition" and "it claims that the disabled person's functional ability deviates from that of the normal human body."[16] Dunn and Andrews explain that the American Psychological Association (APA), the organization behind the highly influential *DSM*, encourages its members to adopt person-first language. The influence of the APA and its *DSM* (which can be considered as the bible of the medical model and which is now in its fifth edition) reaches beyond the professional guild. When people are first diagnosed with autism, they and their caregivers hear the person-first language of the psychologist and other professionals. This is how many learn about autism and the world of professional services. It is at this point that Botha et al. argue that the shift from person-first to identity-first language is most important because it is not a cultural shift made by the neurodiversity movement but a *paradigmatic* one: it is a shift away from a paradigm that sees autism as a pathology (as in the medical model), as expressed by the person-with-autism language.[17]

Even though many learn about autism through a medical diagnostic process, often followed by professional support services influenced by the person-first language of the medical model, many of those on the autism spectrum later prefer to adopt an identity-first way of describing themselves. Their intention is to emphasize the human dignity and value of every human being, which is notable given that was also the original intention behind person-first language. However, because the person-first language is used in medical and professional support settings, it has pathological overtones.[18]

The debate between person-first and identity-first language is ongoing, and there is still one caveat that we should mention. Even in discourses that advocate the use of identity-first language, there is the realization that opinions on this issue differ even within the autism communities. Two points need to be kept in mind. The first is simply that opinions differ and that some still prefer person-first language. Second, academic papers suggesting that the use of identity-first language is based on surveys among autism communities need to be read carefully. The outcome of such surveys does not yield a 100-percent preference for identity-first language. For example, one such often-cited paper is by Lorcan Kenny et al., who present their research on the language endorsed or preferred by people in the autism community in the United Kingdom. A first important finding was the wide range of terms being used, such as "autism," "has autism," "autism spectrum disorder," and "autistic." A second important finding was that "the most highly endorsed terms were 'autism' and 'on the autism spectrum,' and to a lesser extent, 'autism spectrum disorder (ASD)' for which there was general agreement [that these were acceptable or even preferred] across groups."[19] A third finding that is noteworthy for our purposes is that the researchers found a contrast between autistic adults, parents, and family members on the one hand and professionals on the other hand when it came to person-first language.

> The term "autistic" was endorsed by a large percentage of autistic adults (61%), family members/friends (52%) and parents (51%) but by considerably fewer professionals (38%). In contrast, "person with autism" was endorsed by almost half (49%) of professionals but only by 28% and 22% of autistic adults and parents, respectively. Also, while a significant proportion of autistic adults stated that they used the terms "autistic person" and "Aspie," only a minority of other participants agreed.[20]

These few highlights from the research by Kenny et al. show the differences among autistic people themselves and between various stakeholder groups. That said, the preference for identity-first language on the part of the autistic people themselves is not only shown by 61 percent preferring this language (which is not an overwhelming majority) but also by the rather low endorsement of person-first language. Together, these figures suggest a fairly strong preference for identity-first language in UK autism communities.

As a critical note, surveys like these often can (or do) include only certain people within the autism community—that is, those who are able to read and write. This excludes a significant proportion of those in the autism community. However, Botha et al. suggest that this does not invalidate the results of these surveys. Rather than dismissing the results, which would deny the autistic people who did participate in the survey their voice, more research that is participatory in nature is needed.[21] Bottema-Beutel et al. argue that continuing the use of person-first language on the grounds that a part of the autism community has not yet been given the chance to express their preference "works to maintain the status quo by allowing nonautistic researchers to avoid engagement with the expressed preferences of many members of the autistic community and discount or minimize their arguments around language choices."[22] We might add that it is not only autistic adults who were able to express themselves in the research of Kenny et al. and that they expressed a preference for identity-first language but also parents of autistic people, which included parents of autistic children who would perhaps not be able to read or write.

Those who advocate identity-first language tend to have a positive view of being autistic. Even if they do not deny the challenges that come with being autistic, they shy away from a pathological view of autism. Often, the argument is to think of autism as part of neurodiversity. While I would argue that we need to be careful of calling everything neurological as that *can* be reductionistic too (see more on this in chapter 3), to think of autism as a form of diversity instead of a pathology is convincing from a theological point of view. To put it slightly differently, when we speak with and about people, it is a good idea not to start with pathology, which by definition implies that there is something wrong (a pathology) with the person. Moreover, a pathological discourse places us immediately in one or another version of a medical model of autism, which (again, by definition) makes us think in terms of treatment or even cure. In chapter 3, I will discuss in depth the underlying problem of a pathology model in terms of the concept of "normalcy." That is followed in chapter 4 by a discussion of how we should start with the acknowledgment of the presence of the other person (autistic or non-autistic), an acknowledgment that opens up ways of relating to each other which a medical model cannot and does not.

Bottema-Beutel and her team suggest that because of the diversity of opinions within autism communities, it is important to listen to the research participants themselves.[23] In the Singapore church where I did research, it was common to use person-first language, but notably this was language used by the parents and leadership, which may have been influenced by the context of the professional care that happens on a daily basis in the St. Andrew's Autism Centre, of which the Chapel of Christ Our Hope is a part.[24] The picture is very different with the UK participants. In the interviews with them, I asked explicitly what language they preferred. For many, it did not matter, but those who were outspoken had a clear preference for identity-first language.[25] Therefore, when I quote the Singapore people specifically in subsequent chapters, this may include person-first language, but otherwise, I will use identity-first language. This was the language preferred by my autistic interviewees; it is the preference expressed by the surveys of autistic people, their family members, and autistic scholars and is, notably, also often used by autistic writers themselves.

Making the choice for identity-first language, and respecting the reasons given by identity-first advocates, also has consequences for other terms commonly used. To that end, I will avoid the use of ASD (autism spectrum disorder) as much as possible, as I do not think that autism should be thought of as a "disorder" in the first place. Commenting on the well-known "triad of impairments" as a way of understanding autism, John Swinton writes that "any attempt to explain human experience that begins by focusing on three difficulties or deficits should be treated with some suspicion."[26] Starting with deficits immediately places the person as someone "other" than that which is considered to be good and the norm, which then easily leads to seeing that person of lesser value. Instead, in chapter 4, I will argue for another, more theologically sound starting point, one that starts from the presence of autistic people. I will also avoid the terms "high functioning" and "low functioning." What is considered "high" or "low" is measured by the ability to keep up with society as independently as possible. As I will discuss in chapter 3, this terminology is based on the "cult of normalcy," a cult we should be critical of, certainly from a theological point of view. A similar argument can be made against describing support needs as "severe" or "moderate." Such terms are catch-all and do not capture the differences between strengths and needs in different areas of life.[27] For example, one can be fluent in five languages but struggle to go to the bakery on one's own. Moreover, a person might require support with particular tasks on one day or for a season but not on another day or for another season. Finally, even though "autism spectrum" seems to be the least controversial term according to Kenny et al.'s research, as we saw above, we need to carefully consider what we mean by that term. When thought of in a two-dimensional way, "spectrum" can be thought of as linear, as a scale from one extreme end of autism to another extreme end. It follows easily that one end of the spectrum would be associated with "severe," "nonspeaking," "low functioning," and probably including learning difficulties. The opposite would then be "mild," "articulate," "high functioning," and probably include above-average intelligence. Not only is any autism profile more complex than such a two-dimensional understanding allows for, but also such a scale from "low" to "high" might have the connotation that people on the "high" end are "almost normal"—that is, non-autistic.

In conclusion, when speaking about autism, we need to keep three principles in mind in order to describe the world with theological faithfulness. In subsequent chapters, it will become clear how each of these three principles is related to a theology of presence. First, we need to listen to autistic people themselves and talk *with* them and let our speech be informed by autistic voices. In this book, I am informed by autistic people whom I have met in the context of my fieldwork, in my personal contacts near and far, and by autistic researchers and their publications. Second, in line with the autism advocacy movement, we need to move away from seeing autism in the first instance as a pathology and honor God-given diversity instead. Third, related to the previous point, we need to be aware of ableism and normalcy and move away from a discourse that is informed by those. This latter point is easier said than done, as ableism and normalcy are so ingrained in culture, society, and in the way many of us have been brought up. It is difficult to see our own biases; nevertheless, we should try to become aware of them and diligently think through autism and worship from a critical and theological point of view.

AUTISM THEOLOGY: AN EMERGING FIELD

The theological study of autism is an emerging field, with the first publications having come out in the 2000s.[28] In 2008, Thomas Reynolds published his book *Vulnerable Communion*.[29] Reynolds' book speaks about disabilities more broadly, but he makes clear that his thinking in the book has been shaped to a large extent by his relationship with his autistic son. *Vulnerable Communion* has been, and still is, influential in the field of disability theology and has much to offer for autism theology. His explanation of the "cult of normalcy" (the way communities function by including that which fits with the norms of their subculture and excluding that which does not) is profound, and I will draw on that concept in chapter 3.[30] In 2009, John Swinton and Christine Trevett edited a collection of essays on autism and religion in a special issue of the *Journal of Religion, Disability & Health* (now the *Journal of Disability & Religion*).[31] One year later, John Gillibrand published his book *Disabled Church—Disabled Society*.[32] As with Reynolds, the theology that Gillibrand develops in his book is shaped by his experiences as father of an autistic son.[33] Gillibrand's book has a political edge in that he critically discusses health-care provision in the United Kingdom. A point to note here is that autism has caused for him, what he calls (following Michel Foucault), an epistemic break—the need to rethink how one sees and acts in the world when "older ways of handling reality [become] inadequate for their task."[34] Gillibrand's experiences of caring for his son showed him the inadequacy of church and society's ability to "handle the reality" of autism. Thus, he argues that autism might become the starting point for a new discourse and new practices.[35] In this book, I take autism as the starting point for liturgical theology.

Between 2010 and 2018, relatively few books and articles were written on autism and theology. Nevertheless, during this period, three resources were published that focused not so much on theology as on practical guidance for churches. In 2011, Barbara Newman revised her 2006 *Autism and Your Church*, a guide to welcoming autistic people in the church.[36] Stephen Bedard published the guide *How to Make Your Church Autism-Friendly*, first edition in 2015 and an updated, second edition in 2017.[37] Perhaps most well known in the United Kingdom are the guidelines *Welcoming and Including Autistic People in Our Churches and Communities* from the Church of England's Diocese of Oxford, written largely by Ann Memmott. The first edition was published in 2008, a second in 2015, and the latest (fourth) edition is dated July 2021.[38] In 2017, Monica Spoor published a small book in which she tells of her own experience of worshipping in an Orthodox church and gives numerous practical tips and insights for fellow autistic worshippers, with notes for non-autistic people.[39] Most recently, at the time of writing this book, Mark Arnold has written a guide in the Grove Youth Series titled *How to Include Autistic Children and Young People in Church: Creating a Place of Belonging and Spiritual Development for All*.[40] As the title says, this resource is focused on autistic children. Each of these resources uses different models of disability, with Newman using language of the medical model, thereby taking the perspective of autism as a disorder. Memmott, by contrast, explains autism as a "brain design difference" that has its own value and does not need to be seen as a *dis*order.[41] Despite differences in their views of what autism is, each of these publications provide helpful practical advice for churches to help them become places where autistic people truly belong.[42]

From 2017 onward, there was a noticeable increase in publications on autism and theology. Not only has the number of journal articles increased during the last couple of years, but there has been a remarkable increase in theological monographs. In 2017, Jennifer Cox published *Autism, Humanity and Personhood*. In her book, she attempts to construct a theological anthropology that is not based primarily on a relational view of personhood but is rooted in the humanity of Christ. Her concern is that some "people with severe autism" (to use her term) "do not engage in reciprocal relationships," and therefore a relational theological view of personhood is insufficient.[43] However, in my view, the turning point in the development of the field of autism theology came with the publication of Grant Macaskill's article "Autism Spectrum Disorders and the New Testament: Preliminary Reflections" in 2018, followed in early 2019 by his monograph *Autism and the Church*.⁴⁴ The article is read widely, as is his book. These publications were preceded by his Christ's College lecture in 2017 titled *Autism and the Bible: Beginning a Conversation*, which has well over ten thousand views on YouTube (a high number in the world of theology).⁴⁵ Also in 2018, Brian Brock published *Wondrously Wounded*.⁴⁶ Brock's scope is wider than autism, but like Reynolds and Gillibrand, the book is strongly informed by his son who carries the diagnoses of autism and Down syndrome. One chapter is specifically focused on autism. The book contains many rich and thought-provoking discussions, including an in-depth discussion of the body of Christ, an image that figures prominently in disability theology and is also referred to in discussions of autism.⁴⁷ In 2019, Summer Kinard published her book *Of Such Is the Kingdom: A Practical Theology of Disability*. Kinard writes from her perspective of being autistic herself and as mother of five autistic children and also from her perspective as a convert to Eastern Orthodoxy.

It is remarkable, then, that in 2021 alone, four books about autism and theology were published in consecutive months. The first book that was published in 2021 (August) is somewhat different in nature to the other three books that followed. Daniel Bowman Jr. wrote *On the Spectrum: Autism, Faith, & the Gifts of Neurodiversity*, which is a personal memoir, written not by an academic theologian but by a professor of English.⁴⁸ The book is not so much driven by an academic research question but by a desire to raise awareness in church and academy about autism and the experiences of a Christian professor who finds his way in a largely non-autistic world. The result is a personal account with detailed descriptions of the blessings and challenges of autism in the world of faith, work, and family.⁴⁹

Stewart Rapley's book *Autistic Thinking in the Life of the Church* was the next one to be published in September 2021. Based on interviews with autistic people, Rapley proposes that autistic people often experience "cognitive dissonance" with their churches, the Bible, God conceptions, and prayer. He pleads for greater awareness in churches of how the "relational bias" in their theology is interpreted by autistic people, which may create this cognitive dissonance, and for churches to engage with autistic people and rethink their theologies to include more nonanthropomorphic God conceptions. A month later, Cynthia Tam's monograph *Kinship in the Household of God* appeared in print. Per the subtitle of her book, Tam hopes to move *Towards a Practical Theology of Belonging and Spiritual Care of People with Profound Autism*. Based on extensive ethnographic work with two families who have a child with, in Tam's terms, "profound autism" and their churches, she explores ways in which faith communities can become places where members with autism truly belong. Also in October, Eilidh Campbell published *Motherhood and Autism*.[50] Campbell notes that all existing theological books by parents of autistic children are written by fathers (see Reynolds, Gillibrand, and Brock above). Raising an autistic child herself and in dialogue with four other mothers of autistic children, Campbell researches the lived experience of mothering autistic children.

One more publication concludes this selected overview of monographs in the field, which is *The Autism of Gxd* by Ruth Dunster.[51] In a way, this is the most radical of the publications reviewed here, as Dunster writes an "atheological" book (which, in part, explains her spelling of "Gxd"), following especially the work of Thomas J. J. Altizer, who speaks about the gospel of Christian atheism. Dunster defines "atheology" as a "way of thought which affirms belief in Jesus, in the light of God having died in the cosmic event of Jesus' Crucifixion; a paradoxical faith where propositional theology is subverted."[52] Dunster develops an autistic theology based on an autistic hermeneutic. Interestingly, she works with clinical views of autism—for example, the theory of mindblindness—but instead of dismissing those views as some autistic advocates would do, she takes them to their radical consequences and applies them to theology. The result is a creative, autistic theology.[53]

It is relevant to note another moment in the development of the emerging field of autism theology—that is, the founding of the Centre for Autism and Theology (so named since 2021; before that, it was called the Centre for the Study of Autism and Christian Community).[54] The center was the brainchild of Professor Grant Macaskill and was founded by him and three other theologians at the University of Aberdeen: Professor John Swinton, Professor Brian Brock, and me. The center aims to be an international hub for theological and interdisciplinary research, in collaboration with faith communities and other third parties. It emphasizes autistic leadership, shown by the fact that Professor Macaskill is codirector and identifies as autistic, as do a number of those who sit on the center's advisory group. The center's conference in 2021 on autism, theology, and the church was an important event in the field, connecting many (autistic) scholars, professionals, and other interested parties, perhaps for the first time on this scale.[55]

As autism theology has only begun to emerge in recent years as an academic discipline, it is worth noting a few things. First, the publications are almost all coming from the Global North/Western world. Since all theology is contextual, it is important to realize that our theologies are colored by our cultural contexts. In chapter 2, I will demonstrate this point more broadly by giving an overview of some of the most important historical developments in the concept of autism. The effect is that voices from other contexts are largely absent. The present book draws on fieldwork in the United Kingdom and Singapore and as such, makes a small attempt to intentionally include voices from non-Western contexts.

Second, compared with some other academic disciplines, in particular those strongly influenced by medical models of disability and mental health, theology can more easily align with the significant movement in autism communities that argues for autism to be seen not as a disability but as a difference. Many publications from different disciplines that study autism use medicalized language, seeing autism as a pathology, and therefore in need of a cure—or if a cure is not possible, will promote interventions in such a way that autistic people can function as "normally" as possible in society.[56] As discussed above, this medical model contrasts sharply with those in the autism communities who see autism as a different way of being in the world, often captured by the term "neurodiversity." In this model, autism is seen as a brain difference (e.g., Memmott uses the term "brain difference" in the Oxford guidelines discussed above) or a difference in neurological makeup. The term is often shared by others who are neurodivergent, such as dyslexic people or those with ADHD.[57] The neurodiversity movement aligns with the social model of disability, which does not deny that people may also have impairments unrelated to their social lifeworld.[58]

In disability theology, it has often been pointed out that the medical model, with its characteristically pathologizing anthropological views, is theologically questionable. Some disability theologians point to characteristics of what it means to be human, which they find, for example, in the idea that all human beings are vulnerable (Reynolds) or have limits (Creamer).[59] The neurodiversity model in which autism is a different way of being, one that is not better or worse than so-called neurotypical ways of being, is not difficult to accept for many working in the field of autism, theology, and church. It is not difficult to see how the affirmation of the God-given value of each person can function as a theological appropriation of the neurodiversity model. Most of the authors mentioned above would shy away from the medical model, and some would perhaps adopt the neurodiversity model. The late Barbara Newman employs language of the medical model, which is perhaps due to the fact that she was an education professional and therefore influenced by the medical terminology, like many professionals. It is remarkable that Jennifer Cox, as a theologian, uncritically adopts the medical model, particularly as her project revolves around the question of a theologically sound anthropology. All other theologians discussed above arguably take a more positive view of autism, in particular those who identify as autistic themselves (Macaskill, Rapley, and Bowman). Of these authors, Daniel Bowman is perhaps most strongly advocating for the neurodiversity model. Indeed, he includes a full chapter in which he advocates the model, and he is involved (as a member of academic staff) with a student group in his university called Students for Education on Neurodiversity. In this book, I will take the insights from the neurodiversity movement into account, especially their argument that being autistic means to inhabit, experience, and understand the world differently than so-called neurotypicals. However, as noted before, there is a risk of viewing our entire humanity through our brains, which seems to me reductionistic.[60] Therefore, I will mainly stay away from the language of neurodiversity and neurotypicality but use autistic and non-autistic instead.[61]

This book joins the emerging dialogue on autism, theology, and church. It does so by studying liturgy and worship through the lens of autism. Given that worship is a central practice of faith communities, it is not surprising that many of the books discussed above touch on liturgy and worship. Gillibrand has a chapter specifically on liturgy. In Macaskill's book, quite a few examples are taken from worship services. Brock includes discussions of liturgy and worship as well, and doxology as a theological and practical concept forms a central tenet of his work. Rapley focuses on the cognitive aspect of autism and faith in which worship services frequently rise to the surface of the discussion. Tam's research centers on faith communities, and again, the worship service is one of the practices that Tam discusses. However, none of these works have worship and liturgy in view as explicit foci of their project, and their primary intention is not to contribute to the specific discipline of liturgical theology. This book zooms in, therefore, on this central practice of faith communities, where others have touched on it but not made it their focus. Moreover, this book wants to contribute to liturgical theology by bringing in the perspective of autistic people through listening intently to the voices of autistic worshippers, to which we will turn now. Liturgical theology is a fundamental theological discipline, as it is the field of research that studies worship as a core practice of the church. By contributing to liturgical theology as fundamental theological discipline, this book in turn contributes to the field of autism theology.

AUTISTIC EXPERIENCES OF WORSHIP

To research liturgy in relation to autism, one must start with the experience of worship services, as described by autistic people themselves. Therefore, in this section, I will present some of these experiences, as described in the existing literature and in the many stories that autistic people have shared with me. These stories emerge both in informal conversations as well as in the interviews I did with autistic people in the United Kingdom and Singapore.[62]

"Church is never that simple for me," said Rachel in the opening quotation of the previous chapter. Rachel is not alone, as anecdotal stories in the literature as well as my interviews with autistic worshippers make clear. At the same time, we need to be careful not to frame the autistic experience of worship only as a struggle. It is not because, in the words of Oliver (one of my interviewees in the United Kingdom), he experiences everything more intensely than other people—both the positives and the negatives:

> So if the music, if something's distressing, it will be far more distressing for me, maybe, than it would be for an ordinary person. But if it was extremely upbuilding, it probably has a greater emotional impact on me than maybe for other things. So the highs would be higher and the lows would be substantially lower.

It is true that most of the stories about worship told by autistic writers, and by most of my interviewees, commented on the more challenging aspects of worship especially. This will be reflected on in what follows, both in this section and further on in this book. Nevertheless, to frame autistic experiences of worship only in negative terms would, first of all, not be true to the holistic experience of autistic people—as was also clear from my interviews and testified to by Oliver. Second, such framing would perpetuate a discourse that primarily pathologizes autism—a discourse that I try to resist, as discussed above. As we proceed with this chapter, we should keep in mind Oliver's helpful comment that both positive and negative experiences may be more intense for autistic people than for most others.

Here is a description of worship by an autistic blogger, Katherine Bale. In her oft-cited article "17 Ways to Make Your Church Autism-Friendly," she writes,

> **Before the service**, I'm sitting in my seat at church: one or more people are talking to me; the band is playing; the minister is walking in;

there's lots of moving visuals on the screens; several people are wearing strong perfume; there's loud noise from the heating system; unpleasant coloured electric light. And I am sitting there unable to filter out sensory information that I don't need, and feeling increasingly tense. By the time the minister starts, I'm not capable of paying attention and it takes a while to be able to calm down and focus. So, there is a lot of hard work for me to do before I can even start to join in with a worship service.

During the service, I find it difficult to concentrate because of distractions. The distractors are normal things that aren't bad in themselves, but I am unable to filter them out. This takes a lot of effort and is stressful because I don't want to miss anything. This is normal for me and many everyday situations are exhausting.

I enjoy the social time following a service, but making the switch from concentration into social interaction is difficult. It takes time to adjust and can leave me feeling on the outside and hoping the friendly person in front of me won't think I'm not interested and go away before I've been able to tune into what they're saying and find the words to reply.[63]

Bale's experience resonates with various points that I have heard in the stories of many other autistic people. First, her description highlights the sensory aspect of worship. Macaskill notes that for those people whose senses work in typical ways, "the significance of this will not be perceived; it will be processed at a tacit level. Those who struggle to participate in such spaces, however, will be painfully aware of the factors at work."[64] Macaskill's use of the phrase "painfully aware" is notable; for autistic people, certain sensory stimuli can literally be painful, which is often different for a non-autistic person. Where the latter may find the smell of certain flowers unpleasant, an autistic person may find it actually painful and may even need to leave the space. At the same time, there can be helpful sensory experiences, such as that described by Margaretta (one autistic Christian whom I interviewed), who says she experiences prayer as tangible "God hugs." Furthermore, Bale's description illustrates that the worship space is a multisensory space. All the senses are involved in worship: there is sound, light and visuals, touch, smell, taste, and movement. When there is a heightened way of experiencing sensory input, the highs can be higher and the lows can be lower for an autistic person. For example, well-performed music might greatly facilitate an autistic person's encounter with God, but a flute that is out of tune might disrupt the entire experience.

A second point to note in Bale's description is the social aspect of church life, including the time before and especially after the service and, on occasion, during the service—for example, when people are asked to greet each other or share the peace. Social interaction is perhaps the topic most commented on in the literature, more than any other difference between autistic and non-autistic people. Church is a social space and navigating social interactions can be very exhausting for autistic people. However, immediately we also need to add that despite the energy and effort that social times take, all the autistic people whom I have spoken to and all the autistic authors whom I have read say that they do want to interact with other people and that they do want to form relationships. In an interview with one nonspeaking autistic Christian, Philip, he told me that people often avoid him because they do not know how to communicate with him. When I asked how he would like people to interact with him, he said, using his spelling board,

> I'd love them to ask me questions; to hang out doing things even if we don't talk. It's okay. I'd love it if the college group (peer age group) invited us to do anything. I think they are preoccupied with being cool. I am not cool but God treasures me.

Philip's answer is related to Bale's plea: "Do not think we are not interested in you, give us time to respond, to find the words" (and in Philip's case, time to spell the words). In her letter to the church, Monica Spoor adds, "You may misinterpret our substandard social skills and trouble with emotions as 'not caring,' but I assure you, we do care. We express it differently, or not at all, but given the chance we will show you, once you know what to look for, that we do care."[65] Similar comments were made by my interviewees. Some autistic people behave or communicate in ways that strike non-autistic people as odd. If these latter people are preoccupied with what is "cool" in the eyes of society, autistic people will soon be marginalized and pushed to the edges of the community. In a Christian community, such marginalization is problematic because Jesus redefined what is "cool" (i.e., what is valuable and treasured) among his followers. The discussion of normalcy in chapter 3 will deal at length with the problem of marginalization based on certain values.

Interestingly, some autistic writers have pointed out the questionable status of what society deems valuable in terms of social interaction. For example, what a non-autistic person might perceive as rude, an autistic person might call honesty.[66] What is more, an autistic person may think of non-autistic persons as hypocrites. Spoor writes, "To us, neurotypicals lie. Almost all the time. They make promises they do not keep. They make assumptions. They say one thing and do the other, their words do not match their expression. And they do not realize how hypocritical this makes them seem to us, because to them it is mostly normal."[67] What Spoor does, and what can be read in writings by other autistic people as well, is turn around the normal expectations of society, and she shows that what the majority of people in society find socially acceptable and normal is of questionable moral status. This is an important point because the onus to adapt is virtually always on the autistic person or anyone else who deviates from the majority norm. By questioning the moral value of that norm, autistic people show that groups might need to look at their norms twice and that perhaps it would be better if the majority changed rather than the minority.

It is worth raising the question of ministry in relation to social expectations. In my interview with Margaretta, she argued that people in professional roles should be allowed to be themselves without expecting them to conform to standard ways of communicating. These roles can be administrative, pastoral, or clerical. Margaretta's point is argued by other autistic people as well. This raises the important question about what communities expect from people in leadership roles, and again, what the basis is for the norms of a community. We will explore this last question at length in chapter 3.

Another point to note in Bale's description is that the experience of worship begins well before the formal start of the service. The worship service is such an overwhelming sensory experience and such a social labyrinth that some autistic people need to consider from week to week whether they will attend this time.[68] Spoor explains that there is a limit to the amount of energy available to cope with sensory and social overload (and Rapley would add, a limit to coping with cognitive dissonance).[69] Daily life might have been exhausting enough in any given week, and the prospect of needing to cope with the intensity of sensory input and social interaction that is typical of most churches might cause a level of anxiety that cautions an autistic person not to go to church this particular time. We are reminded again of Rachel's words:

> Normal people just go to church and don't think any more about it. They just get in their car or walk, they go through the door, they do the service, and they go home. And it's never that simple for me.

Preparing for the worship service starts long before the formal or informal opening words of the liturgy. Spoor writes that she starts to think about the Sunday worship service on Thursday.[70] By the time the worship service starts, autistic people might have had to spend considerable energy already to cope with social expectations, sensory input, and trying to make sense of the world in general.

A final point, which Bale hints at and which came out clearly in some of my interviews, is that some autistic people need a longer processing time than the typical speed of social interaction or of the worship service itself allows for. Autistic people may need time to process what their conversation partner has just said and then more time to find the right words to respond. They may also need time to move from one element in the liturgy to the next, more time than the liturgical leader allows for. For example, Margaretta plays in the music group in her church. She told me that she likes most of the service, but she does not like it when there is

> an overly quick transition between one thing and another. So like if we're, like if the pr-, if we launch into hymns straight after the sermon, and I'm still thinking about the sermon, and then the number of times I've spectacularly messed up the first verse of the, the hymn after the sermon because my brain's not switched over yet.

Interestingly, when I asked Philip what a worship service would look like when designed from an autistic perspective, the first thing he said was that there would be a lot more silence. Surely, that would help with processing what takes place in the liturgy? That is not to say that all services should be contemplative—there were some people whom I interviewed who would like that, but some others certainly would not. Even without turning the worship service into a contemplative liturgy, churches might think of ways in which more processing time can be allowed. Furthermore, another of my interviewees, Rose, suggested breaking the service into different parts to allow people to join only for certain parts. This could help to create space for processing what is happening in each part of the service and create ways to avert sensory overload.

Bale's description of her experience of worship services highlights points that are mentioned in the literature and that surfaced in my interviews regularly. While some autistic people are hyposensitive in some areas (i.e., needing more sensory input), most comments were about sensory hypersensitivity (i.e., being overstimulated by certain sensory input), leading to sensory overload. A tension exists between, on the one hand, the longing for social interaction, participating in the community, and friendship and, on the other hand, the mutual lack of understanding and communication between autistic and non-autistic people.[71] This lack of understanding is not only because of the differences in communication style but also because non-autistic people might find autistic people not "cool," to use Philip's words. In chapter 3, I will discuss the concept of "normalcy" that, I suggest, lies at the root of this non-autistic perception of autistic people, and in the subsequent chapters, I will argue that Christian communities need to use other standards to determine whether to interact with someone. Bale highlighted, furthermore, that (the preparation for) worship starts well before the formal start of the service. The heightened experience of sensory input and anxiety about social interaction, therefore, also start well before the service. Finally, a point that is less frequently highlighted in the literature but is nevertheless important is that many autistic people need processing time in worship and in social interactions. All of these points need to be taken into account when we think about liturgy and how the community conducts its worship services.

Recently, I was asked in a podcast interview how far faith communities should go in making sure that autistic people can participate in worship services. I answered by returning the question, how far do we want to go to make sure all members of the body of Christ—in which all members, and especially those whom society considers "weaker," are indispensable (1 Cor 12:22)—belong? In addition, we need to say two more things. First, it is unrealistic to imagine a worship service in which all of the needs of all people, autistic or non-autistic, will be met all of the time. Nevertheless, sometimes small changes that have hardly any impact on others can go a long way for an autistic person. Second, throughout my interviews, there was a sense of generosity toward non-autistic members. In the words of Alex:

> What works for me doesn't work for anybody else. . . . I hate to crush other people's enjoyment of it. I'd like to think there's maybe one or two things that you [as the researcher] will find, and you, it could maybe be mainstreamed into church as an improvement out of this [research], and even if it looks like we're reaching out a little bit to people on the autistic spectrum and saying, you know, we get you. Would be nice.

Autistic people realize that compromises need to be made. However, the onus to adapt has been on the autistic people for so long, as the above descriptions of worship experience reveals. It is my hope that through this book, we might find a few things that can be brought into the mainstream of the church with the help of some practical examples. But beyond that, I hope also to analyze the root cause of the absence and ignoring of autistic people in churches and to give a liturgical-theological answer. I hope that answer will inspire Christian communities to think through their worship practices and make improvements for autistic people. Nevertheless, Alex calls for one thing more than anything else—a call I have heard and keep hearing from many autistic people: people in churches reaching out to autistic people and saying, "We get you." Church is "never that simple" for Rachel, nor for most autistic people, but churches can make a concerted effort to understand Rachel and her autistic peers a little bit better. In the process, the church will discover that their autistic members are indispensable indeed.

CONCLUSION

In this chapter, I have presented three elements that impact the context of this study in important ways. I have argued for the use of identity-first language in this book, while occasionally using person-first language when this was the preference expressed by my interviewees, particularly in Singapore (chapter 6). I also argued for moving away from a pathological view of autism, without denying the real challenges autism can bring for autistic people themselves and their families and caregivers. Furthermore, I have sketched the emerging field of autism theology by reviewing some important publications and events. Given the recent emergence of the discourse, it is not surprising that there is a gap in the literature when it comes to a substantial treatment of liturgy and worship. Because worship is a central practice of church life, some publications have touched on this, but robust research specifically on liturgy and autism is lacking. This book starts to fill this gap—not as the end of the discussion but very much as the beginning.

The third section of this chapter presented several stories of the experience of worship by autistic people. Feminist practical theologian Elaine Graham writes, "Bodies offer a 'vantage-point' from which the complexity of human nature, as creator and creation of culture, can be experienced and analyzed. Bodies are the bearers of important narratives."[72] Worship is an embodied experience, as for example the above discussion of the sensory aspect of worship demonstrates. To add the words of Graham, worship culture is experienced and created through the body. When bodies are different from the majority culture, for example, autistic bodies, then these bodies offer a unique "vantage point"—indeed, autistic people often comment that they experience the world (including church and worship) differently from non-autistic people. The stories above made this clear. In this book, we will try to listen to autistic voices (or bodies) to see in what ways that leads to new insights and analyses of church communities and their worship. In order to listen and to understand well, we will need to start with the question of what autism is. This question is surprisingly hard to answer, as the next chapter will demonstrate by reviewing the history of autism as a concept that is continuously "in the making."

2

How Autism Came to Be

The Problem of "Autism Is..."

Autism has been perceived, diagnosed, and discussed in different ways throughout history. Stuart Murray, in *Representing Autism*, analyzes contemporary cultural representations of autism (from the 1990s to the mid-2000s) through fiction, film, and various other media.[1] Each of these representations has historical antecedents, grounded in research and autism advocacy. Looking at the historical development of autism helps us to understand better the ways in which autism is conceptualized today and why we may hold to certain views of autism.

In the preface, Murray discusses a photograph that is on the front cover of his book. The photograph was taken in 1966 by Jane Brown at a school for children with learning disabilities, and it depicts two girls on a swing boat. Murray discusses the picture in relation to the many questions it raises. Are the girls sad? Have they "retreated into themselves"? Are they actually enjoying themselves? Each of these questions betrays a particular view on autism and, more broadly, on disabilities. The answer to the question of what autism *is*, therefore, reveals as much as, or even more, about the ones answering the question within their cultural and historical context as it does about autism itself. The first purpose of the chapter, therefore, is to make us aware that what we might think about the shape and identity of autism is determined by certain theories and that these theories are not the only possibilities for understanding autism.

Taking a skeptic's view, does it follow that all answers are relative and nothing "true" can be said about autism? Arguably, such skepticism is not justified. Perspectives have changed and are changing over time, yet all of them are still perspectives on something that is recognizable as a particular condition.[2] In other words, autism is not merely "in the eye of the beholder" but a real and particular way of being in the world. As we will see in this chapter, autism research has shaped the concept of autism as much as it has tried to understand it.[3] Therefore, research cannot be ignored but should be appreciated for what it does to shape the understanding of autism. For the purposes of this book, research will be listened to in order to hear the ways in which it can help to demonstrate the value of autistic worshippers as indispensable members of our faith communities. As Murray concludes his discussion of Brown's photograph, "Above all . . . the girls in Brown's photograph are *present*, and it is the fact of their presence that needs to be reckoned with, understood and listened to."[4] It is indeed the presence of autism that causes us to wonder, reflect, research, and theologize. The presence of autism in the church, in the worship service, is one to be "reckoned with, understood and listened to," and we may add that this is to appreciate both the challenges and the gifts that autism may bring to the church. Moreover, even if the way autism is perceived does reside in the eye of the beholder, then it is even more important to be aware of (at least to some extent) the various perceptions because they all have their influence in academy, society, and church alike. Ian Hacking points out that the different perspectives—some based on "thin" and others on "thick" descriptions—"make up" different autistic people.[5] Sometimes different perspectives can be held by one and the same person.[6] It is important, therefore, to be aware of the perspectives at work (the "making up of people") in the study and cultural appropriation of autism, in order to see more clearly the possible contribution of a theological perspective and its overlap with other perspectives. This is the second purpose of this chapter.

The history of autism is not an easy read. Some views on autism are denigrating and dehumanizing. Nevertheless, as renowned autism scholars Sue Fletcher-Watson and Francesca Happé write, "The often-upsetting history of autism research and practice is essential reading for anyone choosing to specialise in the field. While we designate it as 'history,' many autistic adults today were raised in this context, and psychogenic theories still have a harmful influence in some parts of the world."[7] Even without "specializing in the field," in order to understand autism and the place it can have in faith communities, it is necessary to have some historical background. Moreover, Fletcher-Watson and Happé point to the pastoral need for understanding what some autistic people might have been through in terms of "harmful influences" caused by misunderstandings—by professionals or wider society. Therefore, even though the history of autism is upsetting indeed at times, it is required reading.

As Murray shows in his book, contemporary cultural representations of autism often reveal vestiges of theories that the academy might view as outdated. Penni Winter, autistic herself, states,

> Autism as a diagnosis—as opposed to the actual condition—has been around since the 1940s and Asperger's since the early 1990s. Yet what have we gained? What real understanding is out there? As we look around in 2012, misconceptions, misunderstandings, maltreatment and downright dangerous fallacies about autism are rife.[8]

Winter goes on to dispel some of the common myths surrounding autism, such as the view that autistic people lack empathy, have obsessive interests, and are "empty." Ultimately, such views reinforce, lead to, or stem from the underlying belief that autism somehow "buries" the real, normal self underneath. Autism, in this way, is seen as subnormal, and consequently the autistic person is seen as of lesser worth or even subhuman. Such a view might sound extreme, and perhaps it is, but unfortunately there are many testimonies from autistic people who have felt (or feel) treated this way. Winter shows that such beliefs underpin the "normalization" discourse and therapies, where the "ultimate goal is simply to rid the individual of any outward sign of their Autism."[9] That is not to say that all therapists buy into such beliefs, of course. Winter recognizes that some parents and therapists have the best intentions for the autistic person to grow "*as an autistic person*," an approach that Winter calls maximization.[10] It is important, however, to be aware of the negative views on autism. Even if the extreme forms of normalization will, perhaps, not be exposed loudly (although they sometimes are), the normalization discourse and its therapies are still very common. The third purpose of this chapter is to create space for a view that debunks unhelpful, negative attitudes toward autism and sees more positive aspects instead. This is not to deny the challenges that autism can bring, either for autistic people themselves or their family members, but that the theological starting point for thinking about autism should not be one that is negatively framed from the outset.[11]

The church is not exempt from misunderstanding autistic people or from harboring questionable views.[12] The extreme form can be seen in spiritually concerning (if not downright abusive) practices such as exorcising the "demon of autism." Less extreme forms, as in "normalization," are very common in churches. Just think of the fact that all people are expected to behave and talk in certain ways, to follow the liturgical and stylistic pattern of that particular worshipping community, or simply to be silent and sit still. The description of the church in Singapore in chapter 6 will demonstrate that it is exactly this kind of "normalization" that keeps many autistic people and their families devoid of a spiritual home. For a pastorally and theologically responsible and for a life-giving response to autism in the church, there is a need to go beyond accommodation and inclusion and instead to foster belonging and value the gifts of autistic individuals. To do this well, it is necessary to look first at the history of autism and see where some popular ideas about autism originate. The fourth purpose of this chapter is to highlight some key developments of this history.

This chapter introduces some key points and names in the history of autism. It does not offer an exhaustive history, nor does it even aim to cover all the important moments in the development of the concept.[13] By offering a few selected names and developments, it aims to introduce the reader to some necessary historical background, but perhaps more importantly, the chapter aims to show how autism is a concept that was not discovered but created. The ways in which autism is viewed today are not only the direct result of much more than a constellation of diagnostic traits but rather of the academic, social, and political context in which those who were writing about autism found themselves. The first section introduces three autism researchers who have shaped the concept of autism more than anyone else: Leo Kanner, Hans Asperger, and Lorna Wing. The second section looks at two factors in the development of autism that cannot be missed: the role of parents and of autistic people themselves. A brief third section offers some reflections on how to interpret the making of the autism concept.

AUTISM IN THE MAKING

The "invention" of the concept of autism is usually credited to Hans Asperger and Chaim Leib (Leo) Kanner. However, the term "autism" was first coined in 1911 by Eugen Bleuler, a German psychiatrist.[14]

Bleuler used the term to refer to a symptom observed in extreme cases of schizophrenia (another term that he coined). In terms of its etymology, Bleuler referred to Sigmund Freud's idea of "autoerotism." Freud used this latter term to "describe hallucinatory thinking in conjunction with self-soothing in a stage of thinking that preceded the infant's engagement with external reality."[15] Bleuler similarly used the term "autism" in relation to the loss of a sense of reality. In this way, autism was related to a pathological process of infantile thinking, one that had to do with some form of inability to connect to the external reality. This in turn was also linked to adult psychopathology because (what was perceived to be) pathological processes of the mind in adults were linked to (normal) infantile mental development, with hallucination being one of the hallmarks of adult psychopathology. Bonnie Evans comments,

> Although Freud and Bleuler's readiness to match pathological thought in adults with normal infantile thought may appear strange, it was, of course, part of a bold new project to think of the origins of mental illness and to frame this in relation to a model of the unconscious understood through the logic of instinctive drives.[16]

Given this origin of the concept of autism, or at least because autism was discussed in these terms, it is not surprising that Freudian psychoanalytical theories had a huge impact on the development of the concept. The term "autism" was used alongside, and sometimes interchangeably with, "childhood schizophrenia," "childhood psychosis," "autoerotism," "subnormality," and "mental deficiency."[17] According to Evans, the Freudian impact lasted until the 1960s, when radically different models of child psychology—and therefore of autism—were developed. It was then also that the concept and condition increasingly gained attention from academics and politicians alike.

Evans argues that the study of autism and the development of the concept were strongly tied in with political, educational, and therefore societal developments. For example, the Boer War in South Africa led some people to believe in "the supposed 'deterioration' of the British race as well as the instabilities of the British Empire."[18] It was therefore of utmost importance to get rid of "feebleminded" persons or "idiots" and "mental defects" in society (at that point in time, these terms included autistic people). This was grist to the mill of the eugenics movement, a movement that exerted a strong influence on policy and research.[19] A second example is the distinction that was made between the mentally deficient and the mentally ill. The former group was considered as societal ballast and institutionalized in so-called colonies. Those interested in child development were not considering children in such institutions as it was thought that nothing could be learned from them. Intelligence tests were being developed (starting with Alfred Binet in France) and refined, and only those with an IQ of 70 or more were deemed worthy to participate in research.

> All psychological measurements and tests from the 1920s and 1930s ... were concerned with the measurement of normal intelligence and normal developmental stages. Any children who did not come up to the listed standards were simply regarded as "backward," merely a less developed version of a normal child, and their psychological processes were not thought to have any intrinsic value in and of themselves. ... The "social" world constructed in these tests was therefore one without any "defects."[20]

Society was structured hierarchically, and research focused on those in the "higher" strata of society.[21] The effect was, as Evans points out, that a "hugely significant section of the population" was left out in psychological studies, a situation that lasted well until the 1950s.[22] These are but two examples, one pointing to the political context and the other to the socioscientific paradigms at work. They show that the concept of autism, or any other medical concept for that matter, did not originate in some neutral vacuum or with so-called academic objectivity but was and is tied in with the wider context.

The early use of "autism" and related concepts by Bleuler and others shows that when Leo Kanner wrote his oft-cited paper "Autistic Disturbances of Affective Contact" in 1943, he did not exactly develop a new psychiatric concept. As a matter of fact, both Evans and Silberman are rather critical of Kanner's role in the debate. In her lengthy book, Evans spends hardly two pages on Kanner's contribution. She argues that Kanner's article did not propose anything new theoretically. The (only) unique feature of Kanner's paper was that it described, in detail, the autistic condition in a particular group of people. The paper was contested, as was his definition of autism. Nevertheless, the reason why Kanner became well known, according to Evans, is that he wrote the first textbook on child psychiatry in the English language.[23] Silberman does discuss Kanner more extensively, pointing to several other contributions Kanner made, but also making the point that Kanner defined autism very narrowly in order to be able to distinguish it from the well-known diagnosis of childhood schizophrenia. Without such a narrow definition,

Kanner could not have boasted the "rarity" of the condition, as something distinct from child schizophrenia. However, his paper did not gain a lot of traction in the beginning, perhaps because he overstated his case. Pushback came from other scholars (e.g., Lauretta Bender and Louise Despert). Kanner was willing to adjust his proposals and soon subsumed his concept of early infantile autism under the childhood schizophrenia banner.[24] That said, in whatever way one evaluates Kanner's work and academic choices, it is undeniable that he became an influential figure in his own time and remains one of the influential names that is associated with autism.

The other name that is usually associated with the origins of autism is that of Hans Asperger. Working at the child clinic hospital in Vienna, Asperger and his team made detailed observation of the behavior of their patients, whom they called *Autistischen Psychopathen*.[25] Asperger proposed this term in his 1944 *Habilitationsschrift*, a major piece of academic writing. He did not claim to use a new term but referred to Bleuler's previous usage.[26] Like Kanner, Asperger described some cases in detail (Kanner described eleven children, Asperger four) and reflected on them at length. Asperger held some views on autism that were more helpful than Kanner, to which we will turn shortly. However, Asperger's paper was largely forgotten about for decades—perhaps partly because it was written in German and not translated into English—before it was "discovered" and popularized by Lorna Wing in the late 1970s and early 1980s.[27] This meant that Kanner was able to dominate the field of autism research up to that point.

Kanner's dominance in the field had consequences for the direction in which the concept developed. Nick Chown and Liz Hughes observe,

> It was Kanner's insistence on infantile autism which was a major part of the disservice done by Kanner to autistic people, and their families and other carers, because it implied that it was something of relevance only to children, thus denying recognition or support to autistic adults for several decades. Another important issue was Kanner's very narrow definition of his syndrome; "extreme autistic aloneness," present from birth, and an "anxiously obsessive desire for the maintenance of sameness," which effectively excluded very many of the children who Asperger would have recognised as being on the autistic continuum. Asperger regarded the range of manifestations of autistic traits as being on a continuum, and that these traits were not uncommon in the population whereas Kanner regarded them as rare.[28]

Chown and Hughes point to what we saw above—that is, the very narrow definition that Kanner used for autism. Furthermore, by limiting the condition to childhood—even by its very name, *early infantile autism*—older children and adults were excluded from the diagnosis. By contrast, Asperger saw that the particular way in which autism comes to expression in an individual might change over time but also that it was a condition that was not going to go away and that it was not something that could be "cured."

Kanner's "hegemony" of the concept had another devastating effect.[29] While Kanner at first believed the condition to be inborn, he kept the door open for another possibility: autism as caused by cold-hearted parents. The theory of the "refrigerator mother," which became especially popular through the work of Bruno Bettelheim,[30] found unequivocal support in Kanner and his close companion Leon Eisenberg.[31] Once again, we can contrast this with Asperger, who also saw family patterns, seeing autistic traits in the parents of some of the autistic children, but described these patterns as potentially helpful because parents and children could find common ground in their unusual ways of thinking and behaving.[32] Asperger described "autistic psychopathology" as that: psychopathology, understood as "abnormality of personality."[33] Autism for Asperger is a disease of the psyche, and he writes about it in medical terms.

Given contemporary views on autism as a (neurological) difference rather than a deficit, disorder, or disability, it should be more than a footnote to the history of autism that Asperger saw some positives of the condition. Yet, as we have seen, it was not more than a footnote for decades. Arguably, the introduction of Asperger's work to the English-speaking world, roughly from the 1980s onward, is related to a more positive look on autism. Based on Asperger's insights, people with average or higher intelligence began to also receive autism diagnoses, just as Asperger included people with an average of above-average intelligence in his sample. Moreover, the children in Asperger's sample did not necessarily exhibit verbal difficulties, again in contrast to Kanner. The (re)discovery of Asperger's work led to widened criteria for the autism diagnosis. From the 1980s, more diagnosed people were better able to speak for themselves, which changed the autism landscape dramatically, as we shall see in the next section. Along with Chown and Hughes, we are left to wonder whether the ideas about the concept of autism would have taken different turns, more beneficial to those who would now identify as autistic, if Asperger's work had been more widely acknowledged sooner.[34]

However, Asperger's legacy has proven recently to be more ambiguous than the above discussion shows. Archival work by Herwig Czech in Vienna, the city where Asperger lived and worked, shows the extent to which Asperger was entangled within the Nazi regime.[35] The emerging picture is not straightforward, which has resulted in different interpretations of Asperger's involvement in the Nazi program and its "final solution"—the killing of anyone who did not have *Gemüt*, and anyone who was not likely to ever going to have Gemüt, by education or otherwise. In her in-depth treatment of Asperger in his sociopolitical context, Edith Sheffer explains the term "Gemüt": it referred to one's capacity of social belonging and one's community spirit. In other words, it referred to "one's fundamental capacity to form deep bonds with other people. It had metaphysical and social connotations."[36] Having Gemüt was essential, not just for one's individual health but first and foremost for the health of the *Volk* (the people). The collective was primary over the individual, and one's value depended on whether one could contribute to the collective, as defined by the Nazi ideology. At the time, German psychiatrists were tasked with diagnosing the people that they saw in terms of their capacity for Gemüt and their potential contribution to the Reich. This is an important aspect of the background to Asperger's theories and actions. The key determinator for access to further treatment became this capacity for Gemüt. With this in mind, some consider Asperger to be a rescuer of children, others a determined perpetrator, while others consider him to be only a passive follower of the Nazi regime.[37]

The emerging picture is ambiguous. For example, it appears that Asperger fought for some children, while there were others whom he was happy to send to Am Spiegelgrund. Am Spiegelgrund was the children's death clinic of Nazi Vienna, where their "euthanasia" program was executed. This was a public secret. While the active killing by neglect, and by injecting a lethal mix of medicine, would perhaps be denied in public, the practice was well known within Viennese medical and psychiatric circles. It is likely that Asperger knew that when he referred some of his patients to Am Spiegelgrund, there was a real possibility that they would not survive the institution.[38] This was not the only way in which historical records show that Asperger was, passively, involved in the Nazi's euthanasia program. Sheffer summarizes Asperger's involvement with the Nazi regime:

> His decisions not to join the Nazi Party and to remain a dedicated Catholic were difficult and unusual choices for someone in Asperger's position, yet he opted to participate in myriad organizations and

institutions that promoted the political tenets, racial hygiene policies, and systematic killings of the Third Reich. High-ranking Nazi Party officials and colleagues deemed Asperger reliable and trusted him with sensitive information. Top euthanasia figures in Vienna included Asperger in their inner circle as well as in the leadership of their field.[39]

The emerging picture is ambiguous. It is a picture of someone who did not actively participate in the killing, but by his involvement in the structures and policies of his day and place—an involvement that *was* active and conscious—his actions had devastating consequences for some of the people in his care. What this means for the contemporary discussion on autism is not yet clear. Asperger has undeniably made an impact on the autism concept, especially since the 1980s and 1990s through the work of Lorna Wing. The diagnostic label "Asperger's syndrome" has already disappeared from *DSM-5* and *ICD-11*, albeit for other reasons. Some would now say they will not use that label anymore, while others continue to refer to themselves as Aspies (see discussion below).[40]

The 1960s were a watershed in the development of the concept of autism. Evans even speaks of the "metamorphosis of autism" that took place in those years and about the "first" and the "new autism." Instead of "affective withdrawal" explained by psychoanalysts, linguistic differences (seen as deficits) became the central feature of autism. New scientific research methods and studies were an important factor in this change of understanding. The first longitudinal studies in autism were conducted, which showed that affective withdrawal often lessened but that autism's impact on language and intellectual performance persisted. The explanation of these two factors was turned around: the linguistic problems were now thought not to be the consequence of social impairments but the cause of them.[41] In a 1968 publication, Michael Rutter, a prominent autism researcher in the second half of the twentieth century, concluded after a review of different theories, "Of all the hypotheses concerning the nature of autism, that which places the primary defect in terms of a language or coding problem appears most promising. It is suggested that many of the manifestations of autism are explicable in terms of cognitive and perceptual defects."[42] However, it was not strictly language that took center stage but handling symbols, which is necessary for, and therefore had repercussions on, the processing of verbal and nonverbal communication and therefore on social interaction.[43] So much is clear to Rutter that "contrary to earlier views, infantile autism is *not* anything to do with schizophrenia, and is *not* primarily a disorder of social relationships."[44] In the first half of the twentieth century, psychoanalytical theories dominated autism studies, in particular in the United Kingdom (in the United States, behaviorism was more popular); it was common for psychologists to speculate on autism as a stage—either normal or abnormal—of development of thought in infants. This changed in the 1960s, when definitions of autism with clear diagnostic criteria were needed in order to conduct epidemiological studies, rather than psychoanalytical theories that lacked empirical evidence. A new era for autism studies had dawned, both in terms of methodologies and the meaning of the concept itself.[45]

Evans sums up the radical shift in perception of autism:

> The new "autism" that was developed during the 1960s had the *exact opposite* meaning of that which had prevailed until the end of the 1950s. Whereas autism and its conceptual cousins—primary narcissism, autoerotism, etc.—had previously always referred to hallucinatory dreamlike imaginary thought that preceded the establishment of realistic thinking, "autism" from the 1960s was used to refer to a *lack* of imagination, a *lack* of hallucinatory thought, a *lack* of creativity and a *lack* of dreams. It was a concept that was predicated on the *absence* of imagination. "Autism" of the 1960s thus became the kernel for describing the development of subjectivity in infants and children, yet it also referred to a state of mind that completely lacked any content or any meaning of its own and which gained its meaning only via the instruments used to measure it.[46]

The first part of this quote underlines pointedly what was discussed above—that is, the reversal of how autism was understood and explained. The second part of the quote, especially the last sentence, is an important addition to this discussion, as it goes right to the heart of what we think a(n) (autistic) human being is—or is not when defined in terms of what is lacking. From the beginning of autism studies, autistic people were not much thought of. On both sides of the Atlantic Ocean, autistic children were readily institutionalized and treated as a burden to society. In the spirit of the eugenics movement of the early 1920s and beyond, they were often sterilized. The distinction between mentally deficient and mentally ill, as we saw above, meant that children in the former category (which included many on the autism spectrum) were not counted worthy to be included in research. The cultural climate changed after World War II. In the United Kingdom, long-stay institutions for children closed, and education for the "ineducable" was established as part of the Mental Health Act 1959.[47] However, the radical shift in theorizing autism, from hallucination to "a state of mind that completely lacked any content or any meaning of its own" can hardly be seen as an improvement in the perception of autistic people. Moreover, to claim that a person's state of mind gains only meaning "via instruments used to measure it" is an instance of highly questionable academic hubris.

It is worth noting at this point that vestiges of this theory are still present today, especially when autistic people are thought to be "empty." Penni Winter sharply criticizes this theory for it views autistic people as "not properly human." It is worth quoting her at length:

> Our lives are definitely, definitely not empty, and *we* are not empty, not soulless, not unfeeling, not devoid of all the things that make a person "human." We live, we laugh, we love, we give, we care, we bleed—oh how we bleed.
>
> The core of Autism is not an emptiness, but a unique way of being, of thinking and feeling, of relating and reacting to the world. *In itself*, this way of being has as much value, as much of a right to exist and to reach its full potential, and as much to contribute, as being neurotypical has. It is simply *different*.[48]

Winter and other autism advocates have an important voice in the contemporary debate. However, in the 1960s, this was not the case, and so, in a real sense, autism was what researchers decided it to be. Although research still has a huge influence on the conception of autism and the subsequent eligibility for financial and other support, the voice of autistic people themselves is much more important now than it was sixty years ago.

The next watershed moment in the understanding and shaping of autism occurred in the late 1970s and 1980s. The landmark publication of this era was the article by Lorna Wing and Judith Gould in 1979 in which they proposed that the key to understanding and defining autism was what came to be known the "triad of impairments."[49] In an additional article published soon afterward, in 1981, Wing argued that "the abnormalities of social interaction, verbal and nonverbal communication, and imaginative activities so consistently occurred together . . . that they could be referred to as 'the triad of social and language impairment.'"[50] Autism now had changed completely, from a stage in child development with links to hallucination into a category of social functioning. From that point on, social development became the driving force for understanding autism. The allure of this theory, as Evans explains, "was due to the fact that it quantified domains of psychological knowledge that had previously been attributed to 'unconscious' mental processes that affected mental function. These processes were now reclassified as kinds of 'social impairment.'"[51] Furthermore, Wing developed tools and measures to aid experimental and quantitative studies. Wing's model was attractive for several reasons, two of them being that it was quite straightforward and had explanatory power. It was soon picked up at both a political and scientific level and became highly influential.[52]

As mentioned above, through the work of Lorna Wing, the views of Hans Asperger were (re)introduced to the world of autism research. Wing discovered the work of Asperger and introduced the term "Asperger's syndrome" in 1981.[53] A decade later, Uta Frith published a translation of Asperger's 1944 publication in a book discussing his views.[54] The views of Asperger, filtered through the work of Wing, Frith, and other scholars became increasingly influential. The publication of *DSM-IV* in 1994 included Asperger's syndrome as a distinct diagnosis, further popularizing its use.

To understand the development of the autism discourse from this moment onward, including a possible explanation for the popularity of the term "Asperger's" in the autistic community, we need to pick up on a point that was mentioned above—namely, that Asperger saw some aspects of the condition in a positive light. As Silverman writes,

> [Asperger] thought that these children could grow to be successful in professional life despite their social oddities, and that they showed no evidence of cognitive disability. Rather, they demonstrated potential for great creativity and originality in their thought processes, "as if they had compensatory abilities to counter-balance their deficiencies," such as their ability to focus narrowly on topics of special interest.[55]

As we saw above, how Asperger's views on the capacities of children should be evaluated is a matter that will need discussion in light of the recent findings about his ambiguous role in the Nazi program that valued people for what they could contribute to society. A utilitarianism—and a nasty one for that—slips into view of autism that is contrary to a theological understanding of what it means to be human. The history of autism should not be reread only in terms of Asperger's position vis-à-vis the Nazi regime but also of what that means for how he saw autism (and other conditions). Whatever the outcomes of such a rereading of history would be, the differences between Kanner and Asperger are important for the history of autism in itself and for understanding the development of the concept, in particular the more positive approach to autism, which in turn impacted the autism communities and neurodiversity movement (to which we shall turn shortly).

One question that is still being debated is Wing's argument that Kanner and Asperger were speaking about the same condition. Whereas Wing saw Kanner's and Asperger's autism as on a continuum of the same condition, this was not accepted by everyone, including Asperger himself.[56] For example, Berend Verhoeff is critical of Wing's views, pointing out that the similarities between Kanner and Asperger notwithstanding, they do differ significantly in some respects. Kanner's infantile autism was closely related to psychotic states, which is very different from Asperger's understanding of the condition as an "abnormal personality." Verhoeff states that "in contrast, Wing argued that Asperger's cases and Kanner's cases were essentially similar. Despite the variations in terms of severity of impairments, Wing argued that both disorders shared a common and essential characteristic: the impairment of two-way social interaction."[57] As we have seen above, social interaction, as part of more encompassing social impairment, is the key to understanding autism, according to Wing. Even if Wing and others have seen more similarities than differences between Kanner and Asperger, the introduction of Asperger to the English-speaking world changed the autism landscape. The understanding of autism widened, with children and adults receiving a diagnosis of autism (or Asperger's syndrome between 1994 and 2013—the life span of *DSM-IV*) when previously they would have fallen outside the diagnostic criteria of autism. However, Asperger's syndrome as an official diagnosis was shelved in less than twenty years, when the *DSM-V*, published in 2013, amalgamated the distinct diagnosis of "Asperger's syndrome" within the all-embracing diagnosis of "autism spectrum disorder."

Even if the official diagnosis of Asperger's syndrome was short lived, since the 1990s, the views of Asperger did not only influence the research community but also the autism community. Asperger's became an identity marker for some autistic people, who still sometimes call themselves Aspies. The significance of the name and diagnosis is demonstrated in an article by David Giles, written at the time that the new classification of autism in *DSM-5* was proposed. Giles analyzed discussion fora of online autism communities in order to find out what their response was to the proposed *DSM-5* change from distinctive diagnoses to an all-encompassing idea of a spectrum. Giles found various responses, with quite a few people supporting or even embracing the idea of a spectrum. Others, however, were concerned that the number of diagnoses would fall, with the consequence of fewer people being entitled to support. Furthermore, some aligned their identity with the specific diagnosis. Giles writes, "Along with diagnosis comes personal identity, and for some, the potential loss of the label brings fears for their own selfhood."[58] For some, being an Aspie had become their identity.

Kristen Linton and her team have come to similar conclusions as Giles. They also point to the fear of underdiagnosis and the subsequent lack of access to support services. Their analysis of the discussion forum on *WrongPlanet*, one of the most well-known online platforms of the autistic community, showed also how diagnosis and identity are interrelated. Even though the online discussion on "higher functioning" was couched in terms of the validity of the *DSM-5* diagnostic criteria, it "can also be perceived as an identity issue among people with AS [Asperger's syndrome]."[59] Linton et al. advise social workers to reassure their clients that their identity is not equal to their diagnosis.

> While some people might relate and proudly identify with AS or AD [autistic disorder], clients should know that, even though their diagnosis may change over time, they are still the same person regardless of their diagnosis. Social workers should remember and remind clients that a diagnosis does not define a person holistically. Social workers may want to reiterate to clients and the community that the ASD diagnosis does not define abilities or disabilities of people who receive the diagnosis and that intelligence is not a part of the ASD diagnosis.[60]

While Linton and her team may be right that a diagnosis in itself does not define a person's abilities, their well-intended comments may in fact invalidate a person's self-image when that person has come to identify him- or herself with a particular "label." The fact that the proposed diagnostic criteria were debated in the autism community demonstrates that the "label" is more than a diagnosis. The diagnostic criteria may change, but an identity has been formed around the label "Aspie," which is sometimes worn with pride. Yet others in the community are happy with the new proposals, seeming to agree with Linton's statement above. Is this because they have claimed a particular identity, as Aspie or otherwise, that they are comfortable enough for the diagnostic criteria to be changed? They know that they will always be Aspies anyway. Perhaps it is not the diagnosis but the identity constructed around that diagnosis, epitomized by a particular label or name, that identifies a person holistically.

This section has introduced some significant moments in the defining and shaping of our concept of autism. These moments are only the tip of the iceberg in the complex history of autism. They serve not only as an introduction to some key points in autism's history, but they also demonstrate that autism is a concept that is socially constructed. That is not to say that there is no meaning in it or that it only exists in the minds of researchers or in the practices of professional support workers, as if there are no distinguishable ways of experiencing and being in the world. What it does mean is that there are different ways of understanding, researching, and responding to this way of being in the world that we call autism and that these ways are often—if not always—influenced by the social, political, national, and academic context of the persons involved. We now turn to one important factor in the history of autism that we have not yet mentioned explicitly but has had, and still has, great influence: parents of autistic people and autistic people themselves.

PARENTS AND AUTISTIC PEOPLE

Our overview of the history of autism, with the aim to show how the concept of autism is shaped by historical contexts, will be deepened by looking at an important factor that impacted the historical development of autism research and available support: the role of parents of autistic people and then of autistic people themselves. Chloe Silverman, in her history of autism, demonstrates the critical role parents have played.[61] This role included parents' political advocacy work for education tailored to the needs of their children as well as parents' participation in research—sometimes being or becoming researchers themselves. Referring to Silverman, Giles claims that "in conjunction with various academics, clinicians and other professionals, it has been the parents of individuals with autism who have shaped the history of the condition."[62] However, the history of parents and autism begins on a rather bleak note. At one time in history, several scholars, including Asperger and Kanner, blamed the parents for being "coldhearted," which was even posited as the cause for autism.

Mothers, in particular, were blamed. For example, in the 1940s, John Bowlby saw maternal deprivation as one of the causes for all kinds of psychological anomalies.[63] Kanner wrote of the parents of autistic children that they themselves "had been reared sternly in emotional refrigerators,"[64] which impacted the way they raised their (autistic) children.

> Most of the patients were exposed from the beginning to parental coldness, obsessiveness, and a mechanical type of attention to material needs only. They were the objects of observation and experiment conducted with an eye on fractional performance rather than with genuine warmth and enjoyment. They were kept neatly in refrigerators

which did not defrost. Their withdrawal seems to be an act of turning away from such a situation to seek comfort in solitude.[65]

The "objects of observation and experiment" is a nod to Kanner's observation that most parents of the children who were referred to him were highly educated and held academic positions. Of course, only those with networks in the upper levels of society would have been able to have their child referred to Kanner. A second thing to note is Kanner's mention of withdrawal from the social environment. It is not difficult to see how such withdrawal plays into the notion of parental coldness. While Kanner may have used the term "refrigerator" first, Donvan and Zucker note that the idea of the "refrigerator mother" was later popularized by Bruno Bettelheim, even if he never used the term himself.[66] Expanding on Kanner's suggestions in his 1967 book *The Empty Fortress*, Bettelheim argued that autistic children in fact wanted to reach out to other people but were hindered by parental failure at a key stage in the children's development.[67] The theory has been discredited now, but it has done much damage to generations of mothers and fathers. Moreover, Murray argues that the vestiges of the theory are present with us today in the way autism is represented in media, film, and literature. Either in the role of bogeyman-like characters or the opposite, as "saviors," parents, especially mothers, play a key role in cultural representations of autism.[68]

However, there is a much more positive story to tell about parental influence on the course of autism's history, even though that story has its own points of critique.[69] It should be noted that Kanner himself left the door open for critiquing the idea of "parental coldness." In the conclusion to his 1949 paper from which I just quoted, he says that "one is also entitled to wonder why some of these parents have been able to rear other children who did not withdraw." Two decades later, Kanner seemingly distanced himself from the theory.[70] Meanwhile, it was to be expected that some parents would push back on the theory. Their passionate advocacy for their children itself discredits the theory of parental coldheartedness, and of course, parents of an autistic child know all too well that they love their child dearly. The story of what is now called the National Autistic Society in the United Kingdom is an example of how parents joined forces to support and advocate for their children.

In 1958, Sybil Elgar visited a school for "severely and emotionally disturbed children." Horrified by how the children were treated, she went back in 1960 to see if anything had changed, which it had not. Two years later, she started her own school in her basement, based on alternative educational principles. It soon grew so popular that they had to look for bigger premises. In 1965, with the help of the Society for Autistic Children, Elgar was able to buy and convert an old railway hostel and continue to develop her groundbreaking program.[71] In the same year that the school was founded, Elgar and the group of parents who supported and collaborated with her founded the Autistic Children's Aid Society of North London, which by the following year was already established as a national body and renamed the Society for Autistic Children. They contested the idea that their children were "ineducable" and advocated with the government to put in place education for autistic children.

The group also became instrumental in raising public awareness and called for improvement of scientific research on autism.[72] One of the pupils of the school was Susie Wing, daughter of John and Lorna Wing—the same Lorna Wing who later made such strides in redefining the concept of autism. The Wings were not only parents of an autistic daughter but were also psychiatrists at the renowned Institute of Psychiatry in London, where much of the autism research between the 1950s and 1970s—a critical period in redefining autism—took place. They joined the society and were key contributors to its work. Their advocacy work with the Society for Autistic Children became a significant factor in the change of education policies in the United Kingdom during that time.[73] In 1966, the society changed its name to the National Society for Autistic Children, followed by another name change in 1975 to the National Autistic Society, which is the biggest autism organization in the United Kingdom.[74] The society's initial logo, a jigsaw piece, became a well-known symbol of autism parent organizations.[75] Meanwhile, just three years after the founding of the Autistic Children's Aid Society of North London, Bernard Rimland, researcher and parent of an autistic child, started a similar organization in the United States together with other parents and researchers. This society was called the National Society for Autistic Children, later called the Autism Society.[76] The story of the National Autistic Society and its American equivalent are two examples of how parent groups have influenced the course of the history of autism.

The instrumental role of parents in the shaping of autism research and policy was not without controversy. In the late 1980s and 1990s, some people who identified as autistic themselves started to criticize the parents' role. A landmark moment occurred in a speech given by Jim Sinclair in 1993 at a conference for parents of autistic children in Toronto. Sinclair had been to such conferences before but felt increasingly uncomfortable at them. This time, he got to the stage and delivered a paper that changed the way of thinking about autism, at least for some. Sinclair's message to the parents was that the problem with autism was not autism itself but the parents' desire to cure it. Sinclair asserted that autism was not something to cure. The grief that parents had was grief for lost hopes and shattered dreams for their child, which came when they learned that their child would probably not reach the common developmental milestones and stages of life. That did not mean that their child was unhappy, hence Sinclair's famous instruction to the parents: "Don't mourn for us."[77] Sinclair argued that autism was not something people *have* but something people *are*.

> Autism is a way of being. It is not possible to separate the person from the autism. Therefore, when parents say, "I wish my child did not have autism," what they're really saying is, "I wish the autistic child I have did not exist, and I had a different (non-autistic) child instead." Read that again. This is what we hear when you mourn over our existence.[78]

Further in the paper, Sinclair drove home the point again: "The tragedy is not that we're here, but that your world has no place for us to be. How can it be otherwise, as long as our own parents are still grieving over having brought us into the world?"[79] In his speech, Sinclair did not deny the parents' grief but assigned to it a different cause—it was grief for the child the parents expected but never got. He suggested, therefore, that this grieving should not be expressed at autism conferences but at bereavement and counseling groups. Moreover, he did not deny that autistic children need support, and he invited parents to give that support. "But don't mourn for *us*."[80]

Sinclair traveled widely to autism conferences with his message, which was welcomed by some and opposed by others. Another development, occurring at the same time and partly at the conferences that Sinclair attended, was that more and more autistic people started to gather and create networks for autistic people themselves. Beyond gathering at conferences, these networks made use of the new technological possibilities that the internet brought. Within time, many digital platforms for autistic people were launched. One of the most well-known of these is WrongPlanet, started by teenagers Alex Plank and Dan Grover. The physical gatherings and the internet fora had two distinct but related features that were missing from any other autism event. At conferences where autistic people gathered, they found an acceptance with each other that was otherwise unknown to them. Often, they would make sure that they had "autism-only" rooms, and by the very nature of autism, all kinds of behavior that was usually socially unacceptable was acceptable here. It was okay to sit quietly in a corner, flap your hands, for example. It was okay to be yourself. Digitally, something similar went on. Because words were the only thing that were visible on the screen, autistic people did not need to comply with unspoken social rules or nonverbal behavior that might be confusing. The internet opened up space for many to interact with others in ways that were otherwise uncomfortable or very difficult.[81]

Sinclair and others who followed his argument were especially critical of the dominant view that autism was a bad thing that needed to be cured. Autism is different, not less, they would say. Their philosophy was one of "neurodiversity." While that term is quite common now, certainly within the autism community, it was coined only in the 1990s. Judy Singer is often credited for having coined the term in an undergraduate thesis. The term was first used in print by Harvey Blume, when he wrote in *Atlantic* magazine in 1998: "NT [neurotypical] is only one kind of brain wiring, and, when it comes to working with hi-tech, quite possibly an inferior one. . . . Neurodiversity may be every bit as crucial for the human race as biodiversity is for life in general."[82] It took quite a while before the term became popular. Certainly, in mainstream society, autism continued to be viewed as a diagnosis to be dreaded. A turning point came when a campaign that played on that negative sentiment was heavily opposed by a group of autistic self-advocates, called the Autistic Self-Advocacy Network (ASAN), founded and led by the young student Ari Ne'eman.

In December 2007, the New York University (NYU) Child Study Center launched its Ransom Notes campaign with the intention to raise awareness about the, in their view, detrimental effects of autism and other, what they called, psychiatric disorders. The Ransom Notes would be all over New York in newspapers and on billboards. Portraying autism as a kidnapper, one such note read:

<blockquote style="text-align:center">
WE HAVE YOUR SON.
WE WILL MAKE SURE HE WILL
NOT BE ABLE TO CARE FOR
HIMSELF OR INTERACT SOCIALLY
AS LONG AS HE LIVES.
THIS IS ONLY THE BEGINNING.
AUTISM[83]
</blockquote>

Another note read:

> WE HAVE YOUR SON. WE ARE DESTROYING HIS ABILITY
> FOR SOCIAL INTERACTION AND DRIVING HIM
> INTO A LIFE OF COMPLETE ISOLATION.
> IT'S UP TO YOU NOW.
> ASPERGER'S SYNDROME[84]

Ne'eman and his group were outraged by the Ransom Notes. The campaign, building on decades of seeing autism as a problem to be solved and a condition to be cured, gave exactly the opposite message to that of the more recent neurodiversity movement. If autism was a matter of neurological difference rather than of disability, then portraying autism as a kidnapper who will confine the person in solitude and social oddity for the rest of their lives was not just grossly mistaken but also highly offensive. Ne'eman encouraged ASAN members to write letters to the NYU Child Study Center and phone them, asking them to withdraw the campaign and apologize. Ne'eman also contacted disability advocacy groups, who joined his cause. He called the newspapers, who covered the story, and he also called the Child Study Center. Although at first, the director of the study center, Harold Koplewicz, refused to apologize for the campaign, saying that "we should stick with it and ride out the storm," soon the campaign was revoked and the billboards disappeared.[85] The significance of the campaign and countercampaign is stated as follows by Silberman:

> For the first time in history, autistics were challenging a conversation about autism in mainstream media without the help of a parent-run organization that claimed to speak for them. The architect of the protest was not a child, a parent, or an "adult patient," but a smart, savvy, and determined policy wonk named Ari Ne'eman, the nineteen-year-old co-founder of the Autistic Self Advocacy Network.[86]

It was the first time but certainly not the last. ASAN successfully countered other campaigns, often in collaboration with other disability advocacy organizations. Moreover, in 2010, Ne'eman was asked to sit on the National Council on Disability by President Barack Obama. ASAN staff members even played a role in the description of autism in the *DSM-5*.[87] Ne'eman and his network of advocates represented the new movement that started with Sinclair in 1993, redefining once more the shape of autism, this time with the term "neurodiversity," and taking a fundamentally more positive approach to autism.

One more factor that needs to be mentioned in the story of autistic people beginning to speak for themselves is the emergence of publications by autistic people themselves. Several people can be mentioned, but for the purpose of this brief historical overview, it will suffice to name one: Temple Grandin. Struggling throughout childhood, Grandin made it into an academic career and became a well-known name in the world of livestock handling in the United States. In 1986, she wrote her first book on autism titled, *Emergence: Labeled Autistic*.[88] It was groundbreaking in the sense that it was the very first book written by someone who identified as autistic, speaking about her own experiences of growing up autistic. However, it was only at a conference by the National Society for Autistic Children (later the Autism Society of America) in 1987 when she was first invited to speak and do a workshop that she became known in the world of autism. Donvan and Zucker comment on the impact of Grandin's talk: "To the parents, hearing her talk about her experience of autism was like suddenly finding an interpreter fluent in a language that had baffled them for years."[89] Grandin published more books of which perhaps the most well-known is her 1995 *Thinking in Pictures*.[90] Her story featured in Oliver Sacks' bestseller *An Anthropologist on Mars*—the title refers to how Grandin explained she sometimes felt.[91] In 2010, a movie about her life was released: *Temple Grandin*. The movie was nominated for fifteen Emmy Awards, and it won seven.[92]

The neurodiversity movement has become one of the major voices in the field of autism research. The slogan of disability advocates and adopted by Ne'eman, "Nothing about us without us," is now an important consideration in autism research and policymaking. Whereas in 1993, it was considered by many non-autistic people implausible that Grandin, being autistic, had obtained a PhD and worked as an academic, thirty years later it is not uncommon at all. This is partly due to the changed and broadened definition of autism in the revised *DSM-III-R* in 1987 and the 1994 *DSM-IV*, which included Asperger's syndrome, but also due to the neurodiversity movement. Giles suggests that the powerful voice of the autism community might have the potential to "challenge medical authority." He continues, "It may be that such communities come to assume centre stage in future debate over diagnostic categories, or even that scientific and medical concerns for such things as diagnostic accuracy are eventually forced to give way to community interests."[93] Such is the shift that has taken place in the relatively short period from the 1940s when autism was considered a distinct condition for the first time to the early decades of the twenty-first century. Meanwhile, there remains a question as to what extent the neurodiversity movement can speak conclusively for those with high support needs. How are autistic people going to speak up when they are, for example, nonverbal or have severe learning difficulties? To be sure, the neurodiversity movement has claimed (with some good reason) that some of their key messages—for example, the message summarized by Sinclair as "Don't mourn for us"—are equally applicable when it concerns autistic people with high support needs. But many of those people are less likely to be involved in conferences and online fora. That said, a generous view of the neurodiversity movement must acknowledge that the movement has played an important part in highlighting the needs and the gifts of that group too.[94]

The self-advocacy turn in the recent history of autism is a cause for celebration. Meanwhile, the need for parent groups remains, as they serve at least two purposes. First, together with the neurodiversity movement (and autistic people who would not perhaps identify with that movement), they advocate for their autistic children. They raise awareness about the condition and petition for support, something that their children cannot always do. Second, many parents of autistic children feel the need to join a group of parents who understand their challenges and joys. They need a safe environment to be able to tell their stories and also simply ask questions about practicalities—for example, where they can find support for certain issues. Sometimes fierce debates take place between the autistic community and parent groups, and parent groups need to listen to the voices of autistic people themselves. In a best-case scenario, both groups can work together on shared goals.[95]

INTERPRETING THE HISTORY OF AUTISM

Two observations are important for interpreting the history of autism and the publications that document that history. First, the brief overview in this chapter shows that different episodes and periods in the history of autism each have their own emphases and sometimes novel ideas. One should be aware of not only overlap and continuity but also of distinctions and discontinuities. Chloe Silverman, in her book *Understanding Autism*, writes, "It is wrong to imagine that understandings of autism have evolved in a linear fashion, from psychogenic to neurological to genetic models."[96] She gives the example of some well-known autism researchers who have been influential in the shaping of the autism concept, pointing to similarities as well as clear differences between them. In other words, "autism has proven almost infinitely mutable."[97] Berend

Verhoeff gives a similar warning to seeing overlap between concepts where it may not be. He discerns two tendencies in the history writing of autism, two that are sometimes combined. The first is to see the history in terms of continuity, as a linear progression in understanding of the condition. In this view, new theories are basically refinements of previous theories. Verhoeff calls such proposals "positivist histories." One of the problems with such histories is that refined diagnostic criteria are seen in fundamental continuity with those before. However, giving the example of the "triad of impairments," Verhoeff points out that

> the *"extreme autistic aloneness"* mentioned by Kanner . . . is nevertheless quite different from impaired sociability, just as impaired social communication is different from the severe deficits in language development that were illustrated by Kanner, such as complete muteness and (delayed) echolalia. . . . An extreme resistance to changes in restricted routines and rituals or changes in furniture arrangements is again in many ways distinct from the "presences of stereotypes or repetitive behaviors."[98]

These examples demonstrate that although at face value, similar behavior is referred to, when one drills down, quite different observations and interpretations—and ultimately different scientific, cultural, and political views—underpin this terminology.

These differences do not need to lead to relativism. Autism is still a condition that is observable, but the "almost infinite mutability" of the concept should make us critical of any essentializing tendencies. Commenting on the intimate connection between the legal and social setting and the changing of concepts of childhood development, Evans affirms,

> This is not to say that autism is merely a "social construct" without any bearing on the reality of psychological development and its atypicalities. . . . Understanding the broader background and setting in which autism developed provides us with a much more detailed and nuanced understanding of what, exactly, autism is and what it has become. This does not aim to invalidate the category. In fact, it confirms its significance and power, as well as the complexities of its meaning.[99]

Silverman, Verhoeff, Evans, and others demonstrate that the history of autism shows distinctions and even radical changes of the concept of autism, implicitly or explicitly shaped by contextual factors. When we understand this, we do not need to conclude that autism is a construct in the minds of researchers without any value. We do need to say, though, that "Autism is . . ." is not a sentence that can be completed by a single phrase. The task in this book is to offer a theological critique on the phrases suggested when they come up in our discussions, especially when they lead to diminishment of people, their experience of worship, and their contribution to the church. This book is not an attempt to formulate a theological "Autism is . . ." phrase instead; rather, the question is what the lived experience of autism has to contribute to faith communities and (liturgical) theology.

The second observation for interpreting the history of autism also comes from Verhoeff. In addition to "positivist histories," he mentions a second tendency in autism histories that we should be aware of—namely, that of creating "essentializing histories." That is the practice of retrospectively diagnosing historical figures with autism. This push quite often comes from the neurodiversity movement. Newton, Michelangelo, and Einstein, to name but a few, are claimed to have been autistic. Essentializing histories aim at validating, transhistorically, the study of autism based on the theory that autism is a genetic condition. However, such studies are based on circular reasoning:

> It is this assumed trans-historical, essential core of today's autism that is being recognized in the many recent examples of peculiar historical figures, and these historical cases, in turn, support the legitimization of the current "tenacious search for autism's essence" at neurobiological levels. It is only in present times that these peculiar historical figures have become part of the history of autism.[100]

Grant Macaskill refers to the same practice in relation to biblical characters. This is similarly problematic for two reasons. First, Macaskill points to the lengthy and detailed process one has to go through today in order to receive the diagnosis of autism, which includes lengthy interviews with the person themselves as well as with family members. All of that cannot be done with biblical characters obviously (nor with Newton, Michelangelo, or Einstein for that matter). Second, such an approach completely misses the point of what the narrative is trying to do: "Doing so neglects the real character, function, and purpose of the narrative and the discourse, which is to *communicate* to its readers something that will shape their own lives in relation to God."[101] That is not to say that the Bible has nothing to offer to our thinking about autism, but diagnosing biblical characters anachronistically (reading contemporary diagnoses back into the Bible) does justice neither to the condition as we know it today nor to the biblical story itself and therefore misses out on what the story in fact might have to say. To think biblically about autism, we need to go beyond an anachronistic identifying of autism in Scripture. Chapter 4 suggests a way to think theologically about autism.

CONCLUSION

The history of autism reveals a concept that has been defined in different ways throughout history. Where some see continuity from Kanner and Asperger to *DSM-V*, others point to the variations in the definition and understanding of the concept over time. What does the autism landscape look like at the start of the third decade of the twenty-first century? Parallel to the raised awareness of autism, research into the condition has increased in number of projects, scholars, disciplines, and money spent. The disciplinary perspectives and goals of research projects can differ widely. Behaviorist therapists still look for ways to adapt or change autistic behavior, although Lovaas' gruesome methods of the 1960s–1980s are fortunately discredited.[102] Brain research looks for differences between the brains of autistic and non-autistic people in order to locate the neurological patterns of autism. Genetic research looks for hereditary causes of autism.[103] Some researchers accept that autism is a lifelong condition and look for ways to support autistic people as effectively as possible, perhaps even highlighting the strengths and benefits of certain autistic traits. Other researchers still look to find the "real" person that they think is hidden in the shell of autism. Relatedly, yet others look for a cure for autism, whether in the form of a drug or psychological treatment. More strands of research could be mentioned. Each of these strands itself encompasses a wide range of variety in research projects and aims.[104]

One of the aims of this chapter was to introduce the concept of autism to those readers who are not familiar with the history of the concept in order to understand better what autism is according to different theories. Another aim of this chapter was to present some highlights in this changing history of the concept of autism and to show that autism—while being real—is also constructed and actively shaped, rather than a fixed condition waiting to be discovered and never changing over time. Some people would have been diagnosed with autism in some eras of the relatively recent history of autism and not in others. As such, some people were denied the support they could have used or even simply the acknowledgment of their way of being in the world. Since the beginning of the twenty-first century, the general public is much more aware of autism, which has reduced some but by no means all of the stigma that surrounds the condition. Public awareness has been raised by autistic people themselves, by parent organizations, and by various kinds of media. In the introduction to this chapter, we mentioned the book by Murray, *Representing Autism*, in which he demonstrates how public awareness is shaped by media but that those media (books, films, internet sites) are also rather unhelpfully perpetuating certain stereotypes. However, these different stereotypes and multiple interpretations of autism in society and academia do not take away from one fact: the presence of autism. That presence leads to theological questions, which we will start to address in chapter 4.

An important aim of this chapter was to create space in the autism discourse to start thinking theologically about autism. That space has been created by pointing out the many ways in which autism has been viewed throughout its history. If autism can be viewed from so many perspectives and if the concept has quite significantly changed over time, then the question of what it means to be on the autism spectrum through a theological lens is relevant and necessary for Christian communities to ask. Autistic people are present—what is their place in the Christian community? What does their presence mean as indispensable members of the body of Christ? In what ways does our view of worship and liturgy change when experienced and looked at through the lens of autism? In the next chapters, I will start to fill the space I have created here to approach those questions from a theological point of view. However, such a task begins by problematizing a statement that I have made just a few lines above: Are autistic people really present in our faith communities?

3

The Tyranny of the Normal
Exposing the Cause of Absence and Ignoring

At the root of why autistic people feel often unwelcome in churches is, I believe, the concept of *normalcy*. To put it simply, normalcy is the set of dynamics by which communities safeguard the boundaries of what and who they deem normal and therefore acceptable. Those who fall within those boundaries can be integrated into or even belong to the community, but those who do not fall within the boundaries either need to change or will be rejected, as will become clear in this chapter. Thus, normalcy results easily in an us-versus-them mentality, delineating subtly but sharply between those who belong and those who do not. In a way, this chapter is not about autism but about communal and cultural dynamics that make autistic people feel that they do not belong. Indeed, writing about disability, Lennard Davis states,

> To understand the disabled body, one must return to the concept of the norm, the normal body. So much of writing about disability has focused on the disabled person as the object of study, just as the study of race has focused on the person of color. But as with recent scholarship on race, which has turned its attention to whiteness, I would like to focus not so much on the construction of disability as on the construction of normalcy. I do this because the "problem" is not the person

with disabilities; the problem is the way that normalcy is constructed to create the "problem" of the disabled person.[1]

We can replace "person with disabilities" in the last sentence with "autistic person": "the 'problem' is not the autistic person; the problem is the way that normalcy is constructed to create the 'problem' of the autistic person."

If one of the keys to understanding the exclusion of autistic people in church is the concept of normalcy, then it is important to explore this concept and its concomitant community or group dynamics. Moreover, one can also question whether some kind of boundary keeping is healthy for the safety of the community. If so, what kinds of boundaries might be good to keep? I will explore this question in more detail in chapter 5, but first, we need to understand the dynamics of normalcy. In order to understand these dynamics, I will start this chapter with some concrete examples of how they are at work both in daily life and in the church. I will then explore how normalcy works by, what Thomas Reynolds calls, an "economy of exchange." An economy of exchange is the concrete outworking of the frameworks that form the backdrop to normalcy; it is the system of reciprocity that governs people's social interaction. After that, I will drill deeper into the history of the concept of normalcy, followed by a discussion of why some (including Reynolds) call it a "cult," exploring the religious element of the cult. Throughout these sections, it will become clear that it is nearly impossible to escape some form of community boundary keeping. The question is, then, how to make sure that that boundary keeping in churches does not turn people into "problems" which then turns people away. That is the question for the final section of this chapter.

THE DYNAMICS OF NORMALCY

Let's start with a definition of normalcy. We can define normalcy as the dominant social dynamics in a given society or group that establish and uphold the group's norms. These dynamics are not just a way of thinking but are deeply ingrained in a community's practices. By its practices, the group expresses—often implicitly, unwittingly, and unacknowledged—what it considers normal and acceptable and thereby what its norms and values are. The term is often used negatively in disability literature, denoting normalcy's excluding, if not oppressive, character toward those who fall outside of the boundaries of the group's norms.

Thomas Reynolds, whose discussion of the concept of normalcy informs this chapter to a large extent, offers an autobiographical account in which he describes how difficult it is for him as a parent not to fall into the trap of normalcy and not to put the expectations of normalcy on his own son, Chris, who is autistic. His discussion is framed in terms of disability more generally, but the dynamics of normalcy that he explores do apply to autism as well. Using the example of parents at young peoples' athletics events, Reynolds shows how parents often project their own expectations, hopes, and criteria for success onto the child: "disappointed parents yelling at their kids to cajole them into performing up to expectations."[2] Or the reverse happens: "Compensating for their own insecurity, parents sometimes obsess over their child's performance in school, athletics, the arts, and so on."[3] Reynolds goes on to say that people with disabilities confront nondisabled people with their own vulnerability, their own sense of loss of control, of not knowing how to respond to the person with a disability. That person then becomes the "other," someone who is "not us."

> We may deem the disabled body abnormal, even monstrous, but it is only because we feel out of control in its presence. Unsure how to interact and elicit a common purpose or meeting point, we appeal to the strength and security offered by the cult of normalcy. Why? Because the encounter has put into question and made unstable the values garnered from a taken-for-granted economy of exchange. The strange and uncanny world of disability has disrupted the familiar and predictable world.[4]

It should not surprise us if this account of Reynolds' own experience and his explanation of the dynamics he observes in himself ring true more widely in the context of our faith communities. It is not difficult, often, to avoid the person with disabilities, or anyone who upsets our illusions of control, our projections of normalcy, and as Reynolds demonstrates, our fears. We feel out of control in the presence of such a person. Therefore, it is easier to "other" the person with autism or disabilities than to enter into a relationship with them. Whereas family members hopefully feel a responsibility toward the person with a disability, in a larger group it is easier—even if uncomfortable—to avoid such responsibilities.

If it is correct to think that those dynamics of fear and exclusion easily creep into the church, then what does that say about the church community? Perhaps it says that the oppressive force of the cult of normalcy is more present in the church community than we might be aware of. This is not to say that church communities are worse than other social groups, but one would hope that churches are governed by other values than that of their surrounding culture when those cultural values conflict with those of God's reign. "So from now on we regard no one from a worldly point of view," the apostle Paul writes to the Corinthians (2 Cor 5:16). One would expect churches to do better than the surrounding culture in valuing people who differ from the cultural norms because churches are so invested in the norm of "loving one's neighbor as oneself" (Lev 19:18; Mark 12:31). Nevertheless, whether we like it or not, often faith communities operate along the lines of the normalcy logic, a logic that reinforces the idea that the more social capital one has, the more we value that person (see section "Practicing Normalcy: Economies of Exchange"). This is not out of malicious intent, just as parents do not project their own hidden fears and hopes (the latter less hidden perhaps) onto their child out of malicious intent. Nevertheless, the harsh reality is, as evidenced by statistics and innumerable stories, that churches often fail to be the places of welcome for those with limited social capital or for those who are deemed to be "different."[5]

The welcome or unwelcome that people experience in church is often keenly felt in the worship service—typically on Sundays—as that is the focal point of many churches' lives. In the way churches worship, the normalcy structures of the group become most strongly expressed, although often unwittingly. For example, some churches will have the expectation—which over time has become an assumption for them—that there is a block of worship songs, in a particular style, played by particular instruments, at a particular volume. Participation is expected in certain ways—again, often that remains unspoken. One might be expected to raise one's hands, close one's eyes, sing along, stand, and this might be talked about as "being in worship." This is a term that, as one autistic Christian told me, an autistic participant (and others) might not understand because it is a rather vague term, especially when no one explains it to you. Because such a term, and the meaning of particular postures and other forms of participation, remain unexplained, a participant needs to infer what is meant, which can be difficult for autistic people.[6] Another example is the silence that is expected during large parts of the service in many churches, which may be difficult for an autistic person who feels the need to hum or jump. When one is not able to participate in the assumed and expected way—the ways determined by the "normalcy" of a group—one may become the object of disturbed and judgmental looks. Some autistic people and their families are asked to sit at the back or in a quiet corner of the worship hall. The back of the church, however, is (both physically and metaphorically) close to the exit.

These three examples, one of parenting and two of worship services, illustrate some of the dynamics of normalcy. That which is, and those who are, other than "our" norm and disrupt our sense of control and security and are too often dealt with in such a way so that "we" can continue in "our" ways of being and doing. The quotation marks around "our" and "we" indicate the sharp distinction between those within ("us/we/our") and those outside of the boundaries ("them/they/theirs") of the norm. Stories of unwelcome and judgment—of being turned into "them," into "others," are told over and over by autistic people and their families. Let us therefore explore the dynamics of normalcy further.

PRACTICING NORMALCY: ECONOMIES OF EXCHANGE

The dynamics of normalcy (in other words, how normalcy "works") can be helpfully explained by what Reynolds terms an economy of exchange. This is "a system of reciprocity that regulates interactions in a community."[7] The word "economy" comes from the Greek *oikonomos*, which is the term for someone who manages a household, but Reynolds uses the idea of a household as a metaphor for the larger community, showing how the economy of exchange is used to steer and give direction to the interactions that take place there. In other words, this economy is not a passive system but something that is lived out in the activities of the community. A household is a place of activity, often of people living together, each with their own contribution and responsibilities. In the household, some behaviors, conversations, opinions, and so on are valued more than others, and the household has its own rhythm in which its members are expected to live.

All of this is embodied, as Reynolds explains:

> Our bodies always negotiate social space by participating in an exchange of goods, whether going to school, playing on a sports team, working in retail, raising children, or meeting for coffee with friends. In every situation, even in the virtual world of cyberspace, we are present to others. That is, we portray or offer something that is recognized and received (or not) as of significance.[8]

As we negotiate this social space, we knowingly or unknowingly ascribe value to others, and others do the same to us, creating this economy of exchange.

Undergirding this process, that which we consider to be of value, is what we might call frameworks. The concept of frameworks was developed by Charles Taylor and describes how our interaction with others is governed by our sense of self and other, alongside a sense of norms and values and a sense of what is right or wrong. When we encounter other people who hold the same values and worldview, we bond. Somehow, we have a precise intuition for those whom we like and do not like, for those with whom we feel at home and for those with whom we do not. But this intuition is not wholly individualistic; it is based on frameworks that are constituted by living together in and as a society. Taylor says that human beings desire to belong as part of "the good." Belonging is needed for a good life in addition to the bare necessities such as food, drinks, shelter, and clothes. "The good is what we find meaningful about life together."[9] However, we do not determine what we find meaningful in some abstract, purely rational way; the frameworks that determine what is "good" are deeply embedded (and embodied, as we saw above) within the culture in which we live. So our relationship to the good is shaped by our belonging to a certain culture. At the same time, we also shape that culture by being part of it: we simultaneously shape and are shaped by the culture to which we belong.

The role of the community in establishing the frameworks and what we intuitively value as "good" is a key point; without the presence of others, we would not have a framework of the good. But the drawback is that in the need to align with the framework of what is considered good so as to belong and be valued, some community members are left vulnerable. The framework always serves the majority, and the minority who do not have the qualities that are valued by the community may find themselves excluded.

Courtney Goto makes this point when discussing "paradigms" (a concept that in her work functions in the same way as framework does in the works of Taylor and Reynolds):

> A paradigm serves a majority of people in a given community.... If it didn't, the paradigm would be challenged and over time it would shift so that the paradigm serves the majority more appropriately. Unfortunately, because a paradigm cannot serve all members of a community equally well, there tends to be a shifting minority whom the paradigm harms, which ultimately undermines the integrity of the community as a whole. While a paradigm protects and enshrines the principles, values, and practices of those who belong to the most dominant groups, it inevitably results in exclusivity and marginalization.[10]

For some, society's thresholds and margins create a safe space: within these limits, we are assured we are acceptable. The paradigm helps us to function and to make sense of situations that otherwise might be even too complex to navigate. However, for the minority who fall outside the boundaries of normal, "the demand for conformity is coercive."[11] This easily leads to a person striving to possess the qualities that are valued by the community.

Such striving might be successful to various degrees, but when such striving is not successful and one does not reach the threshold qualities of the "good," certain things start to happen. First, the community will reject the person (or praise them when they, despite being below the threshold in some regards, manage to reach outstanding results in other areas—in autism a typical example is the "savant" who has some extraordinary skill). Second, those who are within the scope of the good become fearful because the other person is different and therefore disrupts the safe boundaries set by the framework that they live by. They confront the community with the fact that the thresholds are arbitrary, that life could be different, that there is a vulnerability to social constructs.

It is worth quoting Reynolds at length at this point, when he explains the above and arrives at his notion of the "cult of normalcy" (I will discuss the idea of a "cult" further below):

> It seems only too natural then that we make judgments and behave in ways that protect and preserve the ideals of a community's framework or value horizon. We come to rely upon these ideals for orientation in the world; they grant a sense of place. Negatively, we place under surveillance or exclude those elements and persons perceived as out of place, that do not fit. They cannot be assimilated or integrated and are in effect deemed an impoverishment, perhaps even something dangerous, because they do not present what we consider familiar or acceptable. In fact, we come to fear such elements and people. Their difference puts conventions into question. . . . Strangeness disrupts the predictable world and so disorients, making us conscious of the extent to which we are vulnerable. Strangeness creates a dissonance that threatens to spoil the fabric of a community's mutually reinforcing sense of the good. The social order is jeopardized. The predictable world is thrown into relief. Because of this, communities develop protective strategies through what I call the "cult of normalcy."[12]

When confronted with a person who does not reach our threshold criteria of the valuable and beautiful, we create—or perhaps better, we reinforce—our "cult of normalcy." The framework of the good constitutes, upholds, and is at the same time protected by the boundaries of normalcy. In other words, even if we are usually unaware of our frameworks, paradigms, norms, values, and assumptions that make up our idea of the normal, "normalcy" is an active dynamic in any group. It is the same dynamic Goto speaks of when she says that the paradigm always serves the majority and excludes minorities. When the paradigm, or framework of normalcy, is disrupted, the group tightens its framework by reinforcing it to safeguard the sense of control and security that the framework gives.

Much is at stake here, not only in terms of the framework but also how it is played out in our daily lives, governed by the economy of exchange:

> By [the economy of exchange] a framework is brought down to earth, so to speak, regulating and reinforcing the perceptions of what qualities are worthy and unworthy, acceptable, and unacceptable. Because it attributes merit, enabling us to purchase recognition by others, an economy of exchange has the power to govern what becomes appropriate and desirable.[13]

The place where this all happens is the body. Reynolds, therefore, speaks about body capital as an indication of the value one can purchase in the economy of exchange. Body capital is measured in aesthetics and functionality. As Wendy Lawson writes, "We have been led to believe, mostly by advertising material promoted via various media, that to have a good life one must be physically handsome, well educated, earn lots of money and not be disabled by personal difficulties."[14] I would add that body capital increases or decreases according to how well one can perform the negotiation in the economy. In other words, while communities value beautiful bodies more than not-so-beautiful bodies (according to the specific community's norms), and therefore beauty indicates a certain body capital, it is not enough to purchase more capital. Or to give the example of nonspeaking autism, we can replace "beautiful bodies" in the previous sentence with "the capacity to speak": while communities value the capacity to speak more than the incapacity to speak, and therefore the capacity to speak indicates a certain body capital, it is not enough to purchase more capital. The way one uses one's bodily characteristics matters a lot. Nevertheless, the more one answers to the community's ideal, the greater one's head start.

Having lived in three different countries, let me give a personal example of how subtly this all works and how this differs from community to community. I was born in the Netherlands and lived there for about eighteen years. I then moved to Belgium, and notwithstanding a little wandering back and forth between the Netherlands and Belgium, I basically stayed in Belgium for another eighteen years. Even though both countries are small and next to each other, with the official language of Dutch being spoken in the Netherlands and in roughly half of Belgium, the cultures differ enormously and the communities' frameworks play out in subtle ways. For example, while in the Netherlands, I am of average height, in Belgium I was known as "the tall one." My body indicated something slightly different from the norm. Furthermore, Belgians regularly commented on my style of dress; I like to wear bright shirts and sweaters. Again, in the Netherlands, this would be perfectly normal. Although it is not exceptional in Belgium to wear bright colors (I bought most of them there), it was nevertheless another slight deviation from the cultural norm. The way I look and dress, especially in Belgium, would often betray my Dutch roots.

However, more is going on. Studies have shown that people in leadership are often taller than the average person. Tallness can therefore be associated with dominance. Power is embodied. It is not difficult to imagine that taller people, in many contexts, have a bodily advantage over others.[15] Naturally, smaller people need to look up to the taller person, which is a more vulnerable posture than looking down (note the linguistic, metaphorical associations with looking up to or down on someone). Knowing these bodily dynamics, I can make use of them, and one might even say that I have the moral obligation of using my height well. In some contexts, I might be tempted to make myself as tall as possible in order to weigh in on the conversation and support my point by my posture. In other contexts, it might be appropriate to make myself smaller as it were and if not possible in terms of height, in other ways make myself less prominently present.

Writing from a feminist perspective, Elaine Graham explains this dynamic:

> Stories of bodily experience that transgress boundaries and unsettle taken-for-granted categories literally bring us to our sense, bring us face-to-face with the artifice of even the most intimate aspects of our world. We realize how the abstract forces of economic, religious, cultural and political power may also be written on our bodies; how the texture of embodiment renders tangible the texts of social construction.[16]

The language Graham uses is similar to that of Reynolds. The person who transgresses our safe boundaries of normalcy unsettles and therefore makes uncomfortable those who deem themselves within those boundaries. The cult of normalcy cannot cope with that which is strange according to Reynolds; in Graham's terms, the "stranger" is the "bodily experience that *transgress[es] boundaries* and *unsettle[s]* taken-for-granted categories" (i.e., normalcy).

The example does not stop there, however, because another layer of the cultural framework is how it affects the perceived value of those who are different. As we saw above, strangeness is difficult to cope with, and indeed, the Belgians and the Dutch have clear opinions about the other. In general, the Dutch-speaking Belgians—that is, the Flemish—do not look that positively at "the" Dutch. The Dutch are loud and arrogant, so the Flemish think. (The Dutch would say they are self-confident—quite another interpretation of the same behavior.) So, to be recognized as Dutch by the way I look (height and dress) is not always all that positive. This example makes it clear that the frameworks of a community's norms and values, what counts as valuable and not, what buys one social recognition or not is both deeply embodied and socially constructed and not only told by the stories that hold up the framework but also lived out in the details of daily life.

"Bodies offer a 'vantage-point' from which the complexity of human nature, as creator and creation of culture, can be experienced and analyzed. Bodies are the bearers of important narratives," Elaine Graham writes.[17] In this book, I am trying to listen to autistic bodies. These bodies offer a different vantage point to analyze human nature and social interactions, but we will also see how stories are often written onto autistic bodies by a non-autistic majority. In a non-autistic majority world, the bodily aspects that are valued and thus purchase power and recognition are typically those of the non-autistic body, including the way a non-autistic body perceives and processes the world, conducts social interactions, behaves, and has preferences. This is no different in worship services. Some bodies are able to sit still, keep quiet, talk intellectually, act sociably, know when and what to do to fit in with the structure and ways of worship services, and can say the set responses. Those bodies fit within the boundaries of what is valued by the worshipping community and therefore have the most body capital; in turn, they can purchase the most social recognition and are perceived, perhaps, to be more spiritual. Some autistic bodies can keep up with this but often at a high cost by masking or camouflaging their real needs.[18] Other bodies cannot keep up with this at all and might face judgment and ultimately rejection by the community. To come back to the examples of normalcy in worship that we saw at the end of the previous section, the person raising their hands at the right moments, though not really knowing why this would be required during this song, might get very tired of "fitting in." The person humming or making sudden noises might break the normative silence of the group at particular moments during the liturgy. The person who needs to pace up and down might disturb the normative sitting quietly in one's spot.[19]

The normative silence or speaking at the right times, the normative sitting still, and all those other written and unwritten rules of the worshipping community seem to be normal for most people in the community. This is so as a matter of fact; if not, those rules would not be part of the boundaries and normalcy dynamics of the community. Nevertheless, Graham points to an important insight when she observes that unexpected stories, written on bodies that might fall outside of the boundaries of normalcy, could in fact serve as the foundation for new stories. The autistic "vantage points" might serve as a "foundation for new moral narratives of hope and obligation."[20] I will come back to this idea. For now, it is important to note that normalcy works by the dynamics of the economy of exchange by which we ascribe value to, and buy value from, each other. These dynamics emerge from deeply embodied frameworks that determine what is taken as the "good" for life and for belonging.

THE "TYRANNY OF THE NORMAL"

Normalcy is an outworking of the frameworks within which we live; patterns of normalcy are often invisible. Normalcy is like culture or, better, is part of and parcel of culture: we live it, we embody it, we know our own cultures, and yet we are seldom aware of our culture, like a fish does not realize that it swims in water. To further become aware of the often unseen dynamics of normalcy, it will be useful to understand the emergence of the concept, which also reinforces the reason why it may be called a "tyranny" or "cult."

Scholars who use the term "normalcy" often refer to Lennard Davis' discussion of the term.[21] He is not the first to use it—in fact, he explores the origins of the word—but he might be one of the first to engage with the term at length in his discussion of disability. To understand the intricacies of normalcy better, I will summarize briefly some of the key points made by Davis.

Davis argues that the concept of the "ideal" preceded our contemporary concept of "normal," the latter entering the dictionary with its current meaning around 1840–1860. However, historically the gods, not humanity, would represent the ideal; the ideal would always be unattainable for a human being and no one would even think of striving to embody the ideal. No one person can be the ideal in themselves—the ideal can only be constructed from human beings by taking one feature that resembles the ideal from a person, combined with another feature of another person, and so forth, as illustrated by François-André Vincent's painting *Zeuxis Choosing as Models the Most Beautiful Girls of the Town of Crotona* (1789, Musée du Louvre).[22] The normal, on the contrary, is exactly that which resembles the majority of the population and it becomes that which people should start to strive for—to be as "normal" (i.e., as average) as possible.

The idea of the normal is intimately related to statistics. Davis points to Adolphe Quetelet (1796–1847) who observed that astrologists used the "law of error" to determine where a star should be located. Astronomers would "locate a star by plotting all the sightings and then averaging the errors."[23] Quetelet suggested that this "could be equally applied to the distribution of human features such as height and weight. He then took a further step of formulating the concept of *'l'homme moyen'* or the average man.... [This] average man was ... both a physically average and a morally average construct."[24] It is worth highlighting that the average person was average both physically and morally. It is not difficult to trace both aspects in contemporary societies' ideas of normalcy: for example, able-bodiedness (which allows a person to contribute to the economy because their body functions "normally") is highly valued, as well as having moral values that align with the society's values at large.

Davis observes that tellingly, the statistics movement in the nineteenth century was intertwined with the eugenics movement. Most early statisticians were eugenicists. One of the key figures in these movements was Sir Francis Galton. Davis quotes Donald A. MacKenzie, who writes that "the need of eugenics in large part determined the content of Galton's statistical theory."[25] Although there is discussion as to whether statistics made eugenics possible or the other way around, it is clear that "both bring into society the concept of a norm, particularly a normal body, and thus in effect create the concept of the disabled body."[26] Davis points to one particularly important contribution to statistics by Galton: he changed the name of what we now know as the bell curve "from the 'law of frequency of error' or 'error curve,' the term used by Quetelet, to the 'normal distribution curve.'"[27] Keeping in mind the Darwinian idea of evolutionary progress, which was a dominant concept in the eugenics movement, we see the significance of changing the name of the curve: it becomes possible to see the extremes of both sides of the curve as abnormal, identifying the middle of the curve as the norm.

However, Galton had to take one more step. Traits like high intelligence or tallness were praised, and so extreme intelligence or tallness were not to be looked on negatively and eradicated by the eugenics movement. The solution to this problem was for Galton to divide the "normal distribution curve" into quartiles, starting at Q1, with most people falling into Q2 and Q3, and the extremely intelligent, to stay with that example, falling into Q4. Seeing the curve in this way, a ranking of Q1–Q4 became possible, and as such, the most intelligent (Q4) became the most desirable. Whereas in earlier times the ideal was only in the realm of the gods and not something to be strived for, "the new ideal of ranked order is powered by the imperative of the norm, and then is supplemented by the notion of progress, human perfectibility, and the elimination of deviance, to create a dominating, hegemonic vision of what the human body should be."[28] We may add, "what the human intelligence, character, social adaptability should be." The hegemony of normalcy was born—the hegemony of the average, which strives toward the ideal. To be in Q1 is to be avoided—to deviate from the norm at that side of the bell curve is judged negatively and can lead to exclusion. To be average, to fall within Q2 and Q3 is all right and, in many ways, the ideal as it allows one to belong to the framework. To have traits that would fall in Q4 is an ideal, but as I argued above, only as long as one can negotiate this social capital well.

Tracing the concept of normalcy to its statistical roots is not a trivial activity. In the introduction to this chapter, I quoted Davis' argument that to speak about *dis*ability is to speak about *norm*al ability, just as to speak about racial injustice (in the Global North/West) is to speak about whiteness. Likewise, to speak about autism is to speak about the normal and normalcy. Ways of being that are seen to be different always need a standard from which they differ. Medical tests and diagnoses feed on such standards, including the acceptable deviation (margins) from the bell curve's middle line. Indeed, statistics are at the heart of the medical model of disability. Writing about intellectual disability, Stacy Simplican shows how statistical measurements have two sides to them. For example, in the U.S. justice system, measuring someone as having an IQ below 70 might prevent them from ending up on death row. However, there is also a reductionism that is implied in such statistical approaches to intellectual ability. The low IQ number soon becomes the stigmatizing yard stick by which a whole person is measured, reducing the person to that one characteristic, failing to see that any individual is a complex person, with their own stories, cultural background, family, hopes, fears, and dreams.[29]

An official diagnosis of autism is obtained through some version of the medical model, with the two dominant diagnostic descriptors found in the *DSM-5* and *ICD-11*, and therefore (statistical) measurement is always part of the diagnosis. The official name is now "autism spectrum disorder," recognizing that autism is a "spectrum" that works out differently in different people but still named a "disorder." The term betrays the concept of normalcy: there can only be a disorder when there is some kind of order, some kind of norm. The autism diagnosis is given only if one deviates from the norm, which is the average or sometimes the ideal.[30] As such, the medical model frames autism fundamentally as a negative way of being.

Once we understand the roots of the normalcy concept and its (often devastating) consequences for those who fall outside of the acceptable deviations from the norm, we understand why scholars speak about the hegemony or tyranny of normalcy.[31] The hegemony of normalcy points to the overruling and (violently) dominant character of normalcy.[32] The assumption is that whatever is normal is good and that which deviates too much from the norm is bad. Here, we come back to Reynolds' statement, following Taylor, that human beings desire to belong—the good is to belong, to belong is the good. Thus, human beings will always hope to belong and therefore try to fit themselves within the boundaries of what is deemed normal.

In this way, the hegemony of normalcy becomes oppressive; it becomes tyrannical. In a 1977 address to parents of children with learning disabilities, Stanley Hauerwas said, "But the demand to be normal can be tyrannical unless we understand that the normal condition of our being together is that we are all different."[33] A little later on, he stated that those with learning disabilities "also help us to see how to be different without regret."[34] In other words, there is an alternative to the tyranny of the normal if we start radically to question and to redefine what is commonly understood by "normal." According to Hauerwas, this is even true when it comes to the power differential between "experts" (doctors) and parents. Whereas the "experts" may view those with learning disabilities as outside of the boundaries of the normal, parents may question this, he says.[35] This relates to our discussion above of the power or hegemony of the medical model to define difference and diagnose it as "disorders." Starting from the love for the disabled person instead of from diagnostic labels changes the power dynamics that come with the tyranny of normalcy.

The terms "hegemony" and "tyranny of the normal" point to the almost inescapable power of the normalcy construct. I have indicated how the rise of the normal was intertwined with the rise of statistics and eugenics and that this resulted in the diagnosis of "disorders," within a medical model that operates to a large extent by statistics. In such a model, autism, as inherently a diagnosis of difference, is inevitably cast as a negative way of being in the world. To set this discussion in the context of liturgy and worship, I now turn to the term that Reynolds adds to the discussion of the "hegemony" and "tyranny" of normalcy: the "cult" of normalcy.

THE CULT OF NORMALCY

Reynolds has been helpful, in addition to Davis, in explaining the concept of normalcy and how that aligns with Taylor's notion of frameworks. Interestingly, Reynolds calls normalcy a cult. Rather remarkably, he does not tell his readers why he chooses to speak of the "*cult* of normalcy." Nevertheless, this word adds a religious layer to the discussion that is particularly helpful for our focus on liturgy and worship. Whereas Reynolds explores the workings of normalcy with the idea of an economy of exchange, I want to go one step further and see what that idea of an economy means when worked out in a religious setting—what does it mean to speak of a "cult of normalcy" in liturgy and worship?

A cult refers to a group of people who is devoted to a particular person or ideology, and in the Christian context, it is often referred to as a sect in contrast to the church. Because the cult is devoted to a particular figure or ideology, the term denotes a form of worship, and as such, the term has an active element to it. In the cult of normalcy, worship belongs to the god Normal and goddess Average, which become the godheads of this cult. We obey the power of the Normal by striving to be as close as possible to the Average (Galton's Q2 and Q3) or even to go beyond (Q4). The law of Moses and the law of the Spirit (Rom 8:2) have been replaced by the law of the Average. Consequently, we start looking down on those who are far removed from the golden middle line (which can include looking down on ourselves if we are not close enough to the Average)—the golden middle line has become the new golden calf, the new object of worship and representation of the god called Normal. Hegemony is now transposed to a tyrannical cult (or sect) to which we sacrifice those who do not pass the threshold of the holy middle or mean. Normalcy turns into a cult when societies—including Christian communities—are devoted to sustaining their boundaries of normalcy at the cost of minorities who do not fit the norm. Then communities are shaping, as well as being shaped into, the image of normalcy.[36] By now, it should be clear that all this is powered by a group's active dynamics, even if these dynamics are worked out in unspoken and unconscious assumptions.

In faith communities, another layer is added to these active dynamics: the norms are often thought to be divinely ordained, which adds to them spiritual power that can be used to end any discussion and makes some groups in the community vulnerable to spiritual abuse. The idea of an economy of exchange explains how normalcy works in society, and I contend that in many ways, this is not different in church communities. Faith communities find themselves within a culture, and they are made up of people who live their daily lives in that culture. Thus inevitably, that influence is brought into the congregation. If that influence goes unchecked, the above analysis of the cult of normalcy—the worship of Average and Normal—quickly applies. When the language of religion is added to the normative boundaries of what is deemed (un)acceptable, those boundaries appear to be spiritually endorsed, giving them a religious, holy, and therefore beyond-critique status.

If this sounds abstract, just think about churches that consider the lack of physical healing of a person in a wheelchair to indicate a lack of faith on the part of that wheelchair user, churches that ascribe clinical depression to a lack of prayer on the part of the depressed person, or churches that consider autism or epilepsy to be demon possession. In such churches, one might encounter disturbing prayer or exorcism practices or, worse, the bestowing of an unnecessary spiritual burden of sin, guilt, and shame on those persons. One might think that these examples represent only specific parts or denominations of the wider church. Even so, the same religious power can be at play in relation to the examples we mentioned in the beginning of this chapter. The judgmental looks on the humming autistic person, the rejection felt by the person who fidgets or needs to jump up and down and cannot possibly regulate his or her body—these forms of exclusion and marginalization can be invested with the same spiritual "authority," expressed in the liturgical norms in church. Stories abound of people having been asked (often via their parents) to leave because of their autistic behavior, as do stories of people who did not have the courage to enter a church because they knew they were going to be rejected—these stories come from across the denominational church landscape.

The language of "cult" helps us to see the above dynamics and that our ideas of what is and is not acceptable in church can easily turn into idols. These replace our worship of the true God who is revealed in Jesus Christ or add the Normal and Average as a god and goddess alongside the true God.[37] However, God is a jealous God who does not permit the worship of anyone or anything else (Exod 20:3–6, 22–23). To do so would be to conflate the Creator with the created—all worship that is not worship of God is worship of something created. Indeed, as the previous section made clear, normalcy is a human construct; it is part of the created and as such, can never deserve our worship. We will need a theological account to dismantle any traces of worship of the Normal. In the next chapter, I will start to develop such an account in relation to the way autistic people—the outcasts in our cult of normalcy—should be an integral part of God's people.

Reynolds' term, the "cult" of normalcy, raises the theological stakes on the concept of normalcy. The only spiritual authority in church is ultimately Jesus Christ, who is the head of the body (Col 1:18). A church that is faithfully following Jesus must critically evaluate its practices and the extent to which they are influenced by societal, liturgical, or other boundaries of normalcy. The exclusion felt by many autistic people should be a loud alarm bell that there is theological work to do. Idols should be expelled. This brings us to the last section of this chapter in which we need to reflect on the possibility of an alternative to normalcy.

NORMALCY AND AUTISM: REVERSING THE FRAMEWORK

Taylor argues that it is not possible to live outside the boundaries of some kind of framework—frameworks that constitute our ideas of what normal is. He states,

> I want to defend the strong thesis that doing without frameworks is utterly impossible for us; otherwise put, that the horizons within which we live our lives and which make sense of them have to include these strong qualitative discriminations. . . . The claim is that living within such strongly qualified horizons is constitutive of human agency, that stepping outside these limits would be tantamount to stepping outside what we would recognize as integral, that is, undamaged personhood.[38]

It seems, then, that we are caught up in systems (frameworks) that are inescapable, that by implication normalcy will exercise its hegemony, and that if we dare to escape the framework, we risk damaging our personhood. Frameworks, according to Taylor, are necessary for having a sense of identity, for answering the question "Who am I?"[39]

However, the fact *that* we cannot escape living against the backdrop of our frameworks does not mean that we have no agency to choose *which* framework we allow to dominate our lives. Moreover, I suggest that we distinguish between a framework and normalcy. When we define normalcy as the outcome of social constructs resulting from the frameworks we live by, the picture is more nuanced than when we conflate the two. Normalcy, as a protective strategy (Reynolds), as the social dynamics that guard the boundaries of who is "in" and who is "out," will perhaps almost inevitably exist. Admittedly, the distinction between the framework and normalcy, as a social dynamic, is subtle, as the framework itself is a social construct (reinforced by normalcy—there is a reciprocity between the framework and the guarding of its boundaries). Nevertheless, making this distinction can help us to conclude that, as Taylor says, we cannot do without frameworks; but we might foster an attitude, a disposition, a spirituality that is not afraid of that or those who are outside of the limits of our own framework, limits set by the cult of normalcy. To give an example, someone who feels the need to move around a lot in the worship service may fall outside the boundaries that are protected by normalcy; however, we can develop a disposition that welcomes this person and people like him or her and get to know them. The typical (sitting still) does not need to be turned into a hegemonic norm. To go one step further, can our spirituality even be welcoming of that or those who confront us with our own limitations and norms? In our example, can we develop a spirituality that actively welcomes and looks out for people whose behavior is deemed unacceptable by the cult of normalcy? The theology of presence and availability that I will develop in the next chapter aims at fostering such a disposition or spirituality.

Questioning one's current framework can be a proactive choice (advocacy movements and books like this one aim at questioning current frameworks when they lead to a cult of normalcy), but often, it is life's circumstances that give rise to such questioning. Only a few paragraphs after Taylor makes his strong claim quoted above, he acknowledges that some people do step out of the boundaries of a framework, which, Taylor says, we would call an "identity crisis." Taylor relates this to a lack of certainty of where one stands and therefore a lack of orientation. "They lack a frame or horizon within which things can take on a stable significance, within which some life possibilities can be seen as good or meaningful, others as bad or trivial. The meaning of all these possibilities is unfixed, labile, or undetermined. This is a painful and frightening experience."[40] This may be frightening indeed, but I would argue that this can lead to a critical evaluation of the framework one is leaving (that evaluation will perhaps already have taken place, given the fact that one steps out of that framework) and to the reconsideration of one's values. Such deconstruction can be painful—giving up one's former certainties and accepting change is seldom easy. However, it creates space for a theological evaluation of the current framework(s) and the construction of a more faithful framework, oriented toward an eschatological horizon—that is, a horizon that is more attuned to the values of God's reign.

The painfully disorienting and frightening experience of finding oneself outside one's previous stable framework is illustrated by John Gillibrand's experience of, and call for, an "epistemic break." Gillibrand, in his book *Disabled Church—Disabled Society*, writes about his autistic son and how his son taught him, and perhaps forced him, to start thinking differently about reality. Gillibrand calls this an epistemic break, which, he explains, happens when "older ways of handling reality became inadequate for their task."[41] In Reynolds' terms of an economy of change—bearing in mind the overlap with Taylor's concept of frameworks—we could paraphrase Gillibrand, saying that the older currency of buying social recognition, valuation, and therefore ultimately the good life became useless in the new reality of raising his autistic son and (literally) buying him support. His experiences made him see that the societal support networks were failing and made him question the framework of society and how that framework played out in a cult of normalcy that did (or does) not put its value on autistic people with certain support needs. When an epistemic break occurs, the old discourse (which narrates the framework) is inadequate; old ways of buying social capital are insufficient, and a new discourse and ways of exchange need to be found.

Gillibrand continues by saying that "the new discourse may well—ironically—originate from the irrational and/or the unspoken."[42] Here, he is clearly thinking of his nonspeaking autistic son, who according to IQ tests would perhaps be thought of as "irrational." We are reminded of Graham's statement earlier, that "bodies are the bearers of important narratives, some of which unsettle superficial or entrenched understandings; and such unexpected stories excite compassion and serve as the foundation for new moral narratives of hope and obligation."[43] Unexpected stories can lead to an epistemic break. In other words, when we start to take the lived experience of autism seriously, our old ways of handling reality and our old discourses will prove inadequate for the task. We are in need of new ways and a new discourse. It is exactly the unexpected but important narratives of autistic people that help to unsettle entrenched dynamics of normalcy and that, importantly, also "serve as the foundation for new moral narratives," indeed, for a revised or new framework.

In an attempt to listen to ways in which autistic narratives and voices can help us to envision a new or revised framework and to counter cults of normalcy that marginalize autistic people, I now turn to the idea of embracing different "normals." Wendy Lawson, author of *Concepts of Normality: The Autistic and Typical Spectrum*, regrets that the concept of normal has become associated with what the majority of people deem normal. This is another way of referring to the bell curve, where most people fall within Galton's Q2 and Q3, a way of thinking that has gained hegemonic status in our communities. Lawson argues that an alternative way of thinking about what is normal is to consider what is normal for an individual.[44] This means that there is not just one "normal," but there are different "normals." Nick Walker, an autistic writer and advocate of the neurodiversity paradigm, concurs. In fact, it is one of the three fundamental principles of the neurodiversity paradigm:

> The idea that there is one "normal" or "healthy" type of brain or mind, or one "right" style of neurocognitive functioning, is a culturally constructed fiction, no more valid (and no more conducive to a healthy society or to the overall well-being of humanity) than the idea that there is one "normal" or "right" ethnicity, gender, or culture.[45]

If we take the perspective of an individual and look at the world through their eyes, things might be normal for them that are not normal for the majority of the people. Both Lawson and Walker argue that the normal of a person in a minority group is of equal value as that of someone in the majority group (although Walker dismisses the term "normal" altogether, a point to which I will return shortly).

In Lawson's book, Estée Klar-Wolfond has contributed a chapter titled "The Mismeasure of Autism." Based on the feminist work of Carol Tavris, she argues that, like women, autistic people are different *and* equal. She continues to argue for Lawson's claim in this book that there is no "one" normal but different "normals." What is normal for an autistic person, therefore, might be different from what is normal for a non-autistic person. However, society takes the latter as the norm (likely because the latter is "typical"), resulting in oppressive and dehumanizing messages to autistic people. Equality is not reached as long as it is not recognized that people have different starting points.[46] It is worth quoting Klar-Wolfond at length:

> My thesis is that the struggle of autistic people, like what happened to women, is the result of this "mismeasurement" against subjective norms.... Neither valued for their neurological difference, nor heard regarding their perspectives on the social implications of their disability, autistic people have been subject to treatment that seeks to normalize them or, as history has shown, institutionalize and segregate that. Given IQ tests and other measures constructed for the typical majority and not originally intended for them (see Gould 1996), autistic people come to be considered "wrong," "abnormal," "sick," "victims" and "hopeless," and are therefore continually set up for failure....
>
> Autism is not an aberrance, but a challenge *and* a way to live and experience the world. This is not "wrong," but atypical, unique, and referred to as a "way of being." In other words, autistic people are "normal" in their own right.[47]

The mismeasurement goes back right to where Davis argues the current hegemonies of normalcy find their roots—that is, the statistical measurement of the average, and therefore of the normal, resulting in moral judgments (see Taylor) of what is deemed good (normal) and wrong (*ab*normal). Again, the typical is turned into the normal and therefore the norm, resulting in normalcy. Klar-Wolfond points out that normalcy is a result of mismeasurement, however correct the statistics may be, because measurements that aim at establishing the average fail to positively account for difference and diversity. The consequences for autistic people—who in various ways would be nonaverage—are devastating. Klar-Wolfond mentions "treatments" that aim to "normalize" autistic people, and a little further back in history, institutionalization was a common intervention. Even with better ways of supporting autistic people, the notions of "wrong," "abnormal," "sick," "victims," and "hopeless" are still very much around, and living in a society that values the nonautistic average, society sets autistic people up for failure.[48]

However, Klar-Wolfond takes on the concept of normal that "overrate[s] independence and normalcy as worthy goals, whilst forgetting that we are all, in fact, interdependent."[49] Instead, we need to realize that it is possible to be different and at the same time require support. Such a realization is implicit in the idea that we are interdependent because interdependence means that everyone requires some kind of support.

If the requirement for support is included in what we think is normal, then those who require specific support do not necessarily fall outside the boundaries of our normal. In this way, we can start to sever the associations of being different and in need of support from judgmental labels of "abnormal," "hopeless," and "wrong." It allows a perception of "autism as a different and *valuable* way of being. Autistic people, much like women, have the right to be, therefore, different *and* equal and worthy of accommodation. They do not have to change themselves into normal-seeming simulacrums."[50] Klar-Wolfond asks her readers to imagine a different society in which autism is valued instead of pathologized, and looked at positively.[51] That means, in effect, a reversal of normalcy, or the realization that there is more than one normal.

At this point, we need to come back to Walker's dismissal of the term "normal." The overall argument that Lawson, Klar-Wolfond, and Walker are making is the same: over against the tyranny of normalcy, we should realize that neurominorities (as Walker terms neurodivergent groups of people) are of equal value as any other group and especially as the majority group. (Here, the comparison with gender and race is helpful again.) In Goto's terms, these authors represent the oppressed minority, and they are advocating a paradigm shift—a shift in framework. The question to consider here is whether it is best to speak of different normals or to dismiss the term "normal" altogether. Walker's argument is that there is no such thing as one "normal" way of being or a normal human being. Just as it would be ridiculous to say that there is a normal race or a normal ethnicity, it is equally ridiculous to speak about a normal neurocognitive configuration. She rather speaks about (neuro)typical. The term "normal" is drawn from the medical paradigm, a paradigm that Walker strongly opposes.[52]

Both the terminology of "neurotypical" instead of "normal" and of multiple "normals" is useful in my view. Walker's argument is strong: there is no such being as *the* normal human being. If one wants to oppose the medical paradigm, one needs to be critical of the paradigm's terminology because that houses the values of the paradigm. The word "normal" already betrays an implicit value system. However, this is exactly where it may be helpful to speak of different normals, as Lawson and Klar-Wolfond do. The use of "normal" should alert us to the value system inherent in the word and its use. Moreover, the dismissal of "normal" in favor of more neutral words such as "neurotypical" risks obscuring the fact that value systems are still at work regardless of the language that we use. An example of this is when people who apparently operate from within a medical paradigm use the words "neurotypical" and "neurodivergent." The change of terminology alone does not change one's underlying value system—important as language is, nevertheless. On the other hand, Walker's proposal itself is based strongly on a particular normative idea: he replaces one "normal" or "norm"—and perhaps "normalcy"—with another (i.e., the norm that there are different normals and that this should be accepted; this is a new framework that can again be guarded with the boundaries of a new normalcy). This goes back to Taylor's point that one cannot live without a framework.

I agree with Walker's observation that the medical paradigm (the dominant paradigm in society, upheld and reinforced by normalcy) often results in social dynamics that are excluding and oppressive. The only way to escape this dynamic is to acknowledge and perhaps promote the coexistence of different paradigms or frameworks. We recall how Goto argues that paradigms are always serving the majority and, of necessity, excluding a minority. To change from one paradigm to another is, therefore, not enough. I assume that Walker will agree, because her overall argument is more or less the same as Lawson's and Klar-Wolfond's. Within the neurodiversity paradigm is the notion of diversity and therefore the existence of multiple norms. To speak of "multiple normals" is linguistically awkward, and the language of the neurotypicality and neurodiversity is becoming more widely accepted. Therefore, one might want to choose the language of neurodiversity over "multiple normals," but it is important to be aware that this too can result in a new normalcy of a single paradigm or framework. The coexistence of multiple possible (and perhaps equally valuable) frameworks should be kept in mind. As the field of neurodiversity studies is upcoming and growing, there is ample space to do so.

The neurodiversity paradigm has a lot to offer in terms of revising the contemporary framework that is heavily influenced by a medical understanding of autism. The notion of diversity as something to be treasured as well as the insight that one can be different *and* of equal value is constructive and moves the discourse beyond the current cult of normalcy. However, when we keep in mind this chapter's opening quotation by Davis, pointing out that normalcy feeds on the idea of disability, we may wonder whether the neurodiversity paradigm moves the discussion sufficiently beyond the cult of medical and statistical normalcy. To explore this further, I now turn to disability theologian Brian Brock.

Brock also searches for a way to move beyond current understandings of disability and autism. Echoing Davis, he notes,

> A *lack* of ability (*dis*ability) is the conceptual foundation of the term normalcy (*not* having a special lack) at the very same time that the lack is designated as a reduction of capacity in relation to the normal. To unhitch disability from such hierarchical social cues is to render it a very different entity. In Paul's eyes Jesus had inaugurated a social order that is, in crucial senses, "beyond" disability.[53]

Here, Brock reiterates Davis' point that the concept of normalcy feeds on that which is deemed not normal in a vicious circle by which normal and "abnormal" continuously feed on each other. As such, a social order—a hierarchical order at that—is created. Brock suggests unhitching disability from these social cues—in other words, from a framework that includes the vicious circle of the normal/abnormal. This changes what we think disability is because it is no longer defined by the normal, nor is the normal any longer defined by what is deemed abnormal; in disability discourse, disability no longer defines ability, nor does the normalcy of ability define disability any longer. Brock refers to Scripture to suggest an alternative—that is, a social order—inaugurated by Jesus that is "beyond" disability. This discussion applies to autism as well, certainly if we realize that autism is considered a disability in the normalcy discourse. The cult of normalcy does not need to define what autism is, nor does autism need to feed the concept of normalcy by being framed as its opposite. It is possible to change frameworks and see autism as a "different entity." Theologically, the framework and the critique of normalcy that we will need to establish is one that aligns with the social order that Jesus announced and lived and made possible. That will be the work of the next two chapters.

Nevertheless, at the beginning of this section, I said that the theological evaluation of our frameworks needs to be oriented toward an eschatological horizon informed by the values of God's reign. The language of eschatology alerts us to the fact that we are living between the inauguration of God's reign and the final consummation of that reign. In other words, we live between the "already and not yet." We should be careful not to lose ourselves in theological niceties, but instead, we do need to acknowledge that autistic people are still marginalized because our societies operate by a cult of normalcy that is not yet redefined by the values of God's reign. A theology framed in terms of the new life of the resurrection should not forget the lament of the cross. At the same time, lamenting is not a passive outpouring of grief—although it is that as well—but an active prayer and claim that the world is not as it should be and an active waiting and hoping for God to expel a cult of normalcy that is wayward and heal any that have been damaged by it. After all, that is the promise of new life.

In conclusion, it may not be possible to escape the fact that we live in certain frameworks, and it is questionable whether normalcy with its discriminatory dynamics can be fully prevented from resulting from any framework. However, it is possible to question the assumptions of the framework one lives in. An epistemic break might lead to new ways of storying, norming, and valuing one's life and the way one's life is lived in a group or society. Furthermore, it is possible to think of different frameworks, or indeed "normals," as coexisting simultaneously. Even if one can align oneself with one particular framework and its norms better than with another, this does not need to result in valuing one framework over another, although sometimes we may want to call out certain paradigms as unhelpful or even harmful (as the neurodiversity paradigm does with the medical paradigm[54]). For autism, it is necessary to break the vicious circle by which autism and "normal" define each other. A theological critique of the current cult of normalcy and a constructive proposal in light of God's inbreaking reign can help us to move beyond that vicious circle, offering an alternative framework that values everyone for who they are.

That the old ways of handling reality, or let us say, handling church, are inadequate soon becomes clear when one talks to autistic believers. In my interviews with autistic churchgoers in the United Kingdom, I heard stories of churches that were welcoming, but stories of churches that failed to appreciate the gifts and needs of autistic people were also noticeably present in the interviews.[55] By contrast, as we will see in chapter 6, we may think of the Chapel of Christ Our Hope in Singapore as a church that takes the call to an epistemic break seriously and tries to find a new framework and a new way of handling reality. A typical phrase that is used by many in the chapel is, "It's okay." The phrase is often used in situations where the norms of society would judge some behavior as unacceptable—for example, the need to fidget or move around; in the chapel "it's okay." As simple as these words sound, they are in effect creating a new discourse and a new framework. "It's okay" means that where certain behavior might have made you lose social capital in the previous framework, here you have not lost anything. The chapel does not claim to be perfect, and there are things that may express older frameworks (it too finds itself in the "already and not yet"). However, by all accounts, this church provides a safe and welcoming place for autistic people and their families—often for the first time.

CONCLUSION

To conclude this section, I will summarize the main points of this chapter and give some examples of how this works out in a liturgical setting. Lennard Davis claimed that in order to talk about disability, one must talk about ability and how normalcy functions in society. When it comes to autism, church, and liturgy, this is no different. For that reason, this chapter has focused not so much on autism as on the dynamics of normalcy that are assumed in and drive group practices and that reveal (and reinforce) the group's framework. Frameworks are important to societies and groups because they give a sense of belonging. A critical analysis of the framework of a group is needed when its resulting normalcy becomes a dominating force, to the detriment of those who do not fit the framework. A shift in framework needs to take into account how normalcy works—that is, the fact that one needs social capital to "buy" social recognition and to participate in an economy of exchange—the more capital one has, the easier it is to gain more. This latter point relates to Goto's statement that the paradigm always serves the majority and therefore almost inevitably discriminates against the minority. In the final section, I questioned the assumptions that make up a particular framework. That questioning centered on experiencing an epistemic break and embracing multiple frameworks or "normals." The neurodiversity paradigm, largely created by autistic and later other neurodivergent voices, offers helpful suggestions, especially with regard to the notion that "different" does not have to mean "unequal," thereby breaking away from the dominant binary of normal/abnormal with its subsequent implicit binary of good/bad. In many ways, the neurodiversity paradigm is a positive alternative to the hegemony of the medical model of disability. However, the neurodiversity paradigm might not be enough to help us to move beyond the vicious circle in which the "normal" and "abnormal" feed on each other because "different" and "typical" still feed on each other in this paradigm, albeit without a value judgment of either. However, Brock's suggestion to unhitch disability (and autism) from this circle by looking at the framework or social order inaugurated by Jesus Christ offers constructive theological possibilities to look for a new framework without denying the pain of marginalization caused by the current cult of normalcy. It is the work of the next two chapters to explore in depth the possibilities of a theological framework and the move away from normalcy as an exclusionary dynamic.

We can now revisit the two examples of worship norms from the beginning of the chapter (see section "The Dynamics of Normalcy").

One example is related to a particular style of worshipping and the other to the norm of silence without disruption. The first step is to become aware that these assumptions and expectations are part and parcel of the social dynamics in the church and are the norm and therefore are normative, easily leading to the protective dynamics of normalcy. The two norms serve the majority of the people in their respective churches well—otherwise, the norms would change. In the first church, the question now is how flexible their style of worship is and especially how flexible ways of participation are. Is it all right not to raise your hands and close your eyes? Perhaps. Is it all right to rock back and forth or flap your hands in order to coordinate the sensory input and/or concentrate on specific aspects of the worship event? At which point will one feel judgmental looks? Is it possible to be different from the majority and still be valued as a member of the community? What if you require some adaptations—for example, in the overall volume or the volume of the snare drum in particular? Should the church make all the adaptations that you ask for?

Similar questions arise in the second church. How does the community respond to the person who jumps up and down and by doing so makes noise during silent moments? How does that community let you feel that you belong to them, that you are a treasured member, and that you are accepted as you are? What are the liturgical values of silence, solemnity, worship styles, and so on? The point is this: the answer to all these questions reveals the community's norms and its framework of normalcy. As we have seen, the problem is not that the community has certain norms and values—in other words, a framework; on the contrary, they make living and belonging possible. Nevertheless, the community needs to be aware of its framework and needs to evaluate it in light of the gospel.

In the section "Practicing Normalcy: Economies of Exchange," I mentioned Reynolds' claim, after Taylor, that normalcy is embedded in the frameworks within which we live and that those frameworks are related to our desire for the "good." According to Reynolds, the desire for the "good" is intrinsically related to the desire to belong. Therefore, he argues that "the basic question of human existence, then, is whether there is welcome at the heart of things. Will I be received and embraced? Is there a voice behind all other voices that says, 'You are precious, and I will be there for you?'"[56] Is this not also the basic question we ask when we come to church? In liturgy, we narrate our existence before and in relation to God. In the worship service, through the liturgical ritual, we navigate our lives and its meaning within the narrative framework of the God who was at the beginning, is now, and forever shall be.[57] In liturgy, we are listening for that "voice behind all other voices that says, 'You are precious, and I will be there for you.'" Our frameworks of normalcy should enable people to hear that voice, instead of creating barriers and obfuscating that voice.

Frameworks are not an abstract, objective, unchangeable given, which means that they could be different to what they are. That gives us the responsibility to consider critically whether the cultural frameworks that we live by are the best possible and to deconstruct the cult of normalcy that reveals and reinforces these frameworks. For Christians, it means to consider them in light of the frameworks offered by the Scriptures and by tradition. Frameworks, and the concomitant protective dynamics of normalcy, are what shapes us, what we believe, what we live by more often than not unknowingly. When these frameworks turn out to exclude autistic people, we need to evaluate critically the thresholds of cultural frameworks and propose a more faithful alternative where needed to enable every person to hear that "voice behind all other voices." For as long as this alternative framework is more of an eschatological "not yet" than an "already," we will need to find ways to follow Jesus that eschew societies' current frameworks and strive to live out God's alternative framework insofar as possible. The "theology of presence" that I will discuss in the next chapter offers a way to do this.

4

Presence and Participation
Toward a Theology of Availability

Stuart Murray observed that the girls in the picture on the front cover of his book were present, as we discussed in chapter 2. Whatever theory of autism one applies to the picture, in the last analysis, the girls are present. This is a simple but profound observation, especially in contrast to the absence of autistic people in church communities. Moreover, even when autistic people are present, they often feel misunderstood or even judged for who they are and how they are present. In the previous chapter, I have argued that at the root of absence, misunderstanding, and judgment lies the cult of normalcy. In this chapter, I will start to respond to the cult of normalcy and its effects by pausing, with Murray, to acknowledge the presence of autistic people. To be present to one another, however, requires a particular quality of presence. I will explore that quality first on the basis of Gabriel Marcel's philosophy of presence and *disponibilité* ("availability" or "disposability"), which I will then put into dialogue with the theological notions of "kenosis," "participation," and "being in Christ." To aid this discussion, let me give two examples of autistic people who are present yet absent in their churches. The examples are fictitious but realistic.

Saint Boniface Church recently welcomed Graham, who identifies as autistic. Welcoming and sensitive as they are, the church leadership decided within weeks to turn down the volume of the music, as they know this might be an issue for autistic people. They acknowledged Graham's presence in this way and tried to care for his needs. They missed one step in this process, however, which was to listen to Graham himself. Had they asked Graham, they would have found out that Graham does not mind loud music, but he gets headaches from the fluorescent lights. The church is well meaning, but they have failed to provide what is most needed for Graham; they have come up with a solution for a problem that does not exist, while remaining unaware of problems that do exist. Graham is present in the sense that the entire conversation takes place because he joined the church, but he is absent in the conversations and decision-making.

The second example takes place just after the worship service, during coffee time. Jenny comes up to a parent (Sophia) and her autistic child (Alysia). Jenny knows that Sophia does not find it easy to raise her autistic child and kindly asks how Sophia's week has been. Jenny and Sophia start to talk about Alysia. Alysia herself does not really join the conversation, although she stands next to her mom. There may be all kinds of reasons for Alysia not to join in, and we may draw on various theories of autism to interpret this scene (just as with the girls on the front cover of Murray's book). We may refer to the idea that many autistic people have difficulties with social communication. We may speculate, relatedly, that Alysia has difficulties with processing information and therefore cannot join in. We may think of sensory issues that put Alysia off—maybe Jenny wears a distinct perfume that Alysia finds painful. We may interpret Alysia's standing back a little as unwillingness to participate in the conversation. All of these might be possible, but referring to our theoretical concepts of autism may obscure another possibility: Alysia is always talked about and this is yet again such a situation—she is simply fed up with it! Again, all of these explanations might be possible; the point is, have Jenny and Sophia tried consistently to involve Alysia herself in the conversation? Have they acknowledged Alysia's presence, and are they present to her?

From these two examples, it follows, ironically, that autistic people can be entirely absent from discussions and practices even if—or actually, because—"we" talk about "them." (Note that although I try to avoid us-versus-them language in this book, here I use it deliberately.) The two examples of Graham and Alysia are slightly different, however. Graham was absent from the meetings and discussions in which it was decided which steps the church would take to be inclusive for Graham, which resulted in him not being listened to. Alysia, on the contrary, was present in this example; she stood right next to her mom. She was not listened to, not because she was absent but because she was ignored. This is a subtle but important distinction, as it informs the concepts that we use to discuss the problem of presence and absence. Although presence might be (and is, as I will argue) the counter to absence, presence is not necessarily the answer to being ignored. One can be present without being present *to* the other, as in the case of Jenny's (and Sophia's) ignoring of Alysia. To counter ignorance, we will need to make ourselves available (Marcel: *disponible*) to the other.

Back to the girls in the picture on Murray's front cover. Murray observes that they are present. Now we take one step further: I am also present. However, as long as I remain a spectator, I am not available to the girls. A spectator is not a participant in the situation or in the other's life. Murray's observation about the presence of the girls is fundamental to our theology of availability, yet in this chapter, we shift our focus to the question of whether I am actually present, whether I am available to the other—whether I move from being a disinvested spectator to an invested participant. This shift also means that in this chapter, I am addressing primarily non-autistic people. Certainly, both autistic and non-autistic people are called to be present to each other, and in that sense, the discussion in this chapter is relevant for both groups of people. Nevertheless, the burden of presence is unequally shared in most communities. By that I mean, autistic people already have to empathize and bridge communication gaps between them and non-autistic people more than the other way around if they want to participate in the life of the community.[1] It is time to shift that burden, or at least to work toward sharing it more equally. Being available to another comes at a cost—autistic people have paid so much of that already.[2] Therefore, even though the concept of presence that I discuss in this chapter applies to everyone, here the summons to be present pertains to non-autistic people more than autistic people. In other words, Graham and Alysia are already present; now it is time for their communities to be present to them.

This chapter starts with a philosopher, Gabriel Marcel. The concept of availability runs through most of Marcel's work, and as such, he can help us to think about the quality of presence. To speak about being present to one another in the Christian community is not new, but I want to tease out what presence might look like when placed in dialogue with autism and the concept of availability. As the field of autism theology is still in its early development, this is an important discussion to have;

being available to each other is one of the keys to creating a worshipping community where everyone is valued, autistic and non-autistic alike.

The concept of disponibilité has strong resonances with the theological concepts of kenosis and participation in Christ. The second part of this chapter deals with these concepts in order to work out Marcel's philosophical concept theologically. The second part not only gives a theological response to the absence and ignorance of autistic people in church, but the theology of presence and availability will also result in a new normal as a response to the cult of normalcy.

INTRODUCING GABRIEL MARCEL

A detailed biographical picture of Gabriel Marcel (1889–1973) is not necessary here, but it is helpful to make some brief comments about Marcel's background and context to understand and appreciate his philosophy. Marcel was born in 1889 in Paris to a lapsed Roman Catholic father and a liberal Protestant mother. As such, he did not receive much of a religious upbringing, but he converted to Roman Catholicism in 1929 at the age of thirty-nine. Interestingly, as Brendan Sweetman notes in the introduction to his *A Gabriel Marcel Reader*, "his conversion did not significantly change his philosophy, although he inevitably came to explore the nature of the transcendent more fully in his works."[3] Indeed, although Marcel touches on spirituality and sometimes explicit discussions about God, he deliberately stays away from theology, wanting his philosophy to be accessible to both religious and nonreligious people.[4] This makes Marcel a good and quite natural conversation partner for theologians, as his philosophy lends itself to the task of theology.[5]

Marcel calls his own philosophy "concrete" and sought to distance himself from existentialism (especially opposing Jean-Paul Sartre's philosophy), which he saw as pessimistic and atheist.[6] Concrete philosophy for Marcel means "to philosophize *hic et nunc* [here and now]," which is evident in his frequent rejection of abstract thought that loses connection with reality.[7] Often, Marcel will work with concrete examples to work out his philosophical thoughts. The concreteness of his philosophy can also be seen in the fact that not only did he write philosophical essays but also plays.[8] In his philosophical work, he sometimes illustrates his points by rehearsing dialogues from his plays. Marcel's concrete philosophy, including his analyses of social situations, does not lead to generalized abstractions but instead "implies an awareness ... of a fundamental mystery."[9] At times, Marcel will argue that that mystery, through being present to and encountering one another, leads to an encounter with God.

PRESENCE

As the example of Alysia, Sophia, and Jenny shows, we can be present in the same room with someone without being really present to them. We can ignore the other, as happened to Alysia in this example. Or, even if we do communicate with the other, this can be done in an instrumental way rather than in a way that establishes a deeper connection with each other. In Marcel's words:

> We could say that the man sitting beside us was in the same room as ourselves, but that he was not really *present* there, that his *presence* did not make itself felt. . . . Something essential is lacking. One might say that what we have with this person, who is in the room, but somehow not really present to us, is communication without communion: unreal communication, in a word. He understands what I say to him, but he does not understand *me*: I may even have the extremely disagreeable feeling that my own words, as he repeats them to me, as he reflects them back at me, have become unrecognizable. By a very singular phenomenon indeed, this stranger interposes himself between me and my own reality, he makes me in some sense also a stranger to myself; I am not really myself while I am with him.
>
> The opposite phenomenon, however, can also take place. When somebody's presence does really make itself felt, it can refresh my inner being; it reveals me to myself, it makes me more fully myself than I should be if I were not exposed to its impact.[10]

This example shows that being absent to one another can have dehumanizing effects. Here, I am not referring to the absence of autistic people in church due to being excluded but to the examples of Graham and Alysia above, where people thought they were being present to them (especially to Graham) but in effect were not. Because of such absence, or perhaps it is better to say, such ignoring, Graham and Alysia are prevented from being themselves in relationship with others. An opportunity for flourishing is being missed, or as Marcel says, they might become strangers to themselves in these situations.

Nevertheless, Marcel also offers a counterexample. A stranger on the train and I may share certain experiences, or we may like similar books or food. This creates a bond: "you too."[11] Marcel puts it rather strongly, saying that this person "has fused into the living unity he now forms with me."[12] We might say that we have moved from spectators to participants—from a disinvested look at each other in passing to beginning to be involved in each other's lives. The recognition of "you too" is important when we think about what it means to be a worshipping community of autistic and non-autistic people together. "You too" has the potential to break the boundaries of autistic *versus* non-autistic (without denying differences that are real and that the cult of normalcy deals with some oppressively) and to recognize each other by shared experiences—in particular, the experience of being loved by God and adopted into God's kinship. We can hear similar theological overtones in Marcel's statement about "the living unity he now forms with me." The theological meaning of this will become clearer later in this chapter when discussing Susan Eastman's concept of the person in which there is a "living unity" not just with one another but also with Christ.

Being present to one another in the way that we have talked about so far can be further explained by the notion of "intersubjectivity." Marcel explains intersubjectivity as follows. Suppose you are lost in a city. You see someone in the street and decide to ask him for directions. This, in and of itself, does not establish intersubjectivity in Marcel's understanding of the concept. Rather, the man in the street is used as an instrument, as a signpost. Marcel's point is that even though we address this person as a "you," we treat him as an "It."[13] There may be nothing wrong with that, but it does not establish intersubjectivity.[14] However, Marcel continues, suppose that it is late at night when you have lost your way, you risk walking around for many more hours if you do not get help, and the neighborhood where you find yourself does not appear to be very safe. If the man in the street is genuinely interested in helping you, then

> I may have a fleeting but irresistible impression that the stranger I am appealing to is a brother eager to come to my aid. What happens is, in a word, that the stranger has started off by putting himself, as it were, ideally in my shoes. He has come within my reach as a person.... This is nothing more than a sort of spark of spirituality, out as soon as it is in; the stranger and I part almost certainly never to see each other again, yet for a few minutes, as I trudge homewards, this man's unexpected cordiality makes me feel as if I had stepped out of a wintry day into a warm room.[15]

In this example, intersubjectivity—what we may paraphrase as "a true and real connection with someone else"—is established with a stranger. The example shows that intersubjectivity can be established even in brief encounters. Indeed, elsewhere Marcel observes that "presence is something which reveals itself immediately and unmistakably in a look, a smile, an intonation, or a handshake."[16] What characterizes such an encounter, however brief or long that encounter is, is a feeling of relief but more importantly, an (inexpressible) feeling of connection. The connection is life giving and energizing. The stranger has put himself in the shoes of the other; he has made himself available to the other.

Marcel deepens his ideas of presence as being available to someone, and the intersubjectivity that originates from that with the notion of "being *with*" someone. The preposition "with" denotes a specific relationship: "My relationship *with* you makes a difference to both of us, and so does any interruption of the relationship make a difference."[17] "Being with," therefore, describes a type of relationship that cannot be captured by spatial categories of interiority or exteriority; rather, it is a "genuine intimacy" that Marcel feels is best expressed by the Latin word *coesse*.[18] We could render this in English literally as "co-being." Marcel argues that "to encounter someone is not merely to cross his path but to be, for the moment at least, near to or with him. To use a term I have often used before, it means being a *co-presence*."[19] This circles back to the "living unity" that we discussed above. The various ways of describing such unity—as "being *with*," as *coesse* or as "copresence"—point to a reality that eludes precise linguistic definitions. There is an intimacy here that is difficult to describe but can be lived by making ourselves available to each other—by being with each other.

This section has started to introduce Marcel's ideas of presence as a specific way of being with each other, which he calls intersubjectivity, and that leads to an "inexpressible feeling of connection." I have made some initial connections between Marcel's concept of presence and our discussion of autism. For Marcel, presence has a certain quality to it that he explains with the word "disponibilité" to which we now turn.

DISPONIBILITÉ/AVAILABILITY

As we have seen, it is possible to be present to someone in a way that either does or does not establish a connection and communion. To be present in a way that communicates something like "I see you; I hear you; I care for you; you are important to me" is what Marcel calls disponibilité. An English translation of the word falls a bit flat of the French meaning, but it is usually translated as "availability" or "disposability." (The latter term should be interpreted as "being at someone's disposal" and not as "being redundant.") When we are available to each other, we are creating community, and by being with each other in this way, we can encounter God.

Marcel introduces the notion of disponibilité together with that of *indisponibilité*.[20] He points out that the literal English translations of these words—namely, "availability" and "unavailability"—do not convey the French connotation, which Marcel says is rather that of

> handiness and unhandiness, the basic idea being that of having or not having, in a given contingency, one's resources to hand or at hand. The self-centered person, in this sense, is unhandy; I mean that he remains incapable of responding to calls made upon him by life. . . . He will be incapable of sympathizing with other people, or even of imagining their situation. He remains shut up in himself, in the petty circle of his private experience, which forms a kind of hard shell round him that he is incapable of breaking through.[21]

Marcel can conclude, therefore, that it is essential for people "to orientate [themselves] toward something other than [themselves], but also to be inwardly conjoined and adapted . . . to that reality transcending the individual life which gives the individual life its point and, in a certain sense, even its justification."[22] This last part is important: self-centeredness contrasts with the point of being human. It seems that Marcel is saying that self-centeredness results in an inward spiral, which is inward looking and increasingly becomes "unhandy"—that is, 'unavailable' to the other and unable to respond to another's needs and perhaps even to another's presence. It is the person sitting in the same room but not understanding me and, in the worst case, making me a stranger even to myself, as we saw above.

Marcel argues that the category of disposability is even constitutive of what it means to be a human being and relates that to spirituality. "I wonder if we could not define the whole spiritual life as the sum of activities by which we try to reduce in ourselves the part played by non-disposability."[23] It seems warranted to conclude on this basis that to be human is to be oriented outward, to be able to give oneself to another. Giving oneself does not make us poorer but actually enriches us.[24] As we saw earlier, giving oneself, presence as disposability, creates connection and communion by which all parties are enriched and become more human.

Marcel discusses presence as availability/disposability in terms of belonging to someone. Suppose I say to my friend, "Jack, I belong to you. This means, I am opening an unlimited credit account in your name, you can do what you want with me, I give myself to you."[25] Marcel is quick to point out that that does not mean I become Jack's slave. On the contrary, instead of losing my freedom, giving myself to the other is an ultimate act of freedom.[26] Furthermore, giving myself to another does not mean that I do not love myself, although Marcel distinguishes between self-love that is egocentric (which is idolatrous) and self-love that regards the self as a "seed which must be cultivated, as a ground which must be readied for the spiritual or even for the divine in this world."[27] Egocentric self-love is complacent with oneself and turns in on oneself, whereas self-love which sees the need for oneself to grow is open toward the other and to influences from outside. It accepts its permeability in which belonging to one another is an opportunity for growth instead of losing one's freedom.

Marcel explores the phrase "I belong to you" further in another essay in the same book, *Creative Fidelity*, this time in relation to the counter-statement "You belong to me." "The latter implies a claim, the former a commitment."[28] When this commitment is mutual, with an attitude of self-love that acknowledges its need to be cultivated, there is mutual growth. Marcel illuminates what happens in such a relationship with the example of a married couple, who have mutually committed to belong to each other. "Since I cease to belong to myself, it is not literally true to say that you belong to me; we transcend one another in the very heart of *our love*. The doubt which threatens to infiltrate each of us is thus abolished to make room for a superior certainty which transcends us."[29] The risk of saying "I belong to you" and of "opening an unlimited credit account in your name" has now become a certainty in a mutual relationship of belonging in which there is true freedom which leads to growth.

Interestingly, Marcel comments every now and then on the connections between his philosophy and spirituality and religion, but typically, he deliberately stays away from theologizing. However, at this point in the discussion, he does make some theological claims. In particular, Marcel recognizes that some literature from Christian mysticism asserts that Christ claims that "you belong to me." Although this claim is arrogant and misguided when anyone else asserts this, "it is precisely because He is not someone else that He can arrogate to himself this right over me, but only to the extent that He becomes more internal to me than myself. It is not in terms of power but in terms of love that this right can be understood."[30] In the language of Scripture, we could say that Christ lives in me or that I have died with Christ and now Christ lives in me (Gal 2:20; we will come back to this later in this chapter)—"He becomes more internal to me than myself." Here, we find our true selves: "To know that I belong to You, to Thou, is to know that I belong to myself only on this condition—what is more, that this belonging is identical to and confused with the only complete and authentic freedom to which I can lay claim; this freedom is a gift; yet it is necessary for me to accept it."[31] It is interesting to note that Marcel switches from the third person to the second person; he addresses God directly as You and Thou. It is in this intimate relationship, understood not in terms of coercion but of love, that we discover who we are.

One might ask at this point how we move from this belonging to God to disponibilité as belonging to someone else, to give ourselves to another. I want to offer two related observations in response to that question. The first is that one of the recurring words in this discussion is "freedom." As we just noted, Marcel equates belonging to God with "complete and authentic freedom." Any relationship with someone else in which we say "I belong to you" finds its starting point in our belonging to Christ. The freedom found in Christ is the basis for the freedom we find in giving ourselves to another. The second observation relates more specifically to the Christian community, where we relate to each other as people "in Christ." It is not just me who belongs to Christ; all members of the faith community belong to Christ. Here, Dietrich Bonhoeffer's reflections on Christian community are exactly to the point.[32] In his book *Life Together*, he writes, "A Christian comes to others only through Jesus Christ."[33] In the Christian community, we relate to each other always through Jesus Christ. The Christian community is not based on any quality of any of its members but constituted solely on the basis that all members are "in Christ."[34] Our disposability to each other rests on Christ's disposability to us. This is why the encounter with each other in this way is an encounter with God.[35]

In the introduction to this chapter, we noted that Alysia, Sophia, and Jenny were present in the same room but not really present—Alysia was ignored even if she was the subject of the conversation. Marcel makes a very similar observation. We have already discussed his example of the person in the room who is present, who may even repeat my words back to me but nevertheless does not seem to notice *me* and thereby can even make me feel a stranger to myself. In his essay "On the Ontological Mystery," Marcel even goes a step further. Even if the other person really wants to listen to me, they can fail to be present:

> The most attentive and the most conscientious listener may give me the impression of not being present; he gives me nothing, he cannot make room for me in himself. . . . The truth is that there is a way of listening which is a way of giving, and another way of listening which is a way

of refusing, of refusing *oneself*; the material gift, the visible action, do not necessarily witness to presence.[36]

The notion of hospitality is helpful to interpret what Marcel is saying.[37] To offer hospitality is "truly to communicate something of oneself to the other"—it is to welcome that person into that space that is meaningful to you.[38] It is not just a space but a space with emotional connections to the people and the things that you care for or who have cared for you. As Thomas Reynolds writes, "In love another person is received as a gift, a presence to which I respond. In turn I share myself with that other person, revealing back to them their own value. Together we then form a bond of reciprocal mutuality by which we reach become more than ourselves alone."[39] At the heart of hospitality, of welcoming the other's presence and reciprocating that presence, there is the giving of oneself—being available, at the disposal of another. The difference is between seeing the other as a presence or as an object.[40] Even if Jenny had talked to Alysia, she could have done this in a way that turned Alysia into an object. Of course, positively, she could have talked to her in a present way: offering herself with the attitude of "I belong to you," making room within herself for Alysia and what she has to offer.

Presence as availability leads to communion, as we have seen, but seeing the other as an object leads to alienation.[41] My friend James, who is autistic and uses a spelling board to communicate, commented sharply in one of our correspondences: "We are treated as projects and not as people who can contribute. Vocation is not discussed. We offer so much." James is not doubting the good intentions of people who want to do something for him and others on the autism spectrum; however, he is saying that he is often treated as an object instead of another presence in a relationship of mutual availability. Being available is a way of being that makes room for the other as a person. It is a way of being in which "doing for" is not the starting point but rather listening to the other, letting go of one's preconceived notions of who the other is and what might be good for them. In that way, autistic and non-autistic people can, instead of turning one or the other into an object, "form a bond of reciprocal mutuality."

That is not to say that forming such relationships is easy. It can be difficult to get along with someone who is like us; it is even more difficult to sympathize with someone who is very different from us. But this is exactly the point, according to Reynolds: the difference of the other, which shows us our own limitations, forces us to acknowledge our insufficiency.[42] Here, we are back to what we noted above, that presence as availability is the opposite of self-sufficiency. The other draws us out of ourselves, lets us orient ourselves outward to another person or another cause. That is why the other makes us more human and why indeed we cannot exist on our own but become who we are only in relationship to others.

In being confronted with our being different than the other, with whom we do not have the resources to sympathize (or so we think), the risk is to fall back to the safety of normalcy. That is why normalcy is an evasive dynamic, which we use, knowingly or unknowingly, to evade or avoid those whom we cannot place within in our boundaries.[43] This is where availability is an alternative response: instead of giving up because of our lack of imagination, we open up ourselves to the other regardless and make ourselves available to them. Reynolds muses, "This is precisely why weakness harnesses a strange power. It breaks through the false pretences that have numbed our sensibilities. It disturbs the normal and in so doing excites the imagination. How so? By rendering us insufficient to ourselves. And the medium of this is our capacity for sympathy."[44] Sympathy is the result of being truly present to one another. "A *shared* sense of mutual vulnerability is the axis upon which this recognition takes place, linking persons together 'as if' they coincided."[45] Sympathy means that we set aside the dynamic of normalcy by which we judge the other. Sympathy precedes judgment, and sympathy itself is preceded by presence—the presence of the other and the call for us to be present to the other.[46] Murray made the simple observation that the girls in the picture of the front cover of his book are present, regardless of the theory of autism with which one studies the picture. We can now see why this is not only a simple but also a most profound observation. The girls are present, and they require that we are present to them. The autistic people in our[47] churches are present, and they require non-autistic people to be present to them. Presence is not an act of charity but a relationship of belonging to each other, by which we are changed and through which "we become more than what we were before."[48]

In summary, the discussion of (in)disponibilité adds rich texture to what it means to be present, for mere presence can be absence in disguise by either ignoring the other or by being turned inward to such an extent that one can be present yet unavailable to the other. For Marcel, the key is to turn outward, with a commitment even to saying "I belong to you." Such a commitment does not neglect self-care, as it is rooted in mutual commitment in which the partners in this relationship participate in each other's lives—a notion that featured in Reynolds' discussion of sympathy and that foreshadows the discussion further below. Marcel uses the metaphor of hospitality to illuminate what it means to be present to one another (although in his philosophy of presence, this is hardly a metaphor but can in fact be a lived reality as part of being available). The host shares of their life with the guest, and the guest does likewise.

In the beginning of the chapter, I stated that Marcel's philosophy lends itself well for further theological reflection. In the next section, I will explore one way in which we can do this, which is to consider the concept of disponibilité alongside the theological concept of "kenosis" (self-emptying).

DISPONIBILITÉ AND KENOSIS

I have argued in the previous section that Marcel's concepts of availability and presence can help us to counter both ignorance and absence with regard to autistic people in worshipping communities. One theological notion that resonates with these concepts is that of kenosis. Just as Marcel argues that one can only be available—and therefore truly present to the other—by turning one's focus outward rather than inward, so in the act of kenosis ("self-emptying"), Jesus turned outward and made himself available to humankind instead of focusing inwardly—that is, on equality with God (Phil 2:7). By considering disponibilité in light of kenosis, the discussion moves from a focus on being present with one another to a focus on God's presence with the faithful community, showing how our intersubjective presence is rooted in the divine gift of God's presence.[49] In the next sections, we will explore how such rooting can be helpfully understood by reflecting on what it means to "participate in Christ" or "be in union with Christ." The indwelling of Christ in the community through the Holy Spirit and the subsequent participation of the believers in Christ leads to a new identity and to a new normal, thereby responding to the problem of normalcy.

The word "kenosis" is usually associated with the passage from Philippians 2:5–11, which I will quote here in full for the ease of referencing (including verses 12–13, NIV).

> [5] In your relationships with one another, have the same mindset as Christ Jesus:
>
> > [6] Who, being in very nature God,
> > did not consider equality with God something to be used to his own advantage;
> > [7] rather, he made himself nothing
> > by taking the very nature of a servant,
> > being made in human likeness.

> ⁸ And being found in appearance as a man,
>   he humbled himself
>   by becoming obedient to death—
>   even death on a cross!
> ⁹ Therefore God exalted him to the highest place
>   and gave him the name that is above every name,
> ¹⁰ that at the name of Jesus every knee should bow,
>   in heaven and on earth and under the earth,
> ¹¹ and every tongue acknowledge that Jesus Christ is Lord,
>   to the glory of God the Father.
>
> ¹² Therefore, my dear friends, as you have always obeyed—not only in my presence, but now much more in my absence—continue to work out your salvation with fear and trembling, ¹³ for it is God who works in you to will and to act in order to fulfil his good purpose.

In discussing this passage, I will lean primarily (but not only) on the exegeses of this passage by John Barclay and Susan Eastman because their writing is evocative for the purposes of this chapter.[50] To start with Barclay, who in fact follows Eastman, one of the first claims he makes is that this passage should be read as a soteriological narrative.[51] Since the nineteenth century, the passage often has been read as an ethical instruction, over and against a purely Christological reading.[52] However, both readings miss the main point, which is that Christ's self-emptying in this drama of salvation is a means to the end of salvation, not the end in and of itself. The passage is also not primarily a call to humbleness, which would be an ethical reading of the chapter; again, this is implied but it is not the main point. When the apostle Paul instructs the Philippians to imitate Christ (v. 5) and to obey (v. 12) and likewise "empty" themselves, and act in humility toward one another, humbleness is not an end in itself but is the means to participate in the salvific drama. In this way, humbleness serves to form a unity together under the lordship of Christ (v. 11). Thus, Barclay steers our discussion of what it means to be available toward each other in a specific way: this is not to be seen as an act of charity, even not just to make this world a better place, but the way we relate to each other in the Christian community has an eschatological direction: God's work of gathering everyone under the reign of Jesus Christ, to the glory of God. When churches want to become places of belonging for autistic and non-autistic people alike, this is not to be seen as charity work toward autistic people but as participation in the soteriological story of Jesus' kenosis, to gather autistic and non-autistic people alike under his reign.

At the outset of our discussion, then, it is important to see that this "Christ hymn"[53] foregrounds God's activity. In the soteriological narrative, God is the main actor, restoring helpless humanity to God's self; Jesus is the one who emptied himself ("made himself nothing," in the words of the NIV), took the form of a slave, a human being, who humbled himself and was obedient to death; God exalted Jesus to the highest place, giving him the name above all names. Only then do human beings come into view, and their action is a response—a response of worship because of Jesus' acts and God's acts in and toward Jesus. The human action is directed toward God in the first place: every knee should bow and every tongue confess the lordship of Christ, to the glory of the Father. That—the lordship of Christ and the glory of God—is the motivation for the way the believers are to interact with each other (vv. 5 and 12–13), patterned on Jesus' "mindset."[54] Being available to each other in the Christian community is rooted in Christ's availability to God and humankind. Without Christ's availability, there would be no Christian community.

Paul's call to the believers to be one in Christ, then, is tied to the believers' unity in Christ. Unity in Christ is a way of glorifying God (vv. 10–11) and an imperative that flows from having the same "mindset" of Christ. Whenever people are excluded because of their neurological makeup, the unity breaks down. Paul is concerned about the unity in the congregation. Unity concerns both unity within the congregation and unity with Christ. Barclay explains,

> If that [eschatological] goal is the unification of all things (*every* knee and *every* tongue) under the lordship of Christ, the momentum toward that end necessitates the unity of the community in its solidarity with Christ. Believers . . . are conformed (*symmorphizomenos*) to his death, in "solidarity" (*koinōnia*) with his sufferings (3:10), and they anticipate resurrection in a body shaped to (*symmorphon*) his glorious body: it is their union with Christ that constitutes the salvific trajectory.[55]

With these and other examples of the language of "with" (*syn/sym*) and "solidarity," Barclay makes a strong case for understanding unity in the community and unity with Christ as intrinsically related and as integral to God's salvific purposes. Making sure that the Christian community is a place where everybody belongs, autistic or non-autistic, is not an optional extra, nor can it be relegated to some churches that have a "special ministry," but it is (or should be) an inherent characteristic of a community of believers that has the same "mindset" of Christ.

When we keep this soteriological thrust of the "Christ hymn" in the forefront of our minds, we can start to look into the instruction to follow Christ in his humbleness. This is often turned into the focus of the passage (wrongly so, according to Barclay), and he points out that "the instruction to look out for the interests of others (2:2–3) is importantly *reciprocal*—a command to *each* and *every* person, as they consider '*one another*' of higher status than themselves . . . *everyone* is at the same time looking out for the superior interests of *everyone* else."[56] For our discussion, this means that it is not just the non-autistic people who need to look after the autistic people; it is also the other way around. To be sure, the onus has been too often on the autistic people in the congregation to, frankly, put up with the non-autistic people. In the introduction to this chapter, I said therefore that I will try to reverse this pattern. However, without backtracking on that reversal, Barclay shows that the emphasis here is on mutuality and reciprocity. The picture that emerges is that of a community in which all members value one another. Moreover, although in Western cultures, or at least in the United Kingdom, much emphasis is placed on equality, Barclay observes that "in paradoxical but characteristic fashion, Paul's path to equalization runs through not a static equality but reciprocal asymmetry (cf. Gal 5:13: 'through love be slaves of one another'). . . . Solidarity arises through mutual commitment, putting the self in service 'for' one another in order to be fully 'with' each other."[57] This is reminiscent of Marcel's discussion of availability as "being with"—a kenotic way of belonging to each other and a giving away of oneself to the other. Such self-giving has huge potential to address the dynamics of normalcy because those are power dynamics. Self-giving, or kenosis, is inherently a giving up of power and, as Barclay says, asymmetrical.

We have seen several instances where Barclay highlights Paul's language of "being with" one another. Just as Christ was "for" and "with" us, so his followers are called to be "for" and "with" one another. Thus, Paul's language helps us to lay a theological foundation under Marcel's "being with." In Marcel's understanding, this "being with" is aimed at the other person, being available and at the other's disposal. Marcel says that indisponibilité comes from being turned in on oneself—selfishness. At the same time, he talks about self-love to guard against an oppressive notion of self-sacrifice. Likewise, Paul does warn against selfishness, but the contrast to that is not a loss of oneself but is to "the 'self-for' that is also the 'self-with,' the self whose commitment to the other is not ultimately at the expense of the self (properly configured) but aims at shared benefit and conjoint flourishing."[58] Note again the relationship to hospitality here, where making room in oneself for the other does not mean to lose oneself but to give of oneself. The shared benefit that Barclay talks about should not be read as if "being with" includes an interior goal, an agenda for self-benefit. Barclay formulates it slightly differently in the next paragraph, where he states, "Christ commits himself to be *for* and *with* humanity so that humanity may share *with him* in the telos of the story. By the same token, where believers commit themselves to be *for* and *with* each other, their goal is not to annihilate themselves, but to share together in the grace of God."[59] We can see how, in Barclay's reading, "being with" and "being for" in Paul's language does very much the same work as Marcel's language of "being with" and indisponibilité. However, there is one important distinction between Paul and Marcel here. Paul connects this "being with" to Christ's "being with" and "being for" humanity, which is the theological ground for relationships in the Christian community. The divine presence and availability precedes human intersubjective presence and availability. A theology of presence and availability starts with God's presence and availability in Christ, who is present in the community through His Spirit, inspiring subsequently our presence and availability toward each other.

This brief discussion shows how we can think of kenosis as Christ's availability to God and humankind. In this theological account, Christ's presence and availability are soteriological—the salvation of humankind and all creation depends on them. A kenotic theology is a theology of incarnation and therefore of God's presence: Emmanuel, God is with us. It is also a theology of obedience to death on a cross, which in the New Testament is strongly linked to salvation. At the same time, a kenotic theology is a theology of resurrection, of new life, which is available to the faith community through the indwelling of Christ by the Holy Spirit. This new life is characterized by unity in the faith community, to the glory of God, which is seen in the mutual availability of the believers. By following Jesus Christ's kenosis, and so relating to each other according to the norm of self-giving love, we can create a new framework in the community—one that does not exclude autistic people but wherein autistic people are self-evidently a part of the community, held in bonds of mutual, reciprocal love. A kenotic theology and praxis are rooted in Christ's availability, but they acknowledge Paul's instruction to have the same "mindset." The imitation of Christ is often thought of in terms of participation in or union with Christ, to which we now turn.

KENOSIS, IMITATION, AND PARTICIPATION

The concepts of "participation in Christ" or "union with Christ" have evoked much debate in the twentieth century, which continues to the present day.[60] I will primarily build on Susan Eastman's interpretation of "participation in Christ," first to discuss how Christ's participation in humanity enables and provides the basis for human participation in Christ.[61] Then, in the next section, I will explore how Christ's indwelling in the faith community through the Holy Spirit results in a new norm, providing a counter to the cult of normalcy as discussed in the previous chapter. The believers' participation in Christ, rooted in Christ's kenotic participation in humanity, provides the foundation for mutual availability in the faith community.

We start our discussion with Eastman's interpretation of Philippians 2:5–11, the passage that figured prominently in our discussion of kenosis.[62] Eastman explains the passage heuristically by using the model of the theater in ancient Rome. Plays, pantomimes, and other such events were often participatory, where the public could be drawn into the play, or slaves or criminals were forced to act certain roles. The actor often became the person they were impersonating (*homoiōma*, "likeness"[63]), even to the point of death (if that was their script/role). Eastman points out that the language that Paul uses in the Philippians passage is that of the semantic field of the theater. Christ participated in the divine soteriological drama, as it were, by taking on the role of the human, indeed to the extent that he became one with the role he played, even unto death.[64] "At the same time," Eastman adds, "God's subsequent exaltation of the divine and human Jesus in verses 9–11, echoing Isaiah 43:23, reveals that Christ has been acting throughout in the divine character."[65] To be clear, Christ was not just playacting as if it all was not real. It was real, and Eastman's explanation of the participation language is a way of being able to distinguish between the divine and human nature of Christ (although Eastman does not make this claim here) and to see how the divine did share in the human condition.[66]

Christ's participation in the human nature enables humanity to participate in Christ. Just as Christ became the "likeness" of the first Adam (and, as Eastman argues, thereby of all humanity[67]), so humanity can now regain their likeness of the image of God.[68] Thus, we find our identity in Christ. With reference to Robert Tannehill, Eastman states it succinctly: "divine participation initiates a reciprocal human participation in Christ." Or in her own terms, "Christ's assimilation to the human condition [initiates] a reciprocal human imitation of God."[69] There is reciprocity here, a mutual imitation, but it is important to see the order in which this happens. Eastman is keen to point out that Christ's participation in humanity comes first. Only God's initiative in this divine drama of salvation enables human participation in the narrative. This helps again to guard against reading this passage as an ethical imperative for Christians without grounding it in the salvific narrative, which is not to say that there is no ethical exhortation but that the exhortation finds its basis and meaning in the story of God and humans.

> To jump too quickly to appropriating Philippians 2:1–13 as an exhortation to the imitation of Christ is, in my view, to miss the point. The movement of the plot is not that of humanity becoming like Christ but of Christ becoming like Adamic humanity. Any talk about imitation must begin by talking about Christ's assimilation to the realm of human affairs, initiating and sustaining a relational bond that restructures the self in relationship to others.[70]

Thus, whatever the creative imitation of the "in Christ mindset" entails within the Christian community, it is rooted in Christ's participation in, and identification with, humanity and creation's suffering. "Christ's movement from difference to similarity, from distance to solidarity, is itself the source of paraenetic power."[71] This is key: the imitation of Christ starts with Christ's imitation of humanity; the strength to imitate Christ does not need to come from human strength but comes from God's power in Christ, as Christ is present in the community through the Holy Spirit. Being present and available to each other in the community starts with Christ's presence and availability to us. Here, we see again the necessity of a *theology* of presence that needs to go beyond the (rich) insights of Marcel's philosophy.

Having emphasized Christ's imitation of humanity before human imitation of Christ, we should now say a little more about the latter. Several authors are keen to point out that to speak only of imitation without participation results in ethical imperatives without sufficient grounding in Christ's love for humanity. Andrew Root, in his book *Christopraxis*, argues that we need to move beyond *imitatio Christi* to *participatio Christi*.[72] Imitation of itself remains too much at the level of human activity, without accounting for God's work for humanity through Christ and the Holy Spirit, which is the grounds on which human imitation of Christ becomes at all possible. Moreover, Root's argument aligns with Eastman's in articulating a double participation—that is, it is Christ's participation in humanity that makes human participation in Christ possible.⁷³ A similar argument is put forward by Douglas Campbell, in an essay on participation and faith in Paul's letters. Discussing the encouragement Paul gives to the Romans in chapter 15, for the "strong" to please the "weak," Campbell points to verse 5 in which Paul grounds this ethical command in the mindset of Christ (note the overlap with Philippians 2) and prays that God will give that mindset to the Roman believers. The verse "explicitly grounds such exhortations in Christ's own way of thinking, and hence in effect in a christological ontology that has been gifted to Christians by God.... To possess Christ's way of thinking *is* to be disposed to love others."⁷⁴ Campbell's mention of a Christological ontology seals the argument that the believers' acting in love, as an imitation of Christ, is rooted in participation in Christ and indeed Christ's participation in humanity. Grant Macaskill makes a similar point throughout his book *Union with Christ in the New Testament*, especially when he says, "Imitation of Christ in love is not a naked act of moral achievement, but a conscious and dynamic participation in God's love for the world" (269). Presence and availability—love—in the Christian community is therefore thoroughly theological. We imitate Christ's love for his people, especially those who find themselves pushed to the margins by participating in Christ's love. To be available, to be present, and to love is not simply a moral command; it is who we are, it is our identity in Christ.

PARTICIPATION: A NEW NORMAL

When, as a community and as individuals in the community, we receive our identity in Christ, it is because of our participation in Christ. Susan Eastman explains this in her discussion of Philippians 2 but also draws on Galatians 2.⁷⁵ This is set within Eastman's broader interpretation of Pauline anthropology in which she argues that Paul's anthropology is not a rigid modern individualism but instead is a view in which people are constituted by each other. Paul's view of his own person, as constituted both by himself and by Christ living in him, is neither passive nor lacking autonomy and "can be grasped only when we realize that his notion of the person is thoroughly participatory and relational."⁷⁶ In other words, who we are as individuals is always influenced by those around us. The boundaries of our personalities are porous, so to speak.⁷⁷ Just as Christ takes on the role of the human being in the divine drama (as we have seen in Eastman's theater analogy for explaining Philippians 2) and identifies entirely with the character he takes on but nevertheless remains fully divine at the same time, so human beings imitate Christ, take on the role of Christ's body in this world, while also remaining fully human.[78] Nevertheless, because of Christ's becoming human, the human being is permeated by Christ, and thus a new identity is constituted in the believer.

Eastman explains this further in her discussion of Paul's statement in Galatians 2:20 (NIV):

> [20] I have been crucified with Christ and I no longer live, but Christ lives in me. The life I now live in the body, I live by faith in the Son of God, who loved me and gave himself for me.

Eastman is quick to point out that the phrase "Christ lives in me" does not mean that there is someone other than Paul now living in Paul's body. It is, rather, that Paul's entire identity has changed, as is made clear immediately in the phrase that follows: "The life I now live in the body, I live by faith." Here, Paul himself is the subject of the verb "live" (in the body; by faith).[79] The phrase is interesting as it points to two contrasting realms in which Paul lives/Christ lives in Paul: he lives in the body, often translated as "flesh," and in the faith, also translated as "trust." Flesh, in Paul's use of the word, is not just the body but has a much wider meaning. Eastman summarizes the meaning of the "flesh" as "both a reference to actions of the body and a relational term, implying enmeshment in, and determination by, a set of damaging constructs and divisive social practices . . . that at their worst tend to oppose and destroy God's new creation—that is, God's new community."[80] Living in faith, on the other hand, means to be part of this new community of believers; the realm permeated by Christ—the community is *in Christ* and Christ is in the community—and indwelt by the Holy Spirit. The new identity of the believers changes everything: it changes to whom they belong (being under the "lordship" of Christ), the social ties they have (see further below), their norms and values, or to use Taylor's terminology, their framework. The new identity is not only a new sense of self but a new way of being in the world.

One may wonder how it is possible to live both in the flesh and in faith at the same time if these two are opposites. Eastman argues that the key is in the clause at the end of Galatians 2:20: "the Son of God, who loved me and gave himself for me." She comments,

> The mode of life "in faith" is therefore precisely as a gift that brings the presence of the Giver into solidarity with the receiver in the messiness of daily, corporeal, social existence in the midst of the present evil age. Paul makes this relationship clear through the third use of

"in" in 2:20: "Christ lives in me." This divine presence is the source of the gift's transforming power, mediated through a mutual indwelling that remakes the receiver in a new relational system characterised by undeserved and thus noncompetitive grace.[81]

I have quoted this at length because much of it relates to the discussion so far. A first point to highlight is that Eastman speaks about the presence of the Giver—that is, the presence of Christ. I have underlined in our discussion that our participation in Christ starts with Christ's participation in humanity. It is the presence of Christ, through the Holy Spirit, in our communities that makes possible any revision of the cult of normalcy in the first place. A theological recalibration of our norms and values depends entirely on God's gracious presence with us.

Second, our existence is corporeal—that is, embodied. The point here is that a revision of our liturgies and communal practices is not up in the air of the theological ivory tower but can only be real if it is lived—that is, embodied. Furthermore, such revision is inherently social (we are "bod[ies]-in-relation to others"[82])—we are the body of Christ together, in community. And yes, that is messy. Daily existence in this world (which Paul calls the "present evil age") is messy because it is life lived in a world that is broken, where social relationships get broken, where we do not always understand each other, and where differences between autistic and non-autistic may get in the way. Nevertheless, "Christ lives in me," Paul says, and that changes everything. The source of living in faith is Christ's presence, a transforming power indeed. We do still live in the flesh in this broken world, but since Christ lives in us, we live transformed lives. To speak with Paul's words: "Therefore, if anyone is in Christ, the new creation has come: The old has gone, the new is here!" (2 Cor 5:17, NIV). The life of a Christian is an embodied living of the already and not yet.

A third point to highlight from Eastman's quotation is that when we live in faith, our relational system is "characterised by undeserved and thus noncompetitive grace." This changes our identity and our relational network. The grace comes from the one who "gave himself over for me," Paul says. It comes from the one who took the form of a human being, even the form of a slave. It comes from the one who took on the role of humanity to the extreme extent of dying in that role: dying a shameful death reserved for slaves and criminals. Kenosis means self-emptying and by implication giving up power. Now, if we have been crucified with Christ, as Paul states, then "to be joined in company with Christ on such a cross is to share fellowship with his companions there, which is surely to suffer the loss of all other sources of identity."[83] This reframes the cult of normalcy entirely. Remember that normalcy has strong social elements. Normalcy allows communities to judge who passes the threshold of what those in the community deem normal. The identity of those in a particular framework is shaped by normalcy, and the social boundaries are set in turn in an everlasting cycle. Normalcy is driven by power dynamics, which is why kenosis—as self-giving and giving up power—can provide a theological answer rather than replacing one cult of normalcy with another.

Listen to Eastman again: with Christ on the cross, the believers share fellowship with his companions there. For those who do not remain spectators but participate in the divine drama, other social ties are created, defying all norms that communities may have without Christ. Surely, the cross is shameful; it is not what anyone would like to associate with, and therefore, it is very unlikely that anyone wants to be associated with those on the cross and their friends. Yet, here is where God's new community finds its focal point. To identify with the cross is the death blow to all other identities that fight for primacy. That is not to say that other sources of identity do not exist anymore. Of course, one still has brothers and sisters, families, colleagues, and so on. However, Eastman argues that for Paul, the "ties 'in the flesh' are mediated by his new life 'in faith.' He has an independent stance toward those old sources of identity; they no longer tell him who he is, but he is free to interact with them."[84] There is a radical change in sources of identity for the believer and therefore in their identity itself. The old self is crucified with Christ, and Christ now lives in the believer—a live still lived in the realm of the flesh but not determined by that realm but by the realm of faith. By being crucified to Christ, the identity of the believer, which is always influenced and indeed constituted by others, is first of all constituted by Christ himself but also by the social ties of the new community.

The new identity of the believer, as found "in Christ," has far-reaching implications for our ideas of "normal" and therefore the dynamics of normalcy. "In this new community there is neither circumcision nor uncircumcision, because all old systems of worth are 'recalibrated.'"[85] Eastman's language here is very similar to our discussion of normalcy in the previous chapter, where I argued that communities have "systems of worth" that need to be recalibrated. Here is one, if not the only, key theological standard for such recalibration: Christ participated in humanity to such an extent that humanity can now participate in him, in his death and resurrection. The believers have been crucified with Christ, and now the resurrected Christ lives in them, through the Holy Spirit who indwells God's new community. This new community lives by new "systems of worth," where laws and practices that are foreign to God's new community need to give way to that new system of worth, a system determined by "the Son of God, who loved me and gave himself over to me." As Eastman puts it, referring to Galatians 5:6, "This new life together is characterized by 'faith working through love.'"[86] God's endless love and grace are the new normal in God's community. To make this point slightly differently, with the words of Macaskill: "Consistently, he [Paul] says, 'this is what you are, so start to live accordingly, because right now you are monstrously inconsistent with it.' The logic is not so much that we have not yet fulfilled our potential but is actually much more scathing: we are doing violence to our identity in Christ with our moral failings."[87] Having died with Christ, the believers *are* a new creation, and any behavior and social practices that are not aligned as such are coming from the old selves. Again, the ethical command to live a new life is not bolted onto what it means to be a follower of Christ—it is the new natural (normal) thing to do because Christ lives in us.

The cult of normalcy protects social boundaries by setting up criteria of who belongs and who does not and what one should do or be in order to pass the threshold of belonging. Eastman's discussion of Paul's letter to the Galatians helps to further explain what a theological response to this might look like:

> In the letter to the Galatians, Paul is combating a kind of *criterialism* about what counts as justification, and therefore what counts for membership in the community of persons constituted in Christ, by reminding his converts of the relationship they already share. The criteria are the works of the law, with circumcision as a necessary mark of belonging.[88]

"Criterialism" is an excellent word for the explicit and implicit rules of normalcy. In the Galatian community, some were suggesting that circumcision should be a criterion of belonging. Paul objects strongly. Eastman continues,

> Paul, however, sets such criteria in explicit opposition to the singular and completely sufficient gift of "the Son of God, who loved me and gave himself for me." . . . This gift is the only criterion by which the Galatians' identity and belonging are established, thereby linking their personal worth directly to the worth of Christ. Henceforth they are to live together in the intersubjective bond of trust established by Christ's love.[89]

Over against criterialism, Paul sets a gift—*the* gift, Christ himself as the ultimate gift of God's love. If circumcision means anything for you, then Christ has died for nothing, argues Paul. The only identity marker and the only marker of belonging is one's allegiance to Christ, grounded in Christ's allegiance to humanity. Someone's worth is not determined by any other criteria that cults of normalcy may put in place but solely by Christ. That love of Christ is expressed toward each other in the community in which each one knows they belong to Christ and to each other. In this way, Christ's love flows through the community.

The kenotic love of Christ inspires a new "mindset" in the community. As Paul says in Romans 8:5–6,

> 5 Those who live according to the flesh have their minds set on what the flesh desires; but those who live in accordance with the Spirit have their minds set on what the Spirit desires. 6 The mind governed by the flesh is death, but the mind governed by the Spirit is life and peace.[90]

Again, mindset includes much more than a way of thinking; it is a way of being. It is not disinvested spectating but participation in the gift. Paul speaks here of "a transformed mindset, incorporating motifs of perception, discernment and judgment that lead to peace among believers."[91] This interpretation by Eastman is instructive for rethinking normalcy for communities that want to be united in Christ by worshipping with autistic and non-autistic members alike. As we have seen in the previous chapter, normalcy has everything to do with "motifs of perception"; normalcy is a constant process or dynamic of "discernment and judgment." Whereas normalcy, as the guarding of the community's boundaries, results in exclusionary practices not in line with the gospel, the transformed mindset (see also Rom 12:1) of the community that is indwelt by the Holy Spirit is to "incorporate motifs of perception, discernment and judgment that lead to peace among believers." Peace here contrasts with exclusion, absence, and ignorance. It is the presence of Christ through God's Holy Spirit that leads to a new mindset, a new framework, and therefore a reframing of what "normal" is. Normal in the community of believers is to be partakers in the divine life through Christ's participation in humanity. Normal is to be captivated by love for each other. Normal is to be filled with the Holy Spirit, individually and collectively.[92]

CONCLUSION

A theological response to normalcy finds its grounding in Christ's presence toward and participation in humanity, in an act of kenosis, and in the subsequent human participation with Christ in the divine life. Being in Christ constitutes the community and the individual believers. This is good news, for it means that the desire to be a community where everyone belongs comes from within, with Christ as the foundation for living together. A practical and liturgical theology that seeks to change the practices of worshipping communities so that autistic and non-autistic belonging is not decided by the cult of normalcy needs to be grounded in the double participation of God through Christ in the community and the community through Christ in God. Grounding our response to normalcy in this double participation constitutes a new identity in Christ for believers.

The aim of this chapter was to find a theological response to the absence of autistic people and the community's ignorance of their autistic members—in relation to the examples of Graham, Alysia, and so many others. In response to the problem of absence, I formulated a theology of presence; in response to ignorance as a particular form of absence, I formulated a theology of availability as a particular form of presence. Gabriel Marcel showed how it is possible to be present yet absent and how this can even estrange the person from themselves. There is a difference between being a spectator and a participant. As with regard to the picture of the two girls on the seesaw on the front cover of Murray's book, we can remain spectators, discussing theories of autism or liturgical theologies. However, just as the girls are present and just as autistic people are members of our communities and therefore present in the community (if they are not absent altogether), so the community is invited to become participants in their lives. We are invited into reciprocal availability, where autistic church members become part of the lives of non-autistic church members and vice versa. Presence does the opposite of estrangement—sometimes it is just a look, a small gesture, a minute of real attention and care that can establish an unspeakable unspoken moment of connection. Availability, disponibilité, means to commit to one another, to say to the other "I belong to you." In the Christian community, when such commitment is expressed by all members of the community, it leads to genuine care for, mutual commitment to, and friendship with one another.

One might object and say that it is impossible to commit to everybody in the community, and perhaps some people do not reciprocate the commitment, making it a draining concept. This is a valid objection, and we should make sure that our theology rings true to reality. This is where the notion of community comes in, as a community of more than two people. Marcel's examples are mostly about two people meeting each other. In our faith communities, usually there are more people. The diversity this brings, and the gifts that can flow between the various members,[93] means that the commitment that Marcel speaks about is more realistic as it can be shared among the members. This is not to weaken Marcel's challenging concept of committing to being with one another; on the contrary, when shared between more than two people, an even richer connection and encounter with one another (and with God) can result.

The notion of hospitality was helpful to further explore availability. When we show hospitality to people, we invite them into our homes or into spaces where we have some sense of ownership. Therefore, when the guest enters our space, we give something of ourselves to the guest. Likewise, just as the guest does not enter an empty space but one filled with our presence, so the guest is not an empty shell coming into our home. Guests bring themselves, and so the room is filled with the presence of host and guest, and host and guest give of themselves to each other by being available to each other. According to Reynolds, this necessarily leads to sympathy, as we start sharing in each other's lives. That also reveals our own weaknesses, as the difference of the other makes us aware of our own limitations—even the limitations to sympathize with the other, which brings us back to the need for a wider community and to the importance of grounding our sharing in each other's lives in Christ's sharing in our humanity.

In the first part of this chapter, presence and availability as responses to absence and ignorance came from the philosophical rather than theological work of Marcel. In the second half of this chapter, I explored how availability finds a theological equivalent but also a deepening in the notion of kenosis. We saw how the passage in Philippians 2, from which the term "kenosis" derives, is above all a soteriological narrative: the gathering of all people and all things under the lordship of Christ Jesus, to the glory of God. According to the apostle Paul, the unity in the congregation is bound up with that narrative, as Christ Jesus is the point of unity of the community. The God-given (neuro)diversity in the congregation still finds unity in Christ.[94]

Nevertheless, the reality is that often, autistic people feel excluded from the community, resulting in sheer absence or in an inability to fully participate in the life of the congregation. In the previous chapter, I have identified normalcy as one of the root causes for this exclusion. Over against criterialism—Eastman's term for what I call "normalcy" in this book—Paul explains that the kenotic mindset of Christ, which should also be the mindset (or way of being) of the believers, is one of regarding the other higher than oneself. We can therefore see how a theology of availability does not only address absence and ignorance but also normalcy as the dynamic that lies at the root of absence and ignorance. Normalcy judges the other by the criteria for belonging as constructed by the community—in churches in the Global North, that usually means criteria of speed, sociability, ability to speak, intelligence, and generally just the capacity to "fit in."[95] Such criteria are the realm of the "flesh" and should be crucified with Christ; the community has new life in Christ because Christ lives in the believers (Gal 2:20).

The theological response to normalcy, by contrast, starts with a gift: the gift of Christ to humanity—the gift of God's love. The passage from Philippians 2 points to a double participation: Christ participates fully in humanity; humanity participates in the life of the divine through Christ. Being in Christ, the believers live a new life, which leads self-evidently to new ways of relating—of being present—to each other. As Eastman points out, the social ties that one has are now seen entirely through one's identity in Christ, which gives freedom vis-à-vis any social and cultural expectations. This new theological norm recalibrates everything that we think regarding what is normal and abnormal and about who should belong and who should not. This is not an ethical command (at least not primarily) but the new normal set by God's standard of love in God's gift of Christ. The Christian community lives this new life when it is attuned to the Holy Spirit, who works in the life of the community, with all its autistic and non-autistic members. Our presence and availability to each other are possible and indeed the new—normal—way of relating to one another because God is present and available to humanity in Christ. This gift of God's love in Christ and through the Holy Spirit enables the community to be present to Graham and Alysia and for them to be present in and to the community.

In the next chapter, we will see how this kenotic theology of availability works out in terms of liturgical theology, followed in chapter 6 by an analysis of how this might look on the ground, in terms of liturgical praxis, by analyzing the worship practices of the Chapel of Christ Our Hope in Singapore.

5

A Temple Community
A Liturgical-Theological Redrawing of "Normal"

"The ongoing prayer of Jesus, and the ongoing word and self-giving of Jesus, shapes our existence and brings *us* to expression."[1] With this statement, liturgical theologian Don Saliers follows the same theological line of thought that we began in the last chapter—that is, grounding (liturgical) theology and the Christian life in the self-giving (kenosis) of Jesus. Liturgy, as the regular prayer of the church, is rooted in the ongoing prayer of Jesus. In liturgy, Saliers says, we do not express ourselves in the first place, but the prayer, word, and self-giving of Jesus shapes us and brings us to expression.[2] In other words, in the liturgy, we discover and are reminded of, time and again, who we are in Christ. The link with our discussion of normalcy and a theological reframing of community boundaries thus becomes clear: because we become who we are through our participation in the liturgy, not just as individuals but as a community, we see each other as we are in Christ—beloved and valued as we are. Jesus' kenosis redefines the framework in which we live (Taylor) and the boundaries around our communities.

That sounds all good, but is it true? Do the many anecdotes and the statistics cited in previous chapters not negate these lofty theological statements? We should not continue with unpacking these liturgical-theological claims without honestly facing the fact that they do not sound true to a lot of people a lot of the time. A few passages from Dan Bowman make the point.

> Coffee hour after the service. Strangers smile wide, pump my hand, ask classic small-talk questions that should be simple but aren't for me:
> "How are you?"
> I don't know, and I'm not sure if they want a real answer. I tend to take things literally, overthink these exchanges. Would they like me to be real—would it reflect better on who we are as a body of believers if I get honest? Because frankly, I'm often not okay.
> Or should I pretend everything's fine like most people do with strangers? If it were me visiting a church, I'd be put off if I got an inauthentic vibe. Then again, I'd be put off if it seemed like they were trying too hard. (I once visited a church where people spoke in the worst evangelical clichés, then thanked one another for being "so transparent.")
> I feel the sweat on my forehead; I slurp my coffee too quickly, burning my tongue.[3]

> The pastor suddenly issues a call to fill the front of the sanctuary, after I've carefully selected the exact seat I need (near the middle, on the aisle): "Don't be shy, everyone move up—yes, that means you! Plenty of good seats up here!" There's unwanted direct eye contact. I'm frozen with fear.[4]

> Someone behind me touches me with no warning and begins praying into my ear. Their breath tingles my skin, which I'd crawl out of if I could. Others lay their hands on my highly sensitive neck, shoulders, and head, startling me, making me cringe . . . making me wish I'd stayed home this morning.[5]

The challenge for the current chapter is not only to draw on the wisdom of Scripture, liturgical theologians, and tradition but also to bring that wisdom into dialogue with the stories of autistic people. The wish "I'd stayed home this morning" is a far cry from the claim that liturgy is the "source and summit of the Christian life."[6] The autistic experience of liturgy raises questions for liturgical theology; likewise, if there is wisdom in the liturgical-theological tradition, one might hope that liturgical theology can somehow speak into stories like the ones quoted from Bowman. In other words, as we develop a liturgical theology of availability, we will need to ask whether the theological truths are also practical truths.

This chapter fleshes out the new norm in Christ, as formulated in the previous chapter, in liturgical-theological ways. In the previous chapter,

I started to formulate a theological response to the problem of normalcy, which I argue lies at the root of the absence of, or the ignoring of, autistic people in worship services. Gabriel Marcel's concept of indisponibilité proved helpful as I began to formulate a theology of availability, of being available to each other in the Christian community. I grounded this theology further in the concept of kenosis, which led in turn to an exploration of participation in the divine life rooted in Christ's participation in humanity. A central image for participating in the divine life is that of the temple—Jesus as temple, the Christian community as temple, and access to the heavenly temple through Christ as high priest. With that image, we are squarely in the realm of liturgy.

Therefore, in this chapter, I will start with a discussion of the temple image as a point of departure for the liturgical-theological response to the problem of normalcy. After this, I will discuss liturgy, following Saliers' kenotic and participatory definition of liturgy. From there, I will explore Christian identity and unity through participation in liturgy and as effected sacramentally, with a focus on baptism. The last major section will suggest ways to not only redefine but also to move away from community boundaries as a response to the cult of normalcy. In this discussion, I will briefly comment on the role of the Eucharist. In the previous chapter, I argued that our identity in Christ constitutes the new norm of a theological framework. The purpose of this chapter is to think through our identity in Christ in terms of liturgical theology. This will hopefully result in a framework that can provide an answer to stories like that of Bowman, from which new stories of belonging can be lived and narrated.

THE CHURCH AS TEMPLE

A well-known image for union with Christ is the apostle Paul's vivid description of the Christian community as the body of Christ, with Christ himself as head of the body. Many disability theologians use the image to argue that every member in the body, disabled or not, has a valuable part to play in the life of the community. Indeed, all parts of the body, and therefore all members of the church, are indispensable (1 Cor 12:22). As such, the image is used mostly to argue for the value of diversity in the church, while being united as one body, and perhaps less to argue for union with Christ. Less widely used in disability theology is the image of the community as a temple. Nevertheless, the temple imagery in the New Testament is one of the predominant images employed in theological discussions of "union with Christ" and in some ways is closely related to the image of the body of Christ.[7] It is therefore a good candidate to provide further flesh to the bones of our discussion of the new norm in Christ. Moreover, the temple as a place of worship is an image that brings us naturally to one of the major aims of this book, which is to study liturgy and worship through the lens of autism and, where necessary, to reframe liturgical theology. To place the temple image at the forefront also contributes to the field of liturgical theology, as this imagery is regularly referred to but not often discussed in depth.[8]

In his detailed study of the temple image in the New Testament, Grant Macaskill observes that New Testament writers present the temple in three different ways.[9] Peter, Paul, and Luke present the church as a temple, a sign of the (new) covenant and a place where God's glory dwells. John, on the other hand, presents Jesus as the temple, and the writer of the letter to the Hebrews talks about access to the heavenly temple. The differences between the uses of the temple image notwithstanding, they share a number of common themes. 1 Peter 2:4–10 illustrates several of these commonalities that are relevant to the purposes of our study.

Peter tells the readers of his first letter (2:4–10, NIV),

> [4] As you come to him, the living Stone—rejected by humans but chosen by God and precious to him—[5] you also, like living stones, are being built into a spiritual house to be a holy priesthood, offering spiritual sacrifices acceptable to God through Jesus Christ. [6] For in Scripture it says:
>
> "See, I lay a stone in Zion,
>   a chosen and precious cornerstone,
> and the one who trusts in him
>   will never be put to shame."
>
> [7] Now to you who believe, this stone is precious. But to those who do not believe,
>
> "The stone the builders rejected
>   has become the cornerstone,"
>
> [8] and,
>
> "A stone that causes people to stumble
>   and a rock that makes them fall."
>
> They stumble because they disobey the message—which is also what they were destined for.
>
> [9] But you are a chosen people, a royal priesthood, a holy nation, God's special possession, that you may declare the praises of him who called

you out of darkness into his wonderful light. [10] Once you were not a people, but now you are the people of God; once you had not received mercy, but now you have received mercy.

The first theme to highlight is that there is a close connection between Christ and the believers; yet at the same time, there is a difference between them, a difference that is maintained throughout the New Testament.[10] While both Christ and the believers are stones that together make up the building, only Christ is the cornerstone.

The second theme to note in this and other New Testament temple passages is the call to imitate Christ (which connects this discussion to one of the central passages for our kenotic theology of availability, Philippians 2:5–13, as I began to outline in the previous chapter). Jesus is the living stone, and the believers are also living stones. Jesus is king and priest, and the believers are "built into a spiritual house," or temple, "to be a holy priesthood" (v. 5) or "royal priesthood" (v. 9). Jesus is the ultimate sacrifice, and the believers are called to offer spiritual sacrifices. Finally, Jesus lived his life in praise of God, his father, and the believers' purpose in life is exactly that as well. However, Macaskill suggests an interesting and important qualification to the call to imitate Jesus. Noting that a theology of imitation, as emerging from the temple imagery, is especially strong in the Gospel according to John, the letter to the Hebrews, and the book of Revelation, Macaskill concludes,

> Crucially, this theology itself proceeds from a common emphasis on incarnational reality: the Word was made flesh, the Son shared in the flesh and blood of his brothers, the one is and was and is to come died as a sacrificial Lamb. While ascribing full divinity to Jesus, the writers take seriously his humanity and the implications that this has for the imitative activity of believers, with a particular emphasis falling upon the necessity of self-sacrifice. These sacrificial elements are not depicted as a simple emulation of his example, however, but as a participation in his own redemptive work.[11]

I have quoted Macaskill at length because this part of his discussion resonates well with my own; incarnational theology connects the temple imagery to our kenotic theology of availability. It does so by pointing to Christ's participation in humanity. Furthermore, Macaskill introduces an aspect of kenosis that we have not emphasized before: that Christ "died as a sacrificial Lamb," and somehow, this is related to the "necessity of self-sacrifice." I will return to this notion at the end of this chapter. For now, I note that Macaskill qualifies the believers' imitation of Christ and of self-sacrifice by distinguishing between imitation and emulation. Imitation should be characterized by participation, rather than emulation, which is simply to copy. In other words, the believers are not called to do exactly the same as Christ did but to participate in his ongoing prayer for the world in the heavenly sanctuary (one of various aspects of the temple imagery) and in his mission to reconcile the world to God (2 Cor 5:18–20).

A third theme that deserves our attention is that the temple imagery points to the (call for) unity in the church. The believers are united with Christ as a body is to the head, as living stones are to the cornerstone, and as a spiritual edifice built on Christ as the foundation; however, in all these images, they are also inherently united to each other. The people are a "spiritual house" *together*; they make up the body of Christ *together*. (The image of the body of Christ is closely associated with the temple imagery, especially in Ephesians and Corinthians, as Macaskill demonstrates.[12]) To think about belonging and exclusion in the context of the church, it might be worth recalling that Jesus was a stone rejected by the builders and yet became the cornerstone (1 Pet 2:4–8). The "living stones" that might be rejected by the community when it is governed by the cult of normalcy may be much more important than the community realizes. If it is warranted to use the image of the rejected stones in this way, then it finds an important parallel in the image of the body in which the "weaker members" are honored and get a prominent place in Paul's theology.

The fourth theme that emerges from a study of the temple imagery in our passage from 1 Peter 2 is the use of references to the Hebrew Bible. Peter refers to Psalm 118:22 (and other texts), which some other New Testament writers do as well (Matt 21:42; Mark 12:10–11; Luke 20:17; Acts 4:11).[13] This shows that the Jewish background of the image is firmly in view but also that Jesus is seen as the fulfillment of prophetic texts from the Hebrew Bible. It allows, and indeed necessitates, a reading of the image in light of the Jewish background of the Hebrew Bible and second temple Judaism.[14] Therefore, it is warranted and necessary to see the temple image in combination with the covenant and the divine glory or presence. As Macaskill states, "Covenant and temple require one another and this is true of the new covenant also. . . . The glory that indwells the temple and that constitutes the inheritance ([1 Pet] 1:4–5) of the church must be seen as an alien reality, a quality of God that is gifted (1:3) to God's people."[15] Therefore, underpinning the mention of the temple by Peter and others, we find the notions of covenant and glory, sometimes explicitly, sometimes implicitly. In the text quoted above, the glory image can be seen in verse 9 ("him who called you out of darkness into his wonderful light") and as the quotation from Macaskill shows, in the wider context. The notion of covenant is explicitly present throughout the passage, in terms like "chosen by God," "a holy priesthood," and "God's special possession" and culminates in the reversal of God's curse on Israel in Hosea: "Once you were not a people, but now you are the people of God" (1 Pet 2:10). The references to the Hebrew scriptures bring themes such as covenant, sacrifice, priesthood, prayer, liturgy, and divine glory into view.

A final theme that pervades the temple imagery in the New Testament is worth spelling out in more detail: divine glory in terms of divine presence. Presence is an important theme in our response to the cult of normalcy. The temple is the place where God decided to dwell in the midst of the Israelites; it is the place of God's glory. In his Gospel, John identifies Jesus as the new temple, the new place where God's glory dwells. The new place of God's presence is a person: Jesus Christ. Imitating Christ, as participating in Christ, means to follow Christ and thereby the presence of God to wherever Christ goes, which was and is to the places and people often shunned by society. This is good news for any marginalized person or group, including for any autistic person who feels excluded by society and especially by the church.

This image becomes even more exciting but also ambiguous and full of tension when we realize that the New Testament writers do not only identify Jesus as the temple but also the believers—for example, as in the passage from 1 Peter that I quoted above. It is good news for the community of believers that they are "a chosen people, a royal priesthood, a holy nation, God's special possession" (1 Pet 2:9). However, this brings into sharp relief the failure of the church when it excludes those on the margins when it celebrates the cult of normalcy instead of the gospel of Christ. As I already commented in the previous chapter and will continue to do in this chapter, the community of believers worships in the time-full tension of the "already and not yet."[16] That can never be an excuse not to follow and be the presence of God to the margins of society, but it calls for hearing the last line of the passage from 1 Peter: "Once you had not received mercy, but now you have received mercy." The ambiguity and tension of this theme (the community as the temple and therefore the place where God is present through God's Spirit) highlights the necessity to speak in terms of participation in Christ. Only when the community participates in Christ, through the power of the Holy Spirit, will it be able to be filled with God's glory and presence.

In sum, the temple imagery is one of the central images of union with Christ. Studying this imagery leads to the theme of unity with Christ and with each other and the need to imitate Christ—not as emulation but as participation. Only a participatory framework can hold the high calling and theological reality that the community of believers is filled with the divine presence, as a body of the head and as living stones integrated with Christ the cornerstone and foundation. The image of Christ as cornerstone, even if at first rejected by the builders, might bring comfort to those "living stones" in the community who feel excluded, whether because they are autistic or for any other reason. At the same time, the image is a rebuke to communities who think they are building with the "right" stones but ignore the stones that seem worthless from a normalcy perspective. (In addition to applying this image to people, we may apply it to actions that from a normalcy perspective seem worthless or annoying, such as taking time to listen to an autistic person who needs considerable time for processing a dialogue or who may use augmentative or alternative communication [AAC].) Finally, the temple imagery has inherent connotations of worship and related themes such as covenant, priesthood, sacrifice, and prayer. These are prominent themes in liturgical theology, which will serve us as we construct a liturgical theology of availability as a response to the cult of normalcy. But first, we will turn to a brief discussion of what liturgy is.

DEFINING LITURGY

Liturgy and worship have a central place in the life of the church, theologically and practically. In liturgical studies, it is common to denote the liturgy, or the liturgical act of worship, as *theologia prima*. The reflection on liturgy and worship is then called *theologia secunda*.[17] Thus, in the first place, theology is worship. Don Saliers puts it this way: "To pray to God is to be a theologian. Thus the gathered church at prayer is doing theology."[18] Because the church is doing theology when it gathers for worship, its worship is of central importance for responding to the cult of normalcy (a form of worship itself, as I argued in the previous chapter) in order to formulate a liturgical theology of availability.

Moreover, in the introduction to this chapter, I referred to Saliers' argument that worship brings the community to expression. In other words, the church is most itself when it worships. This idea is affirmed by several liturgical theologians. Kimberly Belcher makes the point forcefully in her discussion of the Roman Catholic rite of infant baptism, to which I will return below. Louis Weil also agrees when he says, "Our gathering is not primarily a matter of function but rather of identity: the whole body of the baptized constitutes itself in diverse communities around the world."[19] Liturgy is not something we simply do (function) but actualizes the community in its identity as the body of Christ, as the temple in which the divine presence dwells. The community's identity in Christ, which rests entirely within the grace of God, is not first and foremost captured by doctrinal statements but in word and sacrament—in the book, the font, and the table. Therefore, Weil says, "Through our worship we must offer the best we can as our response to God's mysterious presence in our lives. This is our purpose in the liturgy, and from this perspective our public worship of God may be claimed as the source and summit of the Christian life."[20] The believers find their identity in the liturgy which is "the source and summit of the Christian life" and which therefore also constitutes the believers' identity as the 'royal priesthood' that belongs to and serves Christ.

With such high claims about liturgy, it is necessary to define liturgy. For the purposes of this book, I find Don Saliers' definition most relevant and helpful, as he defines liturgy in terms that are strongly participatory and kenotic, which fits well with the kenotic theology of availability and participation that I am advocating.

> Christian liturgy . . . is the ongoing prayer, proclamation, and life of Jesus Christ—a sacrifice of thanksgiving and praise—offered to God in and through his body in the world. That is, Christian liturgy is our response to the self-giving of God in, with, and through the One who leads us in prayer. The community is called into being to continue that prayer on behalf of the whole world. So we must continue to gather in praise and thanksgiving about the book, the baptismal font, and the eucharistic table in order to know a home.[21]

Later in his book, Saliers expands his definition of liturgy to include "worship that shows creation and human history as the arena of God's glory."[22]

Several points are worth highlighting in this definition, as they relate to and further inform our discussion. First, according to Saliers, liturgy is first of all Christ's work.[23] He is the "One who leads us in prayer"—a point that relates to the temple image of Hebrews, in which Jesus Christ is depicted as our high priest, as the One who intercedes for us, as he already did while living on earth (John 17). Furthermore, Christian liturgy is "a sacrifice of thanksgiving and praise" (a phrase that refers to the eucharistic prayer in traditional liturgies), which

Saliers fills in as "the ongoing prayer, proclamation, and life of Jesus Christ." Thus, before Christian liturgy is about the community doing anything, it is about Christ's prayer, his proclamation, and his life. As Saliers comments on his own definition, it "highlights the christological nature of Christian worship."[24]

The second point is related to, and follows logically from, the first: Christian liturgy is characterized by the community's participation in Christ. As Christ prays, he calls his community to participate in and continue his prayer. Gordon Lathrop points out that much of the liturgical renewal in the past one hundred years is aimed at emphasizing the participation in the liturgy of all who attend the worship service.[25] Here, we can see how our theology of participation from the previous chapter starts to play out in worship. Just as Christ participates in humanity, which enables our participation in Christ, so the Spirit of Christ is present to us. Thus God, through the Holy Spirit, is the primary actor in liturgy before any action on our part.[26] Lathrop calls this a paradox: "The fully active assembly is, exactly at the same time, profoundly receptive, receiving all that comes with the presence and gift of God."[27] Worship is a wonderful active dynamic of participating in Christ and joining in Christ's intercession before the world in the heavenly temple, being stirred by the Holy Spirit, bringing worship to God while at the same time receiving God's presence.

Third, Christ's prayer is "on behalf of the whole world." I am not sure whether Saliers intends a play on the word leitourgia here, but it is hard to miss the meaning of leitourgia as "the work *on behalf of* the people."[28] Christian communities do not worship for their own sake, but it is "thanksgiving and praise offered to God" and "on behalf of the whole world." Liturgy, therefore, is a work in two directions: offered to God and intentionally looking outward to the world and carrying its concerns before God. Saliers' expansion of his definition, quoted above, emphasizes that the whole of creation and human history are within the purview of the liturgy, "as the arena of God's glory." Nevertheless, liturgy is not without its effects on the community itself. We already noted above that in worship, the community finds its true identity. Saliers concurs when he expresses almost poetically that "the book, the baptismal font, and the eucharistic table" are where Christians "know a home."

A final point to note in Saliers' definition is the self-giving of God—in other words, kenosis. Liturgy is "our response to the self-giving of God in, with, and through the One who leads us in prayer." One of the reasons why Saliers' liturgical theology is attractive for our purposes is because he keeps coming back to God's self-giving as prior to our liturgical acts throughout his book. Saliers quotes Geoffrey Wainwright, another influential voice in liturgical theology: "In worship we receive the self-giving love of God, and the test of our thankfulness is whether we reproduce that pattern of self-giving in our daily relationships with other people. Of course, the test already begins with our attitudes and behavior as brothers and sisters in the liturgical assembly."[29] Saliers highlights the relationship between thanksgiving and grace in this quotation to support his point that liturgy is always about thanksgiving (*eucharistia*).[30] To make the connection with a kenotic theology of availability, I would like to highlight the threefold self-giving in Wainwright's quotation: the self-giving of God to humanity, our self-giving to those around us, and the self-giving toward our brothers and sisters in Christ. This not only aligns with Saliers' definition of liturgy but also brings into view our self-giving (availability) to our fellow members in the community of believers. Wainwright seems to say, "If you cannot live a kenotic life within your own community, how would you be able to do so in the wider world?" Importantly, our self-giving is participatory: it is rooted in God's self-giving.[31] The community is reminded of God's self-giving in the liturgy: "Praying with the church is thus a continual reminder and a training in the narratives and images that focus God's self-giving as the primal gift—the primary sacrament."[32] The community needs that reminder time and time again, in a slow process of formation, so that any notion of availability to one's neighbor is rooted in the primal gift of God's kenotic availability to the world.

One aspect of liturgy that is missing from Saliers' definition quoted above but certainly not from his theology is that liturgy and worship are trinitarian, with a significant role for the Holy Spirit. The trinitarian nature of liturgy is attested widely in the literature, as is already clear, for example, from Lathrop's comments on liturgical participation above. In liturgy, the believers join Christ in thanksgiving, praise, and intercession to God. As Saliers already said, liturgy is Christological, and it is Christ's Spirit who enables our prayer. Saliers points to the tension between the biblical invitation to pray boldly and yet we do not even know what to pray. Here, the temple image from the book of Hebrews recurs: "Therefore, brothers and sisters, since we have confidence to enter the Most Holy Place by the blood of Jesus . . . let us draw near to God" (Heb 10:19). Nevertheless, we need the Holy Spirit to pray for us as we do not know what we ought to pray for (Rom 8:26–27). Saliers concludes with a kenotic comment on the role of the Holy Spirit in prayer: "The boldness comes from taking God seriously and from the promise made in Christ that the Spirit will come to the aid of our weakness. Thus we have no access to God apart from God's gracious self-giving and empowering life poured out. . . . We receive the Spirit's continuing intercession."[33] The Spirit enables our prayer.

It is worth pausing briefly to think about the not knowing what to pray for. Earlier in his book, Saliers argues that gratitude helps us to see how things really are. That leads him to describe prayer as "a double journey—at once toward the mystery of God who invites relationship, and into the deep places of our own human self-understanding."[34] Liturgy, as the act of giving God thanks and praise, is an act in and through which we discover more of who God is and who we are. Here is an interesting connection with normalcy because the cult of normalcy rests for a large part on us not knowing that normalcy is at work in our communal practices. Indeed, as Saliers says, we do not know ourselves. In the liturgy, in the double journey, we dive deeper into the mystery of God and start to know ourselves more truly in light of God's story about our lives and about who belongs, instead judging based on our own measures of belonging. Saliers argues that because we do not know ourselves and even cannot know ourselves fully in the liturgy, we need the Holy Spirit to enable our prayer and indeed to intercede for us. The logical priority of invoking the Holy Spirit "for all other modes of liturgical prayer" provides the "'grammar' of how to speak of God."[35] If we are serious about redrawing the boundaries of normalcy, it starts by confessing not only the sins of exclusion that we know of but also the fact that we often do not know how and even that normalcy might be at work in our communities. It starts by asking the Holy Spirit to intercede for us, and the only way to make any progress is to be fully dependent on God's self-giving by participating in the prayer and work of Jesus.

In sum, liturgy has a central place in the life of the Christian community. Jesus Christ is the primary leitourgikos, leading us in prayer, interceding in the heavenly sanctuary before the throne of God. Our acts of worship, therefore, are acts of participating in Christ's prayer and work for the world, enabled by Christ's participation in humanity, and continued presence in the community through the Holy Spirit, who prays for us because we do not know what we ought to pray for. Liturgy, then, is trinitarian, and we can only participate because the Holy Spirit enables our participation. In worship, we discover more of the mystery of God, but we also come to know ourselves better. Consequently, liturgy changes our attitudes toward our fellow members of the community and is directed both toward God and toward the world. We will now further explore how participation in liturgy and the sacraments shapes our identity in Christ, which forms the basis for a liturgical response to the cult of normalcy.

LITURGICAL AND SACRAMENTAL PARTICIPATION

The definition of liturgy makes clear that the liturgical act is participatory. Indeed, participation is a concept that surfaces regularly in liturgical studies in various ways. In liturgy, the believers participate in the liturgy of Christ—his ongoing prayer and work. In another sense, participation is often commented on in light of the well-known phrase, the "full, conscious, and active participation" of the faithful in liturgy.[36] This phrase is from a seminal document on liturgy, *Sacrosanctum Concilium*, which emerged from the Vatican Council II and which further says that such participation is "demanded by the very nature of the liturgy." We are reminded again of the centrality of the liturgy in the life of the church. Interestingly, with reference to the text from 1 Peter 2:9 which we discussed above, the next line in the document reads, "Such participation by the Christian people as 'a chosen race, a royal priesthood, a holy nation, a redeemed people' (1 Pet 2:9; cf. 2:4–5), is their right and duty by reason of their baptism." The reference to the passage from Peter evokes the temple image again, and as a royal priesthood, it is the faithful community's duty to serve as such. Moreover, *Sacrosanctum Concilium* adds a word that is highly relevant to our discussion: it is not only the believers' duty but also their "right" to participate in the liturgy—that is, to participate in the ongoing prayer of Christ as members of the community. When autistic people wish they had stayed at home (see Bowman's story in the introduction) and next time very well might do, has the community denied the "right" of these believers? In this section, I will explore the meaning of liturgy as participation in the divine life by exploring briefly how participation in the liturgy leads to identity formation, followed by a longer discussion of participation in and through baptism. This will have consequences for "the full, conscious, and active participation" of all believers, as will become clear.

Participation in Liturgy as Identity Formation

Participation in liturgy leads to change. To participate in liturgy is to come into the presence of God, to bring all our hopes and dreams and fears and anger and doubt and sorrow and loneliness before God and there, connect those with God's hopes and dreams and fears and anger and doubt and sorrow for creation. In liturgy, our stories find a place in God's story.[37] In light of God's story, our stories change, and therefore we change. In worship, Christians are joined together and become more than just a gathering of individual believers but become the royal priesthood, the body of Christ, the temple of the Holy Spirit. Moreover, in Saliers' words, "worship is participation in God's very life."[38] When our lives are so closely connected with God in worship, joining Christ in his ongoing prayer and work for the world, it is inevitable that we change and become more who we are as individuals and as a community.

The change that takes place in liturgy results inevitably in a certain way of living. Liturgical scholars often comment on the relationship between liturgy and ethics.[39] Throughout his work, Saliers is keen to point out that liturgy is the ongoing formative foundation of the ethical life. Ethics is not so much a list of rules and obligations but the formation of character, attitudes, and dispositions over time.[40] In the previous chapter, I have emphasized along similar lines that the call to be available to each other (an ethical claim) is not an extrinsic command but follows inherently from participation in the life of the divine. We now see that such participation is part and parcel of what liturgy is about; the act of worshipping is to participate in the prayer of Christ. In liturgy, we learn to perceive the world in new ways, as the sacred creation of God, intended to praise God in thanksgiving in all it does and is. When perceiving the world in this way, it changes how we relate to our neighbor and to all of creation. All of creation is sacred, and therefore, all people are sacred, created, loved, and valued by God. In liturgy, we learn to see each other in this way—autistic and non-autistic alike. Participating in liturgy will (or should) affect how we relate to each other; it forms our individual and communal identity over time.

At this point, it might be helpful to return to Charles Taylor again. In chapter 3, I referred to Taylor's argument that we live in certain frameworks, as he explains in his book *Sources of the Self*. These are always moral frameworks by which the community determines what is good—that good includes the need for belonging to a community. In another work, *A Secular Age*, Taylor argues along similar lines that communities and individuals have a "social imaginary."[41] Societies, he says, are not organized according to grand theories but rather shaped through stories, narratives, symbols, and embodied practices. The term "social imaginaries" denotes "the ways in which [people] imagine their social existence, how they fit together with others, how things go on between them and their fellows, the expectations which are normally met, and the deeper normative notions and images which underlie these expectations."[42] That is not to say that theories cannot have any influence, but usually, theories have that influence through a long process of "trickling down" into the social imaginary of the larger population; in that process, the theory is shaped by the practices as well as the other way around.[43] Social imaginary has to do with understanding a situation—knowing what to do and how to act—without perhaps even being able to put words to it.[44] It is like intuiting your way in the neighborhood you grew up in without necessarily knowing the street names.[45] As James Smith states succinctly in his discussion of social imaginary in relation to liturgy and formation, "The imaginary is more a kind of noncognitive *understanding* than a cognitive *knowledge* or set of beliefs."[46] The point that liturgical theologians make (with or without reference to this concept or to Taylor's work), and that we will further explore in this chapter, is that liturgy shapes our social imaginary. For example, Sarah Barton argues that

> our practices of worshiping God shape our imagination about who belongs in the baptized body. And the liturgies that pattern Christian worship teach us which bodies belong. Worship calls forth embodied participation that can bear witness to a community's implicit beliefs about who God is, who human beings are, and how to live as the baptized body.[47]

In other words, when participating in Jesus' prayer and work, in the patterns of the liturgy, in our embodied worship, we learn to imagine the world anew, including who belongs.

Just as the kenosis of Jesus is firmly set in the "mystery of salvation," as discussed in the last chapter by reading the passage from Philippians 2, so the identity formation that takes place in and through our worship is shaped by this mystery. In liturgy, the participants are caught up in the salvific story of God in Christ. In the words of Kimberly Belcher, "Soteriologically, then, the sacraments facilitate the formation of an identity that enables their participants to enter into the trinitarian mystery of salvation: to become conformed to Christ and be filled with the Holy Spirit."[48] Given that the mystery of salvation (soteriology) is trinitarian and the sacraments enact and lead the community into that mystery, the identity formation through the sacraments—and it is no stretch at all to apply this more broadly to the entire liturgical act—is trinitarian. Belcher continues, "The sacramental regimen alters the fabric of Christians' whole identity. The sacraments, beginning with initiation and eucharist, are seen as efficacious in creating a Christian identity—a project in which the Trinity cooperates with human beings."[49] In the next section, I will explore a bit more how this is so when discussing a few elements of Belcher's theology of baptism. The point to note here is that in worship, we encounter and participate in the trinitarian life, which is concretized in water, bread, and wine and in each other as Christ lives in us and which "alters" our whole identity.

Crucially, identity is a formational process, not a static status quo. At the heart of that process is the liturgy in which we participate in the trinitarian soteriological story, but it continues throughout our daily lives. Belcher states, resonating with Taylor's concept of a social imaginary, "Efficacious engagement focuses on how human beings are involved in the world: orienting in it, responding to it, and altering it. World-formation, rather than self-understanding, is human identity."[50] Efficacious engagement with sacraments, and by extension the entire liturgy, is a process that starts in the liturgical act, in the public worship service, but continues after the people have been sent out into the world. The symbolism of a traditional Western church building is that we enter through the door in the west—the west symbolizing the world, which without God is chaotic and messy. We pass the baptismal font, and in some traditions, the faithful dip their finger into the blessed water and make the sign of the cross on their body as a reminder of their baptism. We sit down in the pews to listen to the Word, and in the next major part of the liturgy, we move to the east—which symbolizes Christ as the morning light—to the altar to be nourished by bread and wine, which, in this sacramental act, becomes to us the body and blood of Christ. The font, the book/Word, the table—in these symbols we discover who we truly are, through the soteriological narrative that becomes concrete materiality, which we feel on our bodies, taste with our tongues and lips, hear with our ears, kinetically sense as we move through the building, ever deeper into the mystery of salvation which culminates in the eucharistic act. However, there is no door in the east. We do not stay at the altar but instead return to our pews, briefly, to hear the words of blessing and sending out, back through the doors in the west, back to be a blessing in a chaotic and messy world, to live the story of salvation with and for those around us.[51] Thus, we become leitourgia, the ongoing prayer and work of Christ in this world; but before we are "orienting in it, responding to it, and altering it," we are orienting in the liturgy, receiving and shaping a "liturgical imaginary," responding to the reality of God, and being altered.

Belcher's comment that human identity is more about world formation than self-understanding is interesting. When we are orienting in the liturgy, our self-understanding is altered in light of understanding a tiny bit more about God. "Understanding" is perhaps the wrong word; "encountering" God may be more correct. In the encounter with God, we not only perceive ourselves anew but also the world we live in as a new "social imaginary." Belcher's comment that identity is about world formation pushes us through the west door again, into the world. However, in the liturgy, we learn to imagine a different world, a world in which creation is sacramental (means of grace, enabling an encounter with God through material reality), a world in which the believers have the task to join the Holy Spirit—first inspired by the Holy Spirit—in the process of sanctifying the world. If identity is indeed about imagining the world through God's eyes and acting on such an imagination, then identity cannot be a status quo but is ever evolving, as Belcher says, as we are caught up in a process of joining the community in public worship and subsequently living our vocation to be Christ's hands and feet in the world.

Baptismal Participation

Much of what I have said so far about liturgical formation becomes even clearer in the sacraments. In most Christian traditions, the sacraments, especially those of baptism and the Eucharist, are primary identity markers. Given that the kenotic liturgical theology of availability that I am developing here is rooted in our identity in Christ (see previous chapter), it is necessary to make a few comments on the sacraments. It is noteworthy that Macaskill, whose work I have drawn from extensively in these chapters, also argues that the sacraments are constitutive for the identity of believers.[52] Moreover, "the entire narrative of Jesus's life, death, and resurrection has a constitutive and not paradigmatic significance."[53] By participating in the sacraments, the believers identify with the Jesus narrative.[54] These comments from Macaskill do not only underline the necessity to discuss the sacraments, but they also show again the inherently soteriological context of the theology of availability.

Space does not allow me to outline a detailed sacramental theology, so here I will restrict myself to baptism. (In the next section, I will make some observations about the Eucharist.) Nevertheless, these comments will help to further substantiate liturgically and sacramentally the argument for participating in the divine life as ultimate response to the problem of normalcy. In this section, I will add more detail to the argument that baptism constitutes the believers' identity in Christ, both individually and communally. With that baptismal identity comes a new way of perceiving each other and the world around us, which is the argument of the last part of this section. In the introduction to this chapter, I said that our theology must ring true to those who find themselves excluded from worship. Therefore, I will start with a story of exclusion and return to another story midway through this section.

Sarah Barton, in her recent study of baptism and intellectual disabilities, tells the harrowing story of Hikari, a person with intellectual disabilities. Hikari describes being "a service assistant for many years," before a member from the church "made it clear that I was inferior to everyone else and did her best to get me off the acolyte list" (Barton quotes Hikari's own words here). Barton reflects on this, following Macaskill, saying that "simply baptizing people with disabilities and verbally declaring that they belong within church communities does not constitute the end of the chapter. . . . Put simply, having disabled Christians present in church communities, even in contexts where they actively participate and lead, is not enough." Instead, it requires a daily "baptismal participation in Jesus' death and resurrection" to participate "in a way of life fully dependent upon Jesus."[55] Hikari's story shows that liturgical participation is not self-evident for people who do not conform to the norms of the surrounding culture. Even when such people find themselves in leadership roles, they remain vulnerable to church members who do not appreciate the gift and contribution of those people. Barton suggests that this is where the community's daily baptismal participation in Jesus' death and resurrection is necessary. In order to begin to understand the full weight of this suggestion, it will be helpful to discuss baptismal identity in more detail.

In line with the theology of participation that I have developed so far, Belcher says, "The heart of sacramentality is the belief that when Christians worship, they participate in God's life, and this belief must be the backdrop for any sacramental theology."[56] We could replace the word "sacramentality" with "liturgy" just as well. Because we are invited to participate in God's life, there is the certainty that "God is at work for us in the sacraments."[57] At the heart of a baptismal identity is the belief that God participated in humanity, which precedes and enables our participation in the divine life.

A good starting point for our discussion is the image of adoption because of what it reveals about the Christian identity of both the baptized person and the community.[58] As Belcher explains, "The community celebrating the baptism of the child is the community of the Trinity because by participating in the ritual act of baptizing the assembly conforms itself to the body of Christ and the temple of the Holy Spirit."[59] Belcher describes baptism as an act of "disappropriating," whereby the community hands over the natural authority of parents over their child to Christ. In this way, "the church enacts its identity as Body of Christ."[60] In baptism, the congregation declares that no member of the congregation belongs to themselves, but all belong to God.[61]

Belcher further explains how in infant baptism the whole church is inscribed into the reality of trinitarian salvation and becoming the body of Christ. One instance at which this becomes clear in the baptismal ritual is the signing of the child's forehead with the sign of the cross. "In writing the cross of Christ on the infant's physical body, the celebrant, parents, and godparents also rewrite it upon the ecclesial body, and thereby, by the shared sign, the infant's body is grafted into the Body of Christ, which the assembly, as if surprised, discovers itself to be in the act of signing."[62] Belcher's ritual and theological analysis shows the interrelationship of community and infant and how that reciprocity reveals the community's identity as body of Christ. The community offers the infant to God in an act of "disappropriating," but in so doing, it receives the child as part of the body of Christ. The sign of the cross signifies that the child belongs to Christ, but it does so as part of the community, and thereby the infant shows the entire community's belonging to Christ. The child is the temple of the Holy Spirit, but again, it becomes part of the larger body of the believers that is the temple of the Holy Spirit. In baptism, the community becomes itself. Gordon Lathrop expresses a similar line of thought with the statement, "Baptism is a personal communal sacrament."[63] In this, he means that the various images of baptism apply not only to the individual but also to the community. Belcher's analysis shows how the community and the individual are intertwined.[64]

Belcher argues compellingly that baptism constitutes the identity of the individual believer as a Christian and also that of the congregation. Belcher's analysis relates to the Roman Catholic rite of infant baptism, but her arguments apply equally to adult or believer's baptism. In that case, there is still the reciprocity between the community and candidate for baptism, still the presentation or letting go ("disappropriation") as it were of the individual and receiving him or her back into the community, still the writing and rewriting of the cross of Christ on the individual and community (in more traditional churches), and so forth. The baptized person(s) and the community become the temple of the Holy Spirit and the body of Christ in the ritual.

This leads us to the notion of a baptismal ecclesiology. Louis Weil explains,

> The model of baptism as the fundamental sacrament of identity in the church is sometimes referred to as a "baptismal ecclesiology"—that is, an understanding of the church that defines Christian community in terms of the common ground that all the baptized members share. This understanding of the church sees baptism as the defining sacrament for incorporation into its life.[65]

In terms of liturgical theology, this is sound reasoning, building on the long Christian tradition of baptism. Nevertheless, what about the stories of autistic people or other people who were or are denied baptism? Barton opens her book with such story of Hallie and her mother, Heather. Heather explained to Barton that they were on a long journey of trying to find a church where they could be part of, but they were constantly rejected.

> Heather explained that the pastors' explanations for these rejections varied slightly, but the root cause was always the same: Hallie was too loud, too disruptive, and too distracting. And besides, *Hallie could never understand what happened in baptism because of her intellectual disability*, as one pastor told Heather. Baptizing Hallie, therefore, *wouldn't really matter*. Heather sighed and with tears in her eyes told me that she and Hallie had not been to a church in months.[66]

Whether Hallie is autistic or not, Barton does not say, but she might have been. In any case, the story could be just as well about an autistic person with (presumed) learning disabilities.[67] If baptism *constitutes* Christian identity, as many scholars claim and for which I have rehearsed several arguments in this section, then such exclusion from baptism is highly problematic. The reason for exclusion from the sacraments is not only misguided as it is based on cognitive capacities as prerequisite for entry into baptism, for which there is little biblical justification. Furthermore, it diminishes the individual person by appearing to deny them *sacramental* participation in the divine life (of course, participation in the divine life is not dependent on human guardianship of sacramental access—God uses but does not depend on human beings), and therefore, it also diminishes the congregation as Belcher's reciprocity argument implies. This argument is not limited to baptism but also applies more broadly to exclusion from confirmation, the Eucharist, leadership roles, and so on. Hikari's story at the beginning of this section is such a story of exclusion, where little biblical justification can be found to justify taking her off the list of acolytes. Rebecca Spurrier sums it up this way: "When congregations fail to recognize persons with disabilities, they also fail to name God adequately."[68] It is through the infinite particularities that characterize human beings that we come to know God more fully.[69] To make baptism—which, after all, is the sacrament of initiation into the community—or other sacraments dependent on cognitive or other capacities is an outworking of the cult of normalcy.[70] Baptism does not depend on human assent but on God's descending to earth; before we can participate in Christ, Christ participated and continues to participate in the human nature.[71] Over against the cult of normalcy, a baptismal ecclesiology must include all God's people.

If it is true that baptism constitutes our Christian identity, whether one can understand this cognitively or not (and who can eventually?) and if it is therefore right to speak of a baptismal ecclesiology in which *everyone* belongs, then this must lead to a new perception of ourselves, each other, and the world around us—a new social imaginary. Indeed, Scripture suggests that it does. Baptismal images in the New Testament all refer to either the passage from one situation to another and/or the passage to something new. For example, the baptized person passes from death to life, is adopted into a new family, puts on new clothes, and is even a new creation.[72] This new life is rooted in the death and resurrection of Christ; Christ's participation in humanity precedes our participation in the divine life.

Barton makes another observation relevant to our discussion: it is not only the case that the baptized person has died to their "old life" and raised to new life, with the resulting different perception of their world and their place in the world, but baptism requires those around the person to see that person differently. As Paul writes to the Corinthians,

> [16] So from now on we regard no one from a worldly point of view. Though we once regarded Christ in this way, we do so no longer. [17] Therefore, if anyone is in Christ, the new creation has come: The old has gone, the new is here! (2 Cor 5:16–17, NIV)

On this, Barton comments,

> Paul writes to the Corinthians that allegiances to external characteristics, perceptible to lenses conditioned by the realm of the flesh, do not establish a foundation for identity in Christ. Put differently,

> culturally and socially lucrative aspects of human identity no longer provide a primary perspective on our neighbors.... Instead, the identity of each person initiated into Christ's body at their baptism becomes the orienting perspective from which Paul encourages us to perceive their identity.[73]

Normalcy blurs our lenses by conditioning them by the realm of the flesh, which cannot be the basis for the believers' identity in Christ. Baptism refocuses our perception, setting the story of the baptized person—and thereby the story of the entire community of believers (remember how Belcher demonstrated the interrelationship between the baptized individual and the community)—into the wider narrative of Jesus' life, death, and resurrection—in other words, in a soteriological and trinitarian framework. In baptism, the believer receives a new identity, which makes all the difference in the world.

Again, this might all sound too optimistic. What about Bowman's stories in the introduction to this chapter? What about Hallie and Heather? Barton is fully aware of this tension and argues that we live in between the reality of having been baptized in Christ but also "still awaiting the fullness of new creation in the final resurrection."[74] In baptism, we learn and anticipate what a new life might look like. Through the story of baptism, by rehearsing the narrative of redemption every time the congregation gathers for worship, by taking part in the symbols of reading the book, by signing our bodies with the baptismal water, by listening to the words from the book, and by eating and drinking and singing, we shape and are being shaped into a new social imaginary. In Barton's words, "practices of baptism become sites where Christian communities practice perception through this Christocentric prism, anticipating 'a new beginning of God's creative work' in the lives of each newly baptized member."[75] Without denying the broken reality in our own lives and around us, a baptismal identity changes the way we perceive reality. The Spirit of Christ living in us enables us to live in new ways, anticipating the "life in all its fullness" that Christ came to bring (John 10:10). Barton can therefore conclude her discussion by stating, "Christocentric identity of new creation primes Christians to anticipate what creative and renewing work the Holy Spirit might be up to in the lives of the baptized, both individually, and as a community of mutual care. This view of Christian identity is deeply anticipatory."[76] As such, a theology of participation, of presence and availability, is a theology of curiosity and anticipation of the work of the Holy Spirit in individuals and in the community in the midst of daily life, whether that means rough reality or smooth celebration—usually, daily life is a mixture of both.

We may call this rooting of our lives in baptism and other liturgical practices that shape our identity a baptismal or liturgical spirituality. Spirituality is, in Don Saliers' often-cited definition, "to be human at full stretch before the mystery of God, in mutuality with neighbor."[77] It is to lay all of our lives before God, kenotically participating in Christ's kenosis, letting our lives be transformed by the encounter with God and with our neighbors. A baptismal spirituality returns to the source time and again, to the living water that comes from Jesus (John 4:10–14), to be refreshed continually in the social imaginary shaped by the liturgy to live that life as well as possible, day by day, in this time of "already and not yet." Barton says that the community's daily repentance and baptismal participation in Jesus' death and resurrection (i.e., a baptismal spirituality) is necessary precisely for imagining anew the roles that people like Hikari have in the community and for staying rooted in that "social imaginary."[78]

In sum, with Belcher we saw how, in baptism, the identity of the individual and the community are intertwined, as seen for example in the image of adoption and the signing of the cross. The resulting baptismal ecclesiology shapes a new social imaginary, to use Taylor's term, which necessitates the belonging of all members to the worshipping community. Together, the believers perceive and live a new life in anticipation of the fulfillment of God's reign, fostered by a baptismal or liturgical spirituality. This section has laid further foundations to address the problem of normalcy, but how is this liturgical theology good news for autistic people and their congregations? Can this liturgical theology help to redraw the boundaries of normalcy? We now turn to these questions.

PURITY REDEFINED

An important image of our union with Christ is that of the temple, as we have already seen and elaborated on in this chapter. The temple image is useful to connect a theology of availability with liturgical theology, rooted in our participation in and union with Christ, because the temple is a place of worship. The three different uses of the temple image in the New Testament—Jesus as temple, the individual and community of believers as temple, and the heavenly temple or sanctuary—have all surfaced at different points in this discussion. However, Macaskill makes an observation that might sound uncomfortable but that we need to take seriously given our frequent use of this image: he notes that being the temple, the community of believers is to be pure and to be a blessing to the world.

Macaskill writes, "These two characteristics of the temple... require a recognition that the church's purity involves categorical separation from the world and its values, as the sacramental community of worship, and a simultaneous concern to bring the blessing of God to that world in its very sinfulness."[79] The language of "purity" raises several questions.[80] First, we need to acknowledge the damage that certain interpretations of purity have done to scores of (young) people. The so-called purity culture has resulted in trauma for a lot of people, especially, but not exclusively, for women.[81] Second, purity as "categorical separation from the world" can be associated with certain strands of Christianity that see the world as all bad, something from which the church should be separated. However, Jesus, who is also the temple, seemed to do rather the opposite.[82] It seems that we need to rephrase the idea of categorical separation and instead speak of a "categorical redrawing of boundaries." I will come back to this rephrased idea soon, showing also that we need to go further than that. Third, "purity" in Christian ethics as preached in churches is often understood as following a set of rules or customs, fostering legalism: do not drink, do not have sex before marriage, do not smoke, be in church on Sunday, and so forth. As we have seen in this book, especially in chapter 3, church is not free from the many expectations that communities, religious or not, often impose on their members. These three objections to "purity" make clear that if we are to take seriously the two characteristics of the temple as identified by Macaskill, we will need to reinterpret radically what we mean by purity. To do so might help to reclaim this term for theology in general and for a kenotic liturgical theology of availability in particular. In fact, redefining purity will bring us to an answer to the cult of normalcy—that exclusionary dynamic of guarding the boundaries that define who is "in" and "out." Thus, a reinterpretation of "purity" will also bring a blessing to the world—the second characteristic of the church as temple.

To redefine purity, I will again start with a story told by Sarah Barton and with her reflections on that story. This will help to redefine the boundaries of the community. After that, I will suggest that we need to go further and actually move away from the discussion of boundaries for which I will refer to the work of Bruce Morrill. Subsequently, I will relate the work of redefining purity to the sacraments with a brief comment on baptism and some more on the Eucharist.

When we rethink liturgy and worship through the lens of autism and in light of our critique of the cult of normalcy, then "purity" might take on a quite different meaning. If to be pure involves the categorical redrawing of the boundaries from the world and its values, then we may look more closely at our practices of inclusion and exclusion. Barton offers a helpful story from one of her participants, Anna, a lay reader. Anna observed that her church celebrated "cultural successes" of children, such as winning awards with the sports team, with the inverse effect that those children in their church who were not able to achieve those cultural successes were never celebrated.[83] Barton argues that baptism into the body of Christ needs to inform new imaginations. In a way that resonates strongly with our discussion of normalcy, Barton writes, "Anna's concerns illustrated for me one danger of an imagination about Christian identity rooted in values of contemporary Western liberal democracies—the restriction of ecclesial celebrations to successes marked by individualized productivity and achievement."[84] As we have explored above, a Christian identity and social imaginary (Taylor's term) is marked by the values of the reign of God, which are values that celebrate the God-given diversity in the church and the world. Purity as categorical redrawing of our boundaries will need to be a redrawing according to those values.

Barton quotes John Swinton, who writes with reference to being baptized into Christ's body, that "within Jesus' body diversity has become the new norm" and indeed, "if the only norm is Jesus, then our task is to live well and to live faithfully with our differences. If difference cannot separate us from Jesus, then it should not separate us from one another."[85] If we are to be "pure," as temple of the Holy Spirit, then it cannot mean that we are a community in which physical, cognitive, developmental, racial, sexual, or any other differences are more important than our common identity in Christ. We can now see the weight of Paul's statement in Galatians 3:27–28 (NIV):

> [26] So in Christ Jesus you are all children of God through faith, [27] for all of you who were baptized into Christ have clothed yourselves with Christ. [28] There is neither Jew nor Gentile, neither slave nor free, nor is there male and female, for you are all one in Christ Jesus.

Being united with Christ through baptism, the believers are "wearing" Christ. Baptism is the ground for unity in the congregation. Being in Christ is the identity that all members embody, and as such, there is no difference between ethnicities, sexes, social status, and we may add, disabled or nondisabled, autistic or non-autistic.

Bruce Morrill helps us to think beyond boundaries of inclusion and exclusion. In a passage closely related to our discussion of purity, he states that liturgical theology is not about demarcating "sacred versus profane."[86] On the contrary,

> in Jesus the categories of sacred and profane break down. Christian liturgy is not a matter of taking believers out of the world for a moment but, rather, of immersing them more deeply in the mystery of God's paradoxical purpose for it over time. Sin is not what happens in the profane world, while sanctification can be found in some exclusively sacred, separate precinct. Rather than the religious division of sacred and profane, the categories shaping Christianity are past, present, and future. The mutually informing ritual activity of word and sacrament draws those present in the Church's liturgical assembly into the memory of God's actions and promises of human redemption, transforming them, through the power of the Holy Spirit, into a foretaste of their promised fulfillment, when God will be all in all (see 1 Cor 15:28).[87]

The first implication to draw from this quotation is that Morrill reframes our discussion of purity by pointing out that Jesus' concern was not first and foremost with drawing lines that determine who is "in" and who is "out"; if this was of concern to Jesus at all, it was rather a concern to invite those whom the religious leaders and the culture of the time had deemed "out" back into the community of worshippers. The sharp boundaries of normalcy were redrawn by Jesus, or better, the existing lines were blurred, if not erased. The focus is not on excluding people but on the invitation to follow Jesus and become part of the divine mystery of redemption and sanctification. To put this slightly differently, Martha Moore-Keish argues that the believers' identity is outside of themselves ("ec-centric") in the triune God. The focus should be on the believers' unity that is constituted by this external identity instead of on the boundaries of who can or cannot belong.[88]

That is not to say that there is no new framework; I have argued throughout this and the previous chapter that being drawn into the mystery of salvation and by participation in the divine life, a new framework emerges. Louis Weil explains that in the first centuries of Christianity, the requirement for baptism was not, in the first place, the ability to repeat propositional belief statements but a profession of faith in one's daily life. Christians were not supposed to be in the army (because you should not kill) or take part in the circus (because it was a place of prostitution).[89] Conforming to Christian ideals, as a requirement for adults seeking baptism, requires a critical stance regarding the practices, norms, and values of the surrounding culture. Note, however, the liberating warning from Weil:

> It is also important to realize that baptism is not a sign of *exclusion* but, in its full implications, of radical *inclusion*. The full vision of baptism is of human solidarity, that all human beings are called to be members of the one family of God. Thus, as a sign, baptism points to something far greater and more comprehensive than the defined parameters of the church, much less of any single denomination.... A baptismal ecclesiology lifts up a radical sign of the unity of all people in their common vocation to be the people of God.[90]

This is an important qualifier to the discussion of incorporation into a community—a qualifier that resists turning this "process of socialization" into a new form of normalcy.[91] Baptism should not be turned into a new instrument of normalcy; instead, its character of an invitation into the life of the divine should be emphasized. Back to Morrill. The defining lines in the community are not those of sacred versus profane, and the focus is not on who is "in" or "out," but in the liturgy, God invites the believers more deeply in the mystery of God's story of salvation.

From that invitation into the mystery of salvific presence follows a second implication of Morrill's thought. The story of God invites us to steer our focus away from a preoccupation with the question of boundaries and where we should draw the boundaries of a potential new framework for belonging. Instead, we are prompted to start thinking in different terms: past, present, and future, as ritualized in the liturgy and especially the sacraments. That is not to say that frameworks, in the sense that Charles Taylor talks about them, do not exist, nor that social groups will not draw boundaries and might fall in the trap of normalcy, but the focus may need to be not on the boundaries of belonging but on the time-full Christian life. This may well lead to suspending lines of judgment over who belongs or not to the eschaton and therefore will be subject to God's final judgment in God's own time. Time-full living in God's story, in which we remember God's deeds in history and look forward with anticipation, in the present, to God's future, moves our attention away from a precise definition of where the boundaries of the Christian community's framework should be drawn. Instead, we are invited to worship God in awe and gratitude and embark on the double journey of discovering more of who God is and who we are (Saliers). As such, the liturgy reminds us time and again of our identity in Christ, both in terms of our participation in Christ and in terms of God's deeds in the past, what God will do in the future, and how that impacts our life in the present. In Christ's reality, human-made distinctions fade in importance when it comes to who may enter the community, who may worship, and who belongs to Christ and therefore to the temple or body of Christ. Through baptism, the believers come to live under the dominion of Christ instead of under the dominion of values contrary to God's kingdom.[92]

This move away from boundary drawing is reinforced by highlighting the kenotic nature of God's participation in humanity and that same nature of the believers' participation in the divine life. It is noteworthy that Morrill moves into a discussion of the concept that we ended with in the last chapter and that has surfaced in this chapter time and again: participation, which I have explored along the lines of kenosis. Participation in sacramental worship, in Christ's leitourgia, means to participate in his ongoing prayer and work for the world. The concept of participation in the divine life shows the inseparable connection between worship and ethics. When we become available to each other, as explored in the previous chapter, there is a radical erasure of boundaries that exclude on the basis of social status, social agility, quick speech, bodily composure, and so forth. In the act of kenotic availability, we give ourselves to one another and perceive Christ in the other.[93] Thus, Morrill contrasts the preoccupation with sacred versus profane discussions (i.e., purity) with participation in the divine life. Kenotic participation in Christ is the antidote to the false boundaries of normalcy.

In this chapter, I have discussed participation and Christian identity primarily in terms of baptism. As we are coming to the close of this chapter, I want to make a few brief comments on the Eucharist—space does not allow for more—because the Eucharist is no less important for becoming who we are individually and communally in Christ. In a way, the Eucharist continues baptism. In fact, all that we have said about the erasure of distinctions based on the cult of normalcy is put forcefully by the New Testament writers, especially Paul. Paul's criticism of the Corinthian practice was about them making distinctions based on worldly values of societal status, resulting in some people going hungry while others were well fed. There is archaeological evidence to suggest that the Corinthian believers met in the houses of the rich members of the congregations, for the practical reason that their houses were bigger and therefore could host more people than the houses of less well-off members. It seems that some members were given a seat at the table in the *triclinium* whereas others had to stand in the *atrium*. Those in the triclinium would have better quality of food, whereas those in the atrium would be given lesser quality food and leftovers—and some would have even nothing (1 Cor 11:21).[94] Paul says that celebrating the holy meal on the basis of distinctions of social honor is diametrically opposite of what the Eucharist is meant to be. He says flat out that what the Corinthians celebrate is simply not the Eucharist at all (1 Cor 11:20).

We need to rethink liturgy and worship, then, recognizing each member of the community as being "in Christ" and as fellow member—even a brother or sister. As referred to earlier, Macaskill points to the fact that Paul's ethical instructions to the church are always grounded in the believers' identity in Christ. "Consistently, he [Paul] says, 'this is what you are, so start to live accordingly, because right now you are monstrously inconsistent with it.' The logic is not so much that we have not yet fulfilled our potential but is actually much more scathing: we are doing violence to our identity in Christ with our moral failings."[95] Any rethinking of our social practices, including those as part of our liturgy and worship, should find their basis in our identity in Christ. Insofar as it is justified to divide people into separate groups—after all, not everyone fitted in the triclinium; some had to stand in the atrium—it should not be on the basis of social values: in Christ, there is neither Jew nor Greek, slave nor free, male nor female, autistic nor non-autistic. Moore-Keish observes that the Eucharist, as a food ritual that forges our unity in Christ and with each other, "signals that we are dependent on something outside of ourselves for life itself" or to a "primal need."[96] Moreover, "not only are we all equally in need of nourishment, but we are all equally in need of mercy."[97] The corporate acknowledgment of this need is the equalizer in the community and pushes the community to find its identity not in self-constructed boundaries but outside itself, in Christ.

Participating in the liturgy, in the sacraments of baptism and Eucharist, redefines the meaning of purity. Morrill's discussion of participation in the divine life, as antidote to a preoccupation with the boundaries drawn by normalcy (as discussion above), finds its climax in his discussion of the Eucharist. Notably, Morrill uses the concept of holiness at the outset of his discussion, which is strongly related to the concept of purity. He writes, "Participation in the Eucharist is partaking in the very holiness of God, a holiness embodied in the person of Christ, whose Spirit sanctifies participants' bodies with graces characteristic of how Jesus executed the will of his Father."[98] Morrill also discusses some key notions of Edward Schillebeeckx's sacramental theology, which attends strongly to suffering. Morrill states that not all suffering is redemptive but only that which is suffering because of the cause of justice, which for Jesus culminated in his death on the cross in solidarity with all who suffer. "From this can be drawn the implication for what it means to participate in, to be a part of, God's life—that is, to be holy. The sanctified person suffers not for the sake of suffering but for the sake of the reign of God, for the sake of that which will ultimately prevail. Schillebeeckx identifies this type of suffering with 'sacrificial love.'"[99] It is remarkable that Morrill links holiness so strongly to suffering. This might seem not so relevant for our discussion of autistic people's belonging to the liturgical community. However, further reflection on this shows that it is.

Morrill, following Schillebeeckx and others, advocates solidarity with those who suffer from injustice, and if autistic people are excluded from the worshipping community because of normalcy, as discussed in chapter 3, then it is only a small step to call that injustice.[100] From a gospel perspective, there is no reason to exclude people on the basis of cultural values such as the ability to sit still throughout the liturgy or the requirement to put up with the sensory preferences of the (non-autistic) majority. Liberation theologians ask us to take seriously the gospel imperative of solidarity with those who are unjustly excluded or oppressed.[101] In our church communities, we need to stand in solidarity with those who are excluded from our worship. The stories of autistic people who report suffering in worship because of sensory overload, social setup, or cognitive dissonance abound. In solidarity with these autistic brothers and sisters in Christ, non-autistic worshippers have the duty to call out this unjust suffering, even if that "sacrificial love" means to prophetically raise their voice and suffer the backlash they might get—no doubt their autistic brothers and sisters will show solidarity in return because they have suffered that backlash many times. Thus, Morrill is right when he connects partaking in the divine life through participation in the Eucharist with suffering for the right cause. To participate in the divine life is to be holy, Morrill states; holiness is expressed in sacrificial love.[102] To love in this way, within and beyond the boundaries of our communities, is indeed fulfilling the priestly role in the temple of living stones—that is, it will bring a blessing to the world.

This section started with the uncomfortable observation by Macaskill that to be a temple of living stones necessitates a "categorical separation from the world and its values." I have suggested that it might be better to speak about a "categorical redrawing of the boundaries," which we can see in the life of Jesus, who came to identify with the world. Moreover, with Morrill, I have argued that the liturgy and the sacraments invite us to steer away from a focus on where the boundaries should be drawn. Instead, we are invited, together with all of humanity, to participate in the ongoing prayer and work of Jesus Christ. Having the same kenotic "mindset" of Jesus (Phil 2:5), we are called to be available to those around us, with sacrificial love, rooted in a liturgical and sacramental spirituality that invites rather than excludes.

CONCLUSION

Throughout the chapter, I followed liturgical theologians in making some grand theological claims. Liturgy does bring us to expression, although that is only true because Jesus Christ is the great leitourgikos in whose prayer and work we participate. The grammar of our liturgical theology, following the argument of the previous chapter, must be that God first participated in human, created life before humanity could participate in God. Worship practices that are based on human values will fall short of the values of the kingdom of God and instead continue the cult of normalcy, where the god Normal and goddess Average reign and determine who might enter the sanctuary and who remains at the outer courts of the temple.[103]

A liturgical theology that is robust enough to respond to the cult of normalcy grounds the identity of the believers in Christ. In this chapter, I have explored this, particularly through the image of the temple in which the community of believers are the royal priesthood (1 Pet 2:9), and the temple is the place of divine presence. I then developed a definition of liturgy that fits well with the temple image, emphasizing that liturgy has a central place in the life of the community. Liturgy is, first of all, the prayer and work of Christ in which the community participates in turn; second, it is kenotic; last, it is trinitarian. Liturgy does not just look inward but is always directed toward God on behalf of the world. This last notion connects the definition of liturgy with one of the functions of the temple—that is, to be a blessing to the world.

Participation in liturgy leads to a change in the way we perceive ourselves, those in our communities, and the world around us. This calls for a baptismal or liturgical spirituality. Such a spirituality is fed by liturgy and lived in daily life. The liturgy draws us into the trinitarian story of salvation, which is not only hopeful and comforting but also challenges us prophetically. A baptismal identity and ecclesiology leads to a critical stance whenever people are excluded, addressing Bowman's and others' stories. It is also realistic: we live in between the "already and the not yet" of the reign of God. Therefore, we must lament and confess our ignorance and excluding practices; however, we also look forward with anticipation, excitement, and curiosity to what the Holy Spirit is doing already and what will be fulfilled when God's reign breaks in.

The temple image brings with it the requirement of purity, a notion that might be uncomfortable for various reasons. Nevertheless, a reclaiming of that notion actually helps us to formulate a response to the cult of normalcy. A categorical redrawing of the boundaries along the lines of the values of God's reign is good news for those who find themselves marginalized by the cult of normalcy. At the same time, Morrill's thinking has helped us to move away from a focus of boundaries in the first place. A liturgical and sacramental spirituality is marked by time-full living, remembering God's deeds in the past, living in the presence of Christ through the Holy Spirit in the present, and looking forward to the fulfillment of God's promises.

In the liturgy and the sacraments, we learn a new social imaginary, a new way of seeing the world, a new calibration of our values. When the community becomes aware of the particularities of their autistic members, it might start to understand its practices differently. To return to Bowman's stories from the introduction to this chapter, at coffee hour after the service, the noninvolved question "How are you?" might be turned into a genuine interest in the other person, into a being prepared to listen to the other person, whether they are doing all right or not. Clergy might set aside their need to talk to full rows of people in the front and allow for the (literal) space autistic members have carefully carved out for themselves. Whenever people touch to greet or to comfort or to pray for someone, first they might check whether that is all right with the other person, respecting the other person's boundaries. Furthermore, when the community's values are aligned according to the values of God's reign, Hikari might well continue to serve as an acolyte. Her particularities are welcomed as part of the God-given diversity that is the new norm in the community. Hallie might receive baptism because the church realizes that cognitive understanding is more of a cultural than a kingdom value. This is what it means to be truly present to each other; this is what a kenotic liturgical theology of availability might look like in practice.

This new framework is what we celebrate every time in the liturgy and what we remember when we sign ourselves with the baptismal water as a reminder of our baptism. It is also what we remember every time we eat the bread and drink the wine, which become Christ's body and blood to us in the Eucharist. A liturgical spirituality is not so much concerned with the boundaries of the community but instead invites people to join in the mystery of God's story of salvation. In that story, we find our identity in Christ, through baptism. Distinctions along the lines of cultural values, even along the lines of biological and neurological makeup fade in importance, as we are all one in Christ (Gal 3:27–38). This is good news for autistic and non-autistic people alike. In the next chapter, I will analyze a church—the Chapel of Christ Our Hope in Singapore—and its worship, where this good news becomes the lived reality of the community of believers. The analysis further demonstrates how a kenotic liturgical theology of availability might be shaped in worshipping communities.

6

Availability in Practice
Autistic Worship in Singapore

Imagine what it looks like to have a church where autistic people are central. Imagine a church where every decision is taken from the perspective of its autistic members, a liturgy in which every element is thought through with autism in mind. This book has first explored why the opposite is so often true in churches. I have identified "normalcy" as the root cause for the ignoring or even absence of autistic people. In chapters 4 and 5, I have responded to normalcy with a kenotic liturgical theology of availability. In this final chapter, I will analyze a church that embarked on a journey first of imagining a church where autistic people are at the core of church life and then of putting this into practice. This Singaporean church is called the Chapel of Christ Our Hope.

This chapter has three aims. First, this chapter aims to "land" the liturgical discussion of the previous chapter in the actual praxis of worship in one particular church by describing a church that has autistic people as its raison d'être and by observing how this church worships. Second, in webinars and conferences, I have noticed that people in churches are often willing to become more inclusive but do not always know how to do so. This chapter offers an example, which perhaps gives inspiration, even though it is not meant as a blueprint to be followed in every detail. Related to the first two, the third aim is to demonstrate the complexity or multilayered nature of worship by presenting a detailed description of worship. By describing the complexity of worship, we can see what worship might look like when we intentionally hope to include autistic people. This may result, again, in some practical examples, but we should also be clear that, although sometimes small changes can have great (positive or negative) impact in terms of enabling autistic people to participate in worship and to feel that they belong, countering the cult of normalcy requires more than a quick fix.

In this chapter, I will describe how and why the Chapel of Christ Our Hope (hereafter "the chapel") originated and how the church functions in terms of its community life and liturgy.[1] The first part of this chapter describes the origins of the chapel and is primarily based on the many conversations I had with Pastor David and on some other interviews that I conducted there. The second part of the chapter describes the liturgy and worship services in the chapel. In these first parts, two things will become clear: (1) in a real sense, autistic people are the raison d'être for this church, and (2) at the same time, the church also recognizes the need to support the family members of autistic people, especially the parents. Therefore, this church (and hence this chapter) is not only about the place of autistic people in the Chapel of Christ Our Hope but also that of their family members. In the last part, I will offer a theological interpretation of the liturgy and community life of the chapel, thereby applying the lens of the kenotic liturgical theology of availability that I developed in the previous chapters.

For the description of worship in the chapel, I will draw on my observations of two worship services of the chapel that I attended, on detailed field notes of my first nine-day visit to this community in February 2020, and on interviews with the leadership and with parents of autistic members from that first visit. In May 2022, I was able to return for a second visit, which had been planned much earlier but delayed by COVID-19. During this visit, I attended two more worship services, and I interviewed five autistic church members on the basis of pictures that they had taken beforehand and discussed with their parents. I had asked them to take pictures of significant things or moments in the worship service. Some of these interviewees had a learning disability and/or limited speech, and therefore, it was difficult to do in-depth interviews. However, because the views of nonspeaking autistic people (as expressed by themselves, instead of by their parents or caregivers) are vastly underrepresented in research, I wanted to make an effort to create a space where their views could be expressed. Despite the communication difficulties, the results were interesting, and I will refer to them in this chapter, alongside the more in-depth discussions that I was able to have with parents and church leaders.

THE STORY OF THE CHAPEL OF CHRIST OUR HOPE

In this first section, I will describe the origins of the chapel. This paradigm-shifting story began in a way that is high and humble at the same time.

High and Humble Beginnings

Presumably, not many churches can trace their origins back to a president suggesting to the bishop at an informal tea party that he should start a project centered on autism, but the Chapel of Christ Our Hope can. It was back in the early 2000s that President S. R. Natan approached the bishop of the Anglican churches in Singapore (John Chew, who was also archbishop of the province at the time), saying he was glad the churches were doing all kinds of social work, including running a hospital, psychiatric and nursing homes, and more. But President Natan wondered, had the bishop thought of doing work with autistic people, in particular with those called, in medical terms, moderate to severely autistic? As bishops do, he started praying and thinking about the idea and discussed it with some senior clergy. David, who later became the pastor of the chapel, remembers, "Some advice came, saying that you don't want to go down that road, because it's a deep hole. It will sap all your energy and your resources. It's a black hole, you don't want to go there." However, a small group started to think about the president's suggestion. It became increasingly clear that in Singapore, with its cultural tendency to value education and perfectionism, very little was in place for autistic people (who would often not answer to those ideals and whose way of being in the world would not be much valued) and their families.[2] The less it seemed anyone was willing to do something for this group in society, the more they started to feel that they should respond to this need. Meanwhile, the president came back and said that the government was willing to finance the project.

Another tea party at which the bishop as well as John Ang, a retired professor in social studies, happened to be present moved the project further along. The bishop asked the casual question, what were the professor's plans for retirement? Ang answered that he had been wanting to do work with autism but never had the time while lecturing at the university. As Pastor David comments, "So we have, we have the

164 | Autism and Worship

government willing to finance, we have a church willing to, I mean, prepared to exercise faith in this and say, 'Yeah, we will do this.' And now we have somebody who has the know-how, right?" Ang became the first CEO of St. Andrew's Autism Centre (SAAC), and the center was the womb from which the chapel was born.[3] Pastor David[4] was the chaplain of SAAC from the very start, and even though the chapel originated only a few years later, from the beginning the idea was to integrate a chapel into SAAC.

The integral place of the chapel within SAAC can be seen not just in the employment of one full-time and two part-time chaplains but also in the architecture and design. One of the theological meanings reflected in the architecture of SAAC is the chapel's central place in the crossover, a first-level outside walkway that connects several of the buildings. Figure 2 shows a map of SAAC. Figure 1 shows the inner garden of the complex; the crossover is most clearly seen in the left side of the picture. The building that is most dominant in the picture (apart from the three high buildings in the background) is the chapel. In Pastor David's words, "The chapel is right in the middle, so it represents the heartbeat of the whole center." At the same time, the architecture of the chapel was kept, in one sense, fairly simple because, as Pastor David

Fig. 1 Inner garden and crossover, view from one of the entrance points

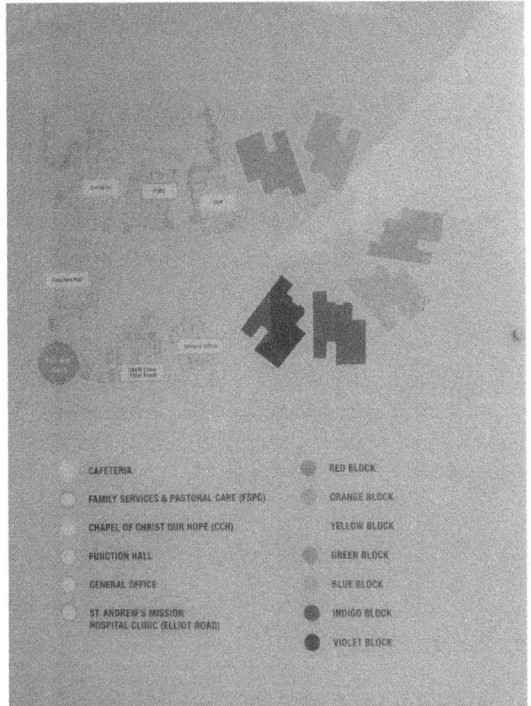

Fig. 2 Map of St. Andrew's Autism Centre

Fig. 3 Either side of the chapel has tall windows in rainbow colors

Fig. 4 Altar with integrated Saint Andrew's cross

Fig. 5 The front of the Chapel of Christ Our Hope, view from balcony

Fig. 6 At the back of the church hall is a small balcony behind a glass wall

Fig. 7 Balcony

explains, "once you understand autism and all that, which I came to learn quite quickly, you keep it simple." While the building is rectangular and seemingly straightforward, "simple" describes the interior design—which, as the figures show, is rather uncluttered—rather than the level of intention and planning.

The description of the building demonstrates how, from the beginning, autism informed the thinking about the chapel and the community it would gather. The attention given to the architecture of the chapel (and the whole SAAC for that matter), considering the needs of autistic people, was also characteristic of other aspects of the planning stages for the new community to be formed. In the words of Carl, a leader of the chapel who was part of SAAC and the chapel from the earliest beginnings, "[Autism] is our focus, that is our mission. Yeah. So everything will revolve around it." One example of that focus was the way that the idea for the chapel was presented to churches around the diocese. Pastor David recalls that the presentation included an explanation of "what autism is, how it impacts the family, how it impacts the siblings, you know, and how is this an issue in society" and then how this new church might address the questions all of this raises. Eventually, thirty-five people joined the core group that started the chapel.[5]

A Paradigm Shift

For the next nine months, the group gathered once a week "to understand autism, to pray, come and pray together, just to condition ourselves, just to get ready to set up this new church plant. How are we going to do things, and so forth."[6] They invited different parents to come and share their story, staff from SAAC, an occupational therapist who talked about sensory issues, a Roman Catholic psychologist who spoke about autism from a spiritual point of view, and so on. They divided themselves into teams, thinking through how they were going to do things. This resulted in a paradigm shift. Pastor David recalls,

> And then we bring ourselves into teams to—we decided okay, this is how we're going to do, we're going to have a hospitality corner, we're going to, lunch is for sure, everybody will have. Then we got to have thought through the whole process, how it will be, the service, we've got to have set boundaries, we going to be structures in front, so that people don't run all the way to the altar. You know, we have visuals, we have this, the sound shouldn't be too jarring, lighting—all kinds of things. And then what happens when the child does this, does that, what will we do? So we talked about some of these things. We—no aggression, nothing, you

know, just let them be. We won't try to struggle with the child like no, right in front of everybody. No, we won't do that, struggling, and just, just letting, learning, learning from the whole experience. I think in the end we realized that this actually requires a paradigm shift. It's a real paradigm shift: how we've been so used to church life that now we have to think differently. Yeah, so it requires a very conscious effort to think differently.

David perfectly illustrates the point that I have been arguing for throughout this book: "we've been so used to church life" *in a particular way and according to particular (cultural) norms* "that now we have to think differently." What David calls a paradigm shift, I have explored in terms of frameworks. It remains a challenging, if not painful, question as to why it is necessary for a paradigm shift to take place in order for a church to be a place where autistic people, and their parents, feel that they can belong. As we will see in a moment, many parents in the chapel (and, by extension, their autistic children) described feeling excluded in other churches, and they felt that they had to leave those churches. On the one hand, one might say that if autism is a different way of being in, experiencing, and understanding the world, it should not come as a surprise that centering a church on autism requires a paradigm shift. On the other hand, one difference between the chapel and other churches, one that stands out for all the people whom I interviewed, is that they feel accepted there. At the chapel, autism—in whatever way it is expressed: need for structure, walking around, making noises—is not an issue. Moreover, the autistic people whom I interviewed all spoke about the friendships that had developed in the chapel, in particular with other autistic people. The chapel models another paradigm, one in which autistic and non-autistic people belong equally—a paradigm to be followed by other churches, however different that might look like in the particular practices of any given church community.

Another way in which the chapel made autistic people central from the beginning was the way in which the chapel responded to the needs of families with autism. Before the chapel itself was started, Pastor David was already chaplain to SAAC and spoke with a lot of parents. It became increasingly clear that the parents often felt excluded from other churches, as the following excerpt from my interview with Pastor David shows:

> D: And then of course I engaged with the parents quite a bit, yeah, so worked very closely with the center [SAAC] to engage the

>   parents. . . . I think after talking, hearing parents, you know, when I had conversations and you hear their story and just so many of them, you realize that yeah, there's a great need for a chapel like this. Because many of them couldn't stay in church anymore. They have to leave church: they try this church, that church, they try many churches . . .
> L: Because of their child with autism?
> D: Yeah, because of the child with autism. So they all had issues with just staying back, yeah, or just being in the church, a sense of belonging. So that's where, that's how this chapel started.

Indeed, several people I interviewed commented on the difference between the chapel and other churches. Many of them had tried different churches but felt people looked at them or shushed them. Even if they were accepted in principle (or in some cases, more accurately, tolerated), often there would be no material provision for people with additional needs. John, another leader of the chapel, commented that some other churches put programs in place, but it could feel very much that "they" (the church or non-autistic people) did something for "them" (autistic people). John described how some churches, especially bigger churches, put on disability "programs" that felt a bit like charitable actions toward those with disabilities. He states, "It's almost like a program, it's almost like the neurotypical people reaching out to the people with disabilities." One parent, Lai Chan, reflected on a church that had tried to care well, saying, "So they just try their very best, and to a point that I see is they're more or less giving a care service instead of including [my son] in like really worshipping God and all that." Jonah said that some churches, in contrast, do not even allow children with special needs to come into the main sanctuary with their parents, leaving them feeling isolated from the congregation and unaccepted. He sharply commented, "People with special kids are treated like pariahs. . . . You go to another place, you don't bother us, we want to listen, only we." It is clear from those comments that a place was needed where autistic people and their families felt that they could truly belong. The chapel tries to be that place, and according to its members, it succeeds in that.

In this way, an informal chat between a president and a bishop over tea instigated a paradigm shift in thinking about what it means to be a church. As a result, the chapel has become a place where some of the least valued people of Singaporean society are being valued and are finding a place of belonging. The chapel prepared to hold its first worship service on Easter Sunday 2012, knowing that the key to the success of the chapel would be the way autistic people and their families would feel. Those people were going to be central in this church. A decade later, we will now turn to what that looks like on a Sunday morning.

WORSHIP AND LITURGY AT THE CHAPEL OF CHRIST OUR HOPE

We begin by paying attention to the liturgy and worship practices of the chapel. First, it is necessary to establish a framework for describing the worship services. We will start with a descriptive model based on an analytical model proposed by Ronald Grimes. However, because worship is a theological act, the description needs to be followed by a theological interpretation; this will be the subject of our final reflections in this chapter.

A Framework for Describing the Worship Service

When asked to describe their worship service, a casual congregant may note the people gathered or the gathering space, but the focus would likely be on what the liturgical ministers do, especially the priest. However, the liturgical ritual contains many more aspects to explore, and it is questionable whether the focus of the description should be on the actions of the leaders of the liturgy—liturgical scholars remind us of the common translation of leitourgia as "the work of the people"—with an emphasis on *all* the people (but see the discussion in the introduction of this idea). Grimes proposes a helpful figure to explore and describe rituals (figure 8), which we will use to give an initial description of worship at the chapel.[7] Grimes is wary of suggesting that this figure is universal and exhaustive; other elements may be added or shifted around. Moreover, all these elements are interrelated, and as such, one may even argue that some elements or parts thereof can be subsumed under other elements. The point is not to come up with a perfect analytical model but with a structured way of analyzing the worship service. When speaking with people in the Singapore church about their worship service, three aspects stood out, which I have included in figure 8. The three aspects were the structure of the service, sensitivity to sensory issues, and movement.

However, an interview with Kim Gek, one of the assistant pastors in the chapel, showcases that the liturgy of the chapel transcends straightforward descriptions. The entire worship service, although it can be broken down into specific elements, is experienced as something more than the sum of its parts (a possibility named by Grimes as well). This is not

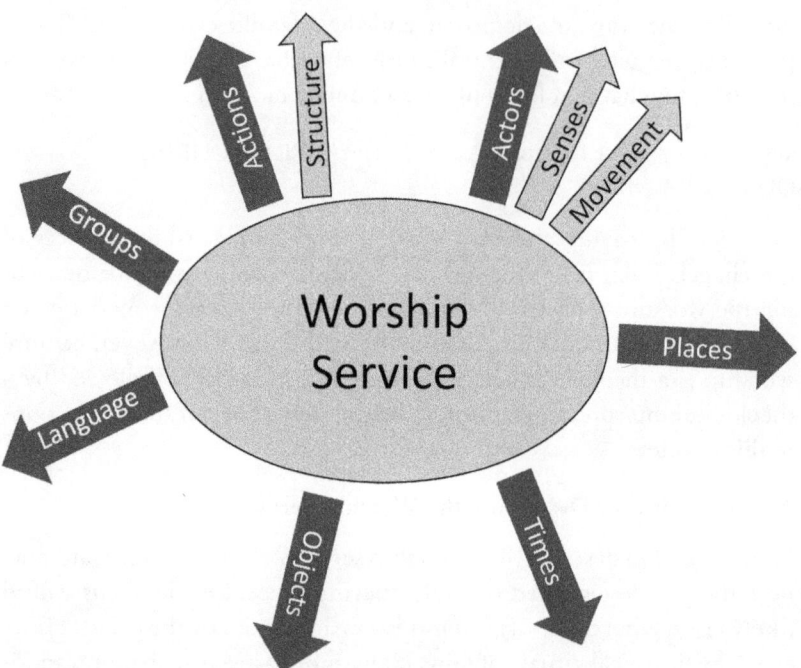

Fig. 8 Elements of a worship service, adapted from Grimes

necessarily reflected in the figure, but it is necessary to include this in the description of the worship service. Kim Gek commented that the liturgy was not different from any other church—that is, a church that follows the same liturgical tradition. I was puzzled by Kim Gek's comment because most people I had spoken to up until that point had said that the church was so different and that also the worship service was different. Kim Gek mentioned the use of pictures and symbols, but other than that, she said the liturgy remains the same:

> I come from an Anglican church as well, so I don't think that is, I don't think that the church has changed itself for them [i.e., autistic people], but I guess it has made allowances to include them. Yeah, I mean, I do go back to my old church as well on the other weeks that I'm not here. Yeah, I don't think that the church liturgy has changed specially for these children, but I guess with the signs and symbols we use, it helps them to know what is happening right now and what's next. . . . But other than that, I don't think that there is—the liturgy of the church have changed, yeah.

If the liturgy does not change, if the order of service does not change, and if the worship songs are the same as in other churches, then what is it that makes the chapel different from other churches? Is it only the use of pictures and symbols, or is it more?

Worship at the Chapel of Christ Our Hope: An Analysis

The description is based on two worship services that I observed in February 2020.[8] On the second Sunday, I was allowed to record what took place in the service, up to the point of the sermon, which helped my observations when analyzing the worship service in more detail at a later point. The sermon was not recorded at the request of the preacher, who was anxious about being filmed. On the first Sunday, I stayed throughout the whole service in the chapel. On the second Sunday, I went out with the autistic people to their own program, Rainbow of Hope, halfway through the service.

The description that follows might raise certain critical questions, and I will point to some of them. However, the purpose of this description is not to critically evaluate what the chapel does well and what needs to be improved. Instead, as mentioned in the introduction to this chapter, the purpose of the description is to show what worshipping with autistic and non-autistic people together might look like as well as the complexity of worship.

In chapter 1, I presented some stories of the experience of worship by autistic people. One of the points that became clear was that preparing for the worship service starts well before the actual start of the worship service. One can debate what the starting point of a worship service is and what the starting point for analysis should be. Does it start with the first words spoken? Or with the main actors' first actions? But then, who are the main actors? Is it those who have formal liturgical roles? From a narrative and theological point of view, this is debatable. Elsewhere, I have argued that the main characters of the liturgical story are God and people (the whole congregation).[9] If one of liturgy's main functions is to bring the people of God together for worship, then perhaps the community-forming aspects of the worship service should be taken into account. So the chatter before the worship service (or, in some churches, the sitting together in silence), as part of community formation, might be a better starting point for analysis. Moreover, one can question what the focus of the analysis of a worship service should be: is it the things that might be experienced and understood, rather than the words that are being spoken? The interviews made clear that sensory issues were taken very seriously in the planning of worship at the chapel. Moreover, some recent scholarship on autism argues that the key to understanding autism is to understand the workings of sensory perception.[10] Therefore, to sensitize the reader to this aspect of worship and to foreground the communal experience of worship, I start the analysis with a fairly detailed description of the sensory environment of the chapel.[11]

Senses

One of the things that can be noted in terms of experience *before* the service starts is the difference in light. Outside, the sun is brightly shining; inside, the colors are softer because of the tall, rainbow-colored windows (figure 3). Bright light enters through the carved-out cross in the middle of the front wall, right above the altar. That said, before entering the chapel, one walks over a path that is shaded by the crossover running right above the path on the ground. In that sense, the difference in light is more gradual than just bright to soft light. Also weather related is the difference in temperature. Singapore is typically hot, with temperatures that easily rise above 30°C. Most people seem to come by car, and it is quite likely that the cars are air-conditioned. The chapel itself certainly is, perhaps even a bit chilly. Other senses might be different inside compared to outside as well, such as smell and sound, although the open back doors before the start of the service and the chapel's spaciousness help to reduce the difference.

What about sensory input *during* the worship service? In terms of *sound*, one can hear people chatting to each other just before the service starts. During the service, sound comes through speakers; the band is plugged in, as are all who use microphones from the front. The band is different each Sunday of the month. On the first Sunday that I attended, the band consisted of a keyboard player, drummer, and guitarist/singer. On the second Sunday, the band was a little bigger: a keyboard player, two guitarists, a drummer, and two singers (one male, one female). The volume is kept reasonably low on purpose. Throughout the service, one can hear some autistic people making noises. Some wear headphones to block the sound. When building the chapel, the walls were designed with sound-absorbing materials. There were no particular *smells* as far as I could tell; no incense is used. Sometimes autistic people can become upset by the perfumes that people may have put on, but I did not hear anyone comment on that. When the Eucharist is celebrated, one may smell bread and wine when taking it.[12] For *taste*, the same can be said.

In terms of *sight*, figures 1 and 3–7 give an impression of what the building looks like. Pastor David noted that in the planning phases for the chapel, he realized that things had to be kept simple. Indeed, there is very little decoration. Pastor David notes that the space is designed to have no distractions and that sensory issues were taken very seriously. The raised front part of the church has a simple but beautiful altar in the middle (with the Saint Andrew's cross worked into it). There is a lectern on one side and space for the band on the other. Above the altar is a large cross (figures 4 and 5). Clergy and liturgical ministers wear simple robes. The main colors are the color of light wood, a dark altar and lectern, and the rainbow colors of the windows. Of course, there are people to see, walking around and going in and out, even a bit after the service has started (10:00 a.m.). During the service, most people just sit down, although during the services I attended, I observed that several people (presumably autistic people) were walking around, jumping up and down the aisle, rocking in their places. During the songs, some people swayed a little or raised their hands.

Touch is difficult to comment on, as it will be different to different people. It is noticeable that the building contains both pews and chairs. The Eucharist was not celebrated on the Sundays that I attended the chapel, but Pastor David told me that at the moment of sharing the peace, people do not do so by handshake but by giving high fives. This gesture was also evident at other moments when people wanted to greet each other with some form of touch. Otherwise, touching each other was avoided (e.g., no "let's hold hands and pray," as happens in some churches). At the particular time when I visited Singapore, shaking hands was explicitly discouraged because of COVID-19—a discouragement repeated by the church. Finally, *proprioception* (the awareness of body movement) is difficult to comment on, as again, this is entirely personal.

Actors and Movement

Starting with the sensory aspects of a worship service in the chapel helps to describe the liturgical act in terms of that which is done by the entire congregation gathered for that purpose. In other words, when we observe the liturgy by describing the various actors, we need to resist the temptation to start with the officiant or Pastor David. All too often, the liturgical act is interpreted as something done *to* the gathered people *by* the liturgical ministers. However, as we have seen in the previous chapter, the liturgy is a communal act in which all the members participate. Starting with the sensory aspects of the service has allowed us to describe these aspects from anyone's point of view, as all people are affected by some or all sensory stimuli. Given the focus of this book on worshipping as autistic and non-autistic people together—that is, a focus on the entire congregation instead of a clerical focus—we continue the description of worship by next describing the people in the pews.

Looking at who is coming to the chapel, perhaps what stands out the most is the presence of many autistic people. Even if not surprising, because everything the church does revolves around autistic members, it is still remarkable to find so many autistic people in one church. Someone in the chapel told me that it can be up to forty or fifty autistic people on a Sunday. Ronald Grimes rightly argues that everyone is an agent, even by showing up or staying away.[13] This is also true for autistic worshippers in the chapel: even if few of them have formal roles in the liturgy, the whole liturgical setup revolves around them. Thereby, in addition to the active role the autistic worshippers have in the worship service, to which we turn next, they also have a passive but influential role in the service.[14]

Other actors include the sound technicians in the back of the church hall, the four people going around with the collection baskets at one point during the service, those who give a testimony, the band, readers, and three robed clergy. The congregation actively seeks opportunities for involving autistic people in specific roles. In one of the bands, an autistic young man is a singer, together with his mom. They also choose the songs for the Sunday when they are singing. Some autistic people are involved in reading the Scriptures out loud or going around with the collection basket. One autistic person delights in sweeping the cafeteria, where lunch is served after the worship service. He often does not even join the worship service because he is so keen to sweep the place. At first, his parents tried to make him attend the worship service, but now they see this as his way of serving God, and they delight in that.

Some people tended to walk up and down the aisles as it is hard for them to remain seated in the same place for so long. This is an aspect of the chapel that was often commented on in my conversations and interviews. There is a wide acceptance of people walking and jumping around during the service. This brings another group of liturgical actors into view: the parents and siblings of autistic people. Families that include an autistic member feel accepted and at home quickly in the chapel because their child can also move around and make noises. In other churches, this is often seen as disturbing, bad behavior, and a sign of bad parenting. The autistic person, their parents, and/or their siblings will get judgmental looks and will be shushed. The result is that these families feel rejected and judged and become spiritually homeless. When they then come to the chapel and see that other autistic people do the same as their sibling or their child, tense feelings are eased, and the chapel starts to be a place of acceptance and eventually belonging. We should note that this dynamic rests on there being a certain number of people who do move around, talk, shout, or make other noises. The more people do so, the less one individual stands out for it. This is one of the advantages of the chapel being centered on autistic people. In other churches, acceptance through the practices of movement and sound making may be harder to realize. In the terminology of this book, even if autistic people are not the largest group of people in the chapel, they are a sizable minority, able to change the paradigm of the majority in a process of constructing a new framework.

Another group of actors that should be noted is families who do not have an autistic family member but who have joined the church anyway—a fact that is sometimes met with surprise on the part of families with autistic members. It is noteworthy that the direction of inclusion is being reversed here by the chapel. Whereas inclusion is often thought of as the act of including those who are different from the norm into the community (without letting the community's norms be challenged), which in practice means that non-autistic people include autistic people, here families without autism are included in a worshipping community where autism is the norm.

In sum, looking at the actors, autistic people are a visible reality in the chapel. The majority of the people have some kind of connection to autism, mostly because they are autistic or live with their autistic family member day by day. Some people are quite easily identifiable as autistic, others less so. But everybody in the chapel has some level of understanding of autism, if only by being part of the chapel, and all express a great acceptance and create together a place of belonging for—in the words of the chapel's motto—"people with all abilities." In this way, the direction of inclusion is being reversed, from autistic to non-autistic inclusion.

Actions and Structure

The structure of a worship service at the chapel is exactly the same every Sunday.[15] It follows a slightly adapted version of morning prayer as used in the Diocese of Singapore.[16] The structure is projected on a screen before the start of the service (figure 9), and at each new element, this element is projected again, sometimes with instructions with regard to posture (for an example, see figure 10). In this way, the structure is very

178 | Autism and Worship

SCHEDULE BOARD

1. Singing
2. Calling
3. Confessing
4. Praising
5. Telling
6. Giving
7. Welcoming
8. Praying
9. ROH & CM
10. Reading
11. Listening
12. Responding
13. Blessing
14. Bonding

Fig. 9 Structure of worship service

(Please sit or kneel)

1. CONFESSING

Fig. 10 Example of a slide with instructions for posture

clear and remains the same. Readers of this book who are familiar with autism will recognize how this aligns with the importance of predictable structures and routines for many autistic people.

On a typical Sunday, when entering the chapel, there will be a buzz, people socializing, walking around, and talking to each other. This is an unstructured part of the Sunday morning gathering, which may be difficult for autistic people who find unstructured social environments challenging, but at the same time, others may enjoy this time of interaction. The robed clergy join in with the informal interaction. Two minutes before the start of the service, the officiant asks everyone to switch off their mobile phones, a request that is accompanied by a slide on the screen. There is no procession. At 10:00 a.m., the officiant takes place behind the lectern, welcomes the people briefly, and invites them to join in with the prayer that can be found in the service bulletin. Next, a song is sung while the lyrics are projected on the screen. Every time a song is sung, people stand. Moving from one element to another often happens seamlessly.

A moment that breaks the seamless flow of the worship service is when those who attend Rainbow of Hope or children's ministry groups leave the worship hall and go to other rooms. Most of them are accompanied by parents. When they leave the building but before going to their groups, they are encouraged to walk around the site twice. Pastor David explained this remarkable practice to me, saying that this allows autistic people to be active for a couple of minutes before needing to sit, listen, and do activities like filling out worksheets. Some autistic people have quite a bit of energy, and this helps to discharge their energy in ways that help them to concentrate on subsequent activities.[17] Walking around the campus garden twice takes about five minutes, although some are significantly faster than others. Some autistic people remain behind in the service to listen to the sermon. Some are involved in Scripture reading and join Rainbow of Hope after they have read.

A Scripture reading done by one autistic person illustrates how the congregation is used to some of the particularities that autism can bring to the worship service. He came up to the lectern, looked for the passage to read on the tablet, and then—in the words of a woman I spoke with after the service—he "froze," not being able to speak. The congregation simply waited patiently. The leader of the service first checked whether the young man had found the passage, looking over his shoulder, and then stepped back, also waiting patiently. The young man eventually read the passage, without much hesitation. He then went out, presumably to his Rainbow of Hope group. The moment of silence was long, a couple of minutes. It is quite likely that in many congregations, people would have started shuffling nervously; someone would have perhaps started asking questions of the reader. However, none of that happened in the chapel. They simply waited, and one could almost hear in one's mind the typical, relaxed "That's okay" from Pastor David or someone else.

Every person I communicated with about the structure of the chapel commented on the importance of the weekly lunch following the service. On the schedule board, this is item 14, "bonding," which happens over lunch. Structurally, the timing is this: after the people attending Rainbow of Hope and other groups leave the chapel, the service for those who stay in the chapel continues with the readings, sermon, a prayer, a song, and the blessing. As soon as the blessing has been received, the people leave the chapel and head for the cafeteria, where lunch is served. Those attending Rainbow of Hope and children's groups do their walk around the garden (see above), go to their groups, and stay there until about twenty to thirty minutes after the service in the chapel has finished. This gives the parents and others an opportunity to have lunch first and have some conversations with each other before the Rainbow of Hope and children's groups join them again to have lunch as well.

This is a structure and a timing that requires some reflection. When I spoke with someone about this structure, before I had visited the chapel, that person asked critically whether it is possible to speak of genuine inclusion if autistic people still need to go to their own program and if they do not join for lunch until half an hour after everybody else. This seems a fair criticism and certainly something I had in the back of my mind when observing this community and listening to people. At this point, listening to the autistic people themselves, during my second visit, proved invaluable. All of the autistic people had taken pictures of their time in Rainbow of Hope. Clearly, this time was significant for them and enjoyed by them. Some had taken pictures of their friends with whom they interacted especially in Rainbow of Hope. When asked what they liked best about the chapel, most mentioned Rainbow of Hope and connecting with their friends. My conversation partner (who raised the question whether the chapel did in fact segregate their autistic members from the community in this way) and I had tried to be sensitive and critically look for (inadvertent) ableism; but the autistic people themselves proved us wrong.[18] In addition, the more I listened, the more I started to see, first of all, how treasured these separated times are by the community, and second, why the structure and timing are set up this way.

For example, Winona, mother of an autistic son, contrasts the lunch with an example of another social activity, a music night at school. During the interval time, parents intermingle and interact with teachers, but she hardly ever gets the chance to do so because she needs to keep an eye on her son. She continues,

> And then, very thoughtfully, the church arranged for us parents to finish the sermon earlier than when the children with autism were dismissed. So we had that precious . . . half an hour, yeah. Or so. And just to be able to have an adult conversation, you know, and for my other children to be able to, like speak to their peers and all that. And then after that, for the, for my child with autism to come together and then we had lunch. So that was like amazing, really amazing.

Many parents (and sometimes siblings too) experience living with an autistic family member as a challenge—and a joy!—and as exhausting at times. Their autistic family members require a lot of attention; some cannot be left on their own and require constant support, and meltdowns or other outbursts of emotion can be taxing. The chapel acknowledges this and wants to be a church not only for autistic people but also for their families. They have listened long and hard to parents and try to be a place where parents can relax for one or two hours a week. For the parents, it is a relief to be able to let their children go to a program where they are spiritually fed and in good hands, to be able to concentrate on the sermon, and to enjoy lunch with other adults without having to constantly keep an eye on their autistic family member. For the same reason, there is not a list of volunteers to provide lunch; instead, it is provided by a professional caterer. There are many factors that help to make the chapel a place of acceptance and belonging, but the lunch is certainly one practice of the chapel that stands out for many.

It is right to critically ask whether the chapel is truly inclusive if some autistic people go out to their own program and join lunch only after half an hour. But from my interviews and observation, two responses to such a question have emerged. First, the chapel is keenly aware that the community is not made up of only their autistic members but that there is also a duty of care, in the widest sense, for the other members too. Rather than driving an activist inclusion agenda, the more appropriate theological question that arises is how Christian communities can be places where *everyone* belongs, autistic and non-autistic alike. Second, being a community where everyone belongs does not mean that all activities need to be done together. Loving, growing, and serving together, to refer to the chapel's vision statement, might mean going out into different groups to enable spiritual growth in the way that is most appropriate for the individuals in those groups. In other words, the question is, how is each person best served in order to grow in love, in serving, and in their spiritual lives? The answer may look different from doing all things together. Moreover, as the interviews with five autistic members of the chapel showed, they very much appreciated having time in Rainbow of Hope with their friends, and they liked this part of the service the most.[19]

Places, Times, Objects, Language, and Groups

In relation to the other elements in the adapted model of Grimes, we can be brief. Above, we have already commented on the *place* in terms of the building and some of the objects one can find in there. It is noteworthy that in addition to what has already been said about the building, at the back of the church, there is a small balcony. The balcony is behind a glass wall, but speakers allow that people can hear everything that goes on in the space below (figures 6 and 7). Those who want to follow the service from there can retreat—for example, if being in a large group is difficult. We have also discussed the *timing* in terms of the moment in the service when those who want to go out to their own groups and the lunch. In total, the service takes about one hour and fifteen minutes from the moment of welcoming people to the blessing. The lunch takes as long as people want to stay, which may be up to an hour or a little bit longer. The standard language in the chapel is English, although people might speak other languages among themselves like Cantonese, Hokkien, Singlish, or Malay. Within the worship service, there is an element of liturgical language—for example, in the prayer at the beginning of the service and the formal text for confession of sins, followed by the words of forgiveness. Even though this is more formal language, characteristic of liturgical language, the clergy makes it sound extempore and not traditional.[20] The songs contain religious language. Pastor David alludes to biblical stories—for example, when prefacing the absolution. Important to note is that at no point is language simplified, as if that was necessary to communicate with the autistic members.

A LIVED KENOTIC LITURGICAL THEOLOGY OF AVAILABILITY

The above description of liturgy in the Chapel of Christ Our Hope shows how one particular church has taken the presence of autistic people to heart and responded by creating a worshipping community where autistic people and non-autistic people are equally valued. The description is based on empirical observation and structured along the lines of a ritual analytical model. Such a description on its own cannot do justice to the theological reality of worship and (as the members would say) to both the presence of people, autistic and non-autistic, and the presence of God. Therefore, in this final section, I will interpret the chapel community and its worship in terms of the kenotic liturgical theology of availability that I have developed in the previous chapters.

The story of the chapel began with the president of Singapore who noted the tension between the absence and presence of autistic people, especially those with a lot of support needs in daily life. Anglican churches have a wide-ranging social care provision; we might interpret the president questioning the bishop over whether the Anglican churches had considered autistic people as a call to the church to face this tension of absence and presence. The negative reactions received by the group of people who started praying and considering the president's question confirms that working with autistic people was going to be outside of the boundaries of the Singaporean societal framework. The attempts to discourage this group from starting this work was normalcy in full swing. However, the group of thirty-five people who eventually started the chapel were beginning to construct a new framework. Their weekly meetings, over a period of nine months, were a form of making themselves available to autistic people by learning about autism and by sketching the contours of a new way of worshipping together with autistic people; through making themselves available, they were shaping and being shaped into a new social imaginary. To become present to the presence of autistic people required, in David's words, a paradigm shift.[21] We may add that it did lead to such a shift or, in Taylor's terms, a new framework in which autistic people are present just like, or even more than, anyone else.

A central feature of the new framework that was emerging was, to use temple imagery, not to throw away (reject) the stones that looked a bit odd, that talked strangely or not at all, or that did not have the shape most other stones do. Instead, they would be valued. Building with rejected stones leads to creative shapes but shapes that are equally strong, if not stronger, as when building with stones that fit the expected shape of normalcy. This is not just theory but is testified to by the members of the chapel themselves. In my interviews with the parents, I asked what it means when Saint Paul says that those who seem "weaker" in the eyes of the surrounding culture are indispensable to the body of Christ. Winona, without hiding the fact that she finds raising Steve, her autistic son, difficult at times, comments,

> And over the years I have learned to submit, submit in the sense that okay, if God wants all of us to be together like this, and he says, Paul says that, you know, every member is important, down to your little toe, little toe nail, whatever, then there is also a place for my child to be here. Maybe because of him, then somebody else's spiritual journey can be transformed, or deepened, or whatever. So who are we to say that oh no, we are not worth like, yeah, being here? So there is a certain value that I think God knows, God knows, yeah, God knows the value of my child. God knows everybody's value. And so I think in a sense that yeah, we are one body, yeah?

The body image helps Winona to see that God has a place for her child in the community. Behind the phrase "then there is also a place for my child to be here," we can hear the pain of the many times that she and

Steve must have felt rejected (Winona indeed says she has "struggled" a lot with other churches that could not "handle" Steve). The pain is almost tangible in this quote, as is the relief of having found a place of belonging. Furthermore, the body image does not only mean that Steve and his family have found a place in the community but also that Steve plays a part in the spiritual formation of other members. Indeed, others comment on how people with autism are transforming the community and are key in the way that they encounter God. A diversity of "stones" makes for a building in which transformation can take place.

John, a leader in the chapel, says that it is exactly because of the autistic members that he has learned what it means to be the body of Christ. "I wouldn't have experienced this kind of body life" without the presence of these members. They have "clearly enriched my experience with God, you know." The diversity within the chapel is a "true example" of the body of Christ, John asserts. He even thinks that it takes a church like the chapel, with its weaker and stronger parts, to put that image into action.[22] John is critical of other churches in Singapore, which he thinks are too homogeneous to be an image of the body of Christ. Jonah, father of an autistic child, is critical of other churches likewise. He says that excluding autistic people means not only that the body of Christ is weakened but also that many families with autistic members remain churchless, without a spiritual community to which they can belong. By excluding autistic people from the church, both the church and the families—not least the autistic people themselves—are impoverished.

The chapel's new framework is grounded in a baptismal ecclesiology, although they would not necessarily use that phrase. As we discussed in chapter 5, a baptismal ecclesiology entails "an understanding of the church that defines Christian community in terms of the common ground that all the baptized members share."[23] That common ground is the identity that every member of the body has in Christ. The theology that I have unpacked in the previous chapters grounds the identity of the community firmly in its participation in Christ, which is first enabled by Christ's participation in humanity. On that common ground, established by Christ's incarnation, belonging does not depend on gender, ethnicity, social status, or (dis)ability (Gal 3:28). That does not mean that such identifying characteristics, including being on the autism spectrum or not, are irrelevant or that they disappear. Clearly, there are still male and female, autistic and non-autistic, people from different ethnic backgrounds, and people of different societal status in the community of believers. The point is that those characteristics should have no role in the dynamics of identifying and guarding the community's boundaries (normalcy). What we can observe in the chapel is that when such boundaries fall away and those who would be absent if normalcy was applied are in fact actively sought out and given a central place in the community, then the community becomes a temple where "stones" of diverse shapes are valued and become present in the community. Availability educes presence; by being present, the other is invited to be present. In the Christian community, the believers find their identity in Christ, which forms the foundational, common ground for being community together.

What does liturgy in such a community of presence and availability look like? The ritual description above shows that liturgy that is based in the concept of kenosis, in the self-giving of God and in turn the self-giving of the believers to God, to each other, and to the world around them, is embodied in many ways. By being attentive to sensory input, for example, the worship space is designed with rainbow-colored windows, creating a pleasantly lighted building. As another example, by knowing that some autistic people have difficulties regulating and controlling their body movement, the community is entirely comfortable with planned and unplanned movement throughout the service, and even a violent outburst can be responded to with a simple "It's okay." The embodied kenotic liturgical theology that pervades the community's worship—whether the members would articulate that in this way or not—creates an atmosphere of well-being and acceptance.

The definition of liturgy that we used in the previous chapter, borrowed from Don Saliers, emphasizes the kenotic nature of liturgy: "Christian liturgy is our response to the self-giving of God in, with, and through the One who leads us in prayer."[24] The chapel is rooted in the self-giving of God, which enables the worshippers there to participate in the ongoing prayer of Jesus Christ, as a response to God's self-giving. Because their identity in Christ is the great equalizer in the community of believers, everybody is invited to take part in that response, autistic and non-autistic alike. Paula, one of the chapel's leaders, observed that the liturgy (in the sense of the order of worship) kept all the members on the same page; but on that page, people are engaged in worship differently. This is a beautiful image of unity and diversity in Christ as expressed in worship. This is an image of responding to God's self-giving with praise, thanksgiving, confession, intercession, and lament—a response marked by the self-giving of the members to each other, allowing for and appreciating a wonderful and indispensable diversity among the members. This is kenotic liturgy in action—the liturgical response to the dynamic of normalcy in action that attempted to discourage the initial group of Christians who started the chapel. This is a kenotic liturgy that shapes and is being shaped by a new framework where, in the words of Don Saliers, we "know a home."[25]

The leaders of the chapel will be the first to say that the chapel is not the perfect church. The description and theological interpretation in this chapter is not meant to hold up the chapel as a church that gets it all right and even less as a blueprint for every church to follow. This church is situated between the "already and not yet" of God's reign, like all churches. However, it is a church that dared to face the tension between the presence and absence of autistic people and, by making themselves available, learned a new social imaginary, which eventually resulted in a new framework that the members try to live out in worship and in their community life. It is a community that tries to follow Jesus in a categorical redrawing of, or even moving away from, boundaries that would otherwise render autistic people absent and ignored. As such, it is a church that lives the kenotic liturgical theology of availability that I have proposed in this book and perhaps an inspiration for other communities of believers to follow.

CONCLUSION

A president and a bishop meet each other at a tea party. . . . It almost sounds like the opening sentence of a joke. Yet this is exactly the beginning of the Chapel of Christ Our Hope, a community that has grown to be perhaps the first in the world where everything revolves around autism. If autistic members are central in the chapel, how does the analysis of the chapel in this chapter demonstrate that? What are some of the points that churches wanting to be more attentive to autism can learn?

The first point to highlight is that autism was central from the very beginning and remained central in all decision-making processes, from the architecture to the planning of worship services and the provision of lunch. At every decision point, the question was asked, "How does this work for our autistic members and their families?" Second, Pastor David said, in an almost throwaway comment, that from the beginning they were clear that they would not correct certain expressions of autism in the worship service: no shushing, no silencing, no prohibiting of movement. This is a powerful counter to the cult of normalcy. Third, the chapel proactively seeks to involve their autistic members in formal and informal roles. Autistic people are not just tolerated or just accommodated, but they play an indispensable role in the chapel, in the first place simply by being there—a presence that invites and requires the presence and availability of the other.

Together, these points contribute to the fourth and perhaps the most important aspect of the chapel: the acceptance of everyone. Again, it should be clear that acceptance here means much more than merely tolerating certain people and even more than inclusion in the sense of making adaptations. This is a community where autistic people *belong*.[26] When these four points are in place, one can see how it subsequently and simultaneously impacts the worship service in its structural elements, with regard to sensory issues, and in taking care of *all* people, including those who are autistic and non-autistic alike. The liturgy becomes a place of safety and rest where everyone is enabled to worship God.

Worship is a theological act in which, by God's self-giving, the community comes to expression and becomes what it is: a holy nation, a royal priesthood, a chosen people, the body of Christ (1 Pet 2:4–10; 1 Cor 12:12–31). The chapel is a place that values the "weaker" members of its body (1 Cor 12:22) and sees that without them, they would be incomplete and not the body that God intended the church to be; indeed, they would fail to recognize God's self-expression through autistic people. This last point is a testimony to the special place that the chapel is, while at the same time, it is an implicit criticism (voiced explicitly by some of the chapel's members) of churches that do not create the space for "weaker" members. The chapel, as a community of believers, responds to God's self-giving by giving themselves to each other and by becoming available. The resulting new framework is a powerful countertestimony to the cult of normalcy.

Conclusion

A Church That "Gets You"

> For me, autism is feeling more. The way I see autism is like when I look at things: I see more than most people do. Or I can hear, when I'm sitting hearing and my hearing seems to be better than most people because I can hear little noises that other people just distract. So the way I see it is if I can hear more and I see more, therefore must be able to experience God more. (Elise)

> I'd like to think there's maybe one or two things that you [as the researcher] will find, and you, it could maybe be mainstreamed into church as an improvement out of this [research], and even if it looks like we're reaching out a little bit to people on the autistic spectrum and saying, you know, we get you. Would be nice. (Alex)

In this excerpt from my interview with Elise, she answers my question as to whether being autistic helps or hinders her to encounter God. She points to the fact that sensory perception often works in particular ways for autistic people. I use the word "particular" deliberately instead of "different." The discussion of frameworks and normalcy in chapter 3 made clear that "different" means, by definition, "different from a certain norm." Moreover, "different" often reinforces the dominant power of and the ascribed value to the norm. If you want to belong, you do not want to be too different unless that difference gains you more social capital—which, in terms of autism, often is not the case. At the core of this book is the questioning of the norms that often operate in faith communities as well as in societies at large. In place of those norms, I have assumed that a particular way of being in the world, even when that differs from the norms of the group, does not mean less valuable. Elise makes clear that her particular way of hearing and seeing may mean that she experiences God more.

I hope that this book has made a valuable contribution to two academic fields: liturgical theology and autism theology. By assuming the value of diversity and the particularities of autism—without denying the challenges that autism can bring for the autistic person and their family and caregivers—I have tried to look at worship practices and liturgical theology afresh. As an academic discipline, liturgical theology has not taken the perspective of autism substantially into account. The distinctive perspective of this book, therefore, will hopefully serve to start a conversation that is much needed. With this book, I also try to contribute to the emerging field of autism theology. The literature overview in chapter 1 showed that over the past few years, the number of publications in autism theology has increased significantly. Nevertheless, substantial academic monographs with a sole focus on autism are few and far between. That is one of the reasons why I have taken considerable time to review some specific debates in the introduction and chapter 1, especially around the terminology we use and the relationship between autism and disability, as well as to write an overview of some key moments in the history of autism in chapter 2. That chapter also created the space to think theologically about autism as a valuable perspective in the autism discourse more broadly.

These first chapters set the stage for responding to the first main question that I have tried to answer in this book: what causes the absence and ignoring of autistic people in faith communities, and what might a liturgical and/or theological response look like? In a way, the history of autism breathes the absence of autistic people because for some, the intention has always been either to cure autism and "normalize" (at this point in the book, the reader should recognize the toxicity of the term) autistic people or, when that proved impossible, to institutionalize them. Seen that way, autism only became present in a bid to secure its absence.[1] In chapter 3, we expanded the discussion to consider the root cause of the absence and ignoring of autistic people in faith communities and in society at large. This discussion revolved around the notion of frameworks (Charles Taylor) and normalcy (Lennard Davis).

I described a framework as a set of values, norms, rituals, and stories by which a group lives. Frameworks are social constructs made up of the values that a community assigns to some things and some behavior, which is why frameworks have a moral value, often claiming a kind of divine origin and endorsement. The framework determines what is good, and part of what is good, or what it means to lead a good life, is to belong. In order to belong, then, one needs to conform to the values, norms, rituals, and stories of the community. That conformation does not rest so much on cognitively consenting as on embodying the values of the framework in daily life. Thus, the framework has boundaries and boundaries need to be protected somehow. This is not necessarily bad; boundaries means that the framework is delineated, which is the only way in which belonging can take place. Therefore, boundaries give a sense of safety. Where the community can go wrong, from a Christian perspective, is when the values and norms of the framework are in conflict with those of God's reign.

This is where normalcy comes into play. I defined normalcy as the set of dynamics by which the community, both consciously and unconsciously, guards the boundaries of their framework of belonging. Normalcy, although grammatically a noun, acts like a verb. In disability literature, the notion of normalcy is virtually always used negatively. The reason for this is that normalcy excludes. The dynamics of normalcy determine who passes the threshold of what is deemed normal—that is, in line with the values and norms of the community—and therefore, normalcy determines who belongs and who does not belong, who is "in" and who is "out." In a society—and the church is deeply influenced by society—that values able-bodiedness, quick speech, emotional control, speed, apt social communication (marked by numerous little lies, inconsistencies, and often superficiality), intellectual virtuosity, and skillfulness, it is not hard to see why many autistic people do not pass the threshold set by normalcy. The normalcy dynamic is not only protective of the framework's boundaries, but it is also evasive: by excluding people who do not pass the threshold, the community avoids being confronted with that which is different from its norms. In that sense, we can say that the normalcy dynamics are born out of fear. It is easier to remain in one's comfort zone than to open up to potential challenges.[2]

The second part of the first main question (what might a liturgical and/or theological response to the absence and ignoring of autistic people look like?) was related to the next question of this study: what does liturgy and corporate worship look like through the lens of autism, and in what ways might that reframe liturgical theologies? I will admit that when I formulated this second question a couple of years ago at the start of my research on autism and liturgy, I expected to find new liturgical-theological perspectives, maybe even perspectives that could help to shift the liturgical discourse somewhat. Perhaps this is why I was puzzled when one of the leaders of the Chapel of Christ Our Hope, Kim Gek, commented that their liturgy was hardly different from other Anglican churches, especially when others to whom I had spoken in that community had said how different the chapel was from other churches. However, I heard the same in interviews and observational studies in a few other churches, where autistic people clearly felt that they belonged—the liturgies, understood as the order of worship and the books and hymnals they used and even the ritual actions, did not change. There was also no simplification of language or concepts in these churches. The answer to the question of how the lens of autism might reframe liturgical theology and the practice of worship apparently lies not at the level of the ordo of the liturgy, nor in liturgical language or ritual actions. This finding is worth highlighting in itself: it does not take a different liturgy to worship as autistic and non-autistic people together.

What changes, then, in our perspective if we look at liturgy through the lens of autism?[3] First, through this lens, we notice the absence or ignoring of autistic people. By applying the lens of autism, we become aware of the cult of normalcy and the endless ways in which normalcy causes a problem for autistic participation in worship and in the life of the community. By listening carefully to the stories and experiences of autistic people, we can see that normalcy is the root cause (or at least one of the root causes) of the absence and ignoring of autistic people. This lens helps us to see that we need a framework that is not constructed according to the norms and values of our society but according to those of God's reign.

A second change in our perspective is to think of liturgy in terms of presence and availability. That was the topic of chapters 4 and 5. In chapter 4, I asked the question, if the guarding of the framework's boundaries by the protective, evasive, and possibly fear-driven dynamics of normalcy leads to the exclusion and, therefore, absence of autistic people in church, then what might a theological response look like? By discussing Gabriel Marcel's concept of disponibilité, I argued for presence over against absence and for availability over and against ignoring. The presence of autistic people summons the community members to become present to these fellow believers. However, it is possible for someone to be present without being available to the other, in which case, the other can become a stranger to themselves, as Marcel explained. By contrast, when someone is really present, or available, to the other, it creates a deep bond between them, even if only for a moment. Such availability contrasts with ignoring people—for example, by not talking to them, not soliciting their views, withholding liturgical roles (even small ones such as reading a Bible passage or lighting a candle), or being unwilling to make any adaptations that would allow them to participate in the worship service. Disponibilité, in contrast, is always oriented outward instead of being turned in on oneself.

The ultimate example of radical availability is seen in God becoming available in Jesus Christ through the incarnation. Through this act of kenosis, of "emptying" himself (Phil 2:7) and thereby becoming available, Christ participated in humanity, as fully God and fully human. Saint Paul invites the believers in Philippi to follow Christ in this way of being, this mindset—a way of being that is not full of oneself but makes oneself available to the other, which leads to the glory of God (Phil 2:5–13). It is Christ's participation in humanity that makes union with Christ, and thus participation in the divine life, possible. Christ's presence in the community, through his Spirit, forms the basis for the believers' presence toward each other. Union with Christ, expressed in various images in the New Testament, such as the vine and the branches, the body of Christ, Christ as cornerstone and the believers as living stones of the temple, makes for a new identity of the believers, both individually and as community. Belonging to Christ means belonging to a new framework—a framework that is governed by the soteriological story in which the relationship between God and people is restored and in which that relationship determines the norms and values of and changes power structures within the community. Following Jesus means a radical redrawing of and even moving away from a focus on the boundaries of the framework.

In chapter 5, I discussed this new identity in Christ along liturgical-theological lines. Liturgical theologians claim that liturgy is theologia prima: when the body of believers gathers for worshipping, it engages in a theological act. Corporate worship is theology in the I-Thou mode, to employ Martin Buber's term. It is in worship, therefore, that the community is most itself. In the words of Don Saliers, "The ongoing prayer of Jesus, and the ongoing word and self-giving of Jesus, shapes our existence and brings *us* to expression."[4] It is clear, then, in a participatory theology, that when the community joins that ongoing prayer of Jesus in its corporate worship, we can perceive the community's identity most clearly.

With Saliers, I defined liturgy as the community's participation in the ongoing prayer and work of Jesus Christ, enabled by the Spirit of Christ, to the glory of God. The theology of availability, rooted in kenosis, comes liturgically to expression by the believers becoming available to one another, rooted in Christ's availability to the believers. The community lives in a new framework, as I stated above, which means that the boundaries for who can participate in the liturgy and in what capacity are categorically redrawn. The new framework leaves no room to exclude (render absent, ignore) autistic people if they do not happen to fit the cultural norms and values of speed, speech, certain social conventions, and preferred ways of sensory processing—norms and values set by a non-autistic majority. To be one in Christ means that belonging does not depend on gender, ethnicity, or social status, as Paul says in Galatians 3:28. We may add, belonging does not depend on processing speed, verbal ability, or social aptitude. By participating in the liturgy and especially by participating in the sacraments of baptism and Eucharist, the community shapes and is being shaped by a new framework with categorically different boundaries, rooted in the story of God's love for and restoration of God's people and all of creation. In liturgy and in the sacraments, we receive and exercise our new identity in Christ.

Thus, when applying the lens of autism, the second change in our perspective on liturgical theology is perhaps less of a *change* and more of a *renewed emphasis* on the theological basis of the community's gathering for worship. That basis is firmly grounded in God's participation in humanity through the incarnate Jesus Christ. This enables the community's union with Christ and participation in his ongoing prayer and work for the world. The presence of Christ through his Spirit enables the believer's presence to each other and to God in thanksgiving and praise, confession, invocation, and lament. Because of the connection between our stories and God's story that we celebrate in worship, "we know a home" in the liturgy.[5] The lens of autism helps the community to see its true identity in Christ; autism helps us to see what it means to be human and what it means to be a community in Christ.

Beautiful as it sounds that in liturgy "we know a home," it contrasts starkly with Dan Bowman's story in which he said he wished he'd stayed at home instead of going to church and with other similar stories where "home" is the place where one lives and not the worshipping community.[6] That contrast leads to the third main question of this study, which is the practical question of how churches can be communities where everybody belongs, autistic and non-autistic alike. We can find one answer in the story and the worship of the Chapel of Christ Our Hope in Singapore. It is the story of a community of believers who was willing to be challenged by those who do not pass the threshold set by normalcy.

By telling the story of the Chapel of Christ Our Hope and analyzing their worship and community life, I have tried to offer an example of how the kenotic liturgical theology of availability that I have outlined in this book is a lived reality in this particular church. The need for a paradigm shift, which Pastor David spoke about, is a challenge for the church: why is a paradigm shift needed (a change of framework and a defying of normalcy) to create a worshipping community where autistic and non-autistic people alike fully belong and are valued? Churches will need to find their identity in Christ and consider their worship as participation in the ongoing prayer and work of Christ in order to be shaped into a new framework. Churches will need to repent of their absence toward autistic people and of perpetuating frameworks and dynamics of normalcy that render autistic people absent from their communities. Churches will need to become present and rooted in the kenotic participation of Christ in humanity, become kenotically available to autistic people who are indispensable members of the body of Christ. In the eyes of society, autistic people may be oddly shaped stones, but they are indispensable if the temple—that is, the community—has to resemble something of the image of Christ who is the image of God (Col 1:15). Oddly shaped stones fit the cornerstone well.

It does not need to take the launch of a new church, as in the case of the chapel, to become a community where autistic people are valued just as much, or even more than (1 Cor 12:24), other members. Again, in the chapel and in other churches that I observed for my research, the liturgy did not change. Puzzling as that observation was for me at first, it is good news because it means that it does not take great liturgical creativity and effort to worship together as autistic and non-autistic believers. Moreover, if the change of perspective that occurs when we apply the lens of autism to our worship practices is to see the problem of normalcy, the need for a change of framework, and if that change does not require novel liturgical theologies but is possible by going back to the very basics of what it means to be a Christian community, then every Christian community should be able to (and want to) embark on this journey. Above, I said that the lens of autism helps us to see the absence and ignoring of autistic people. However, by applying the very lens of *autism*, it also leads to the same bottom line that Stuart Murray comes to in his discussion of the picture of the two autistic girls on the seesaw: looking at it from within any framework, in our congregations autistic people are present. Many autistic people I spoke to expressed a desire to belong to and participate in the worshipping community, as is also testified to by the stories of Dan Bowman, Monica Spoor, Katherine Bale, and others.[7] The question is, what framework will be the most conducive for non-autistic people to be present to their autistic fellow "living stones" of the temple; what framework enables a community where autistic and non-autistic people are of equal concern to one another (1 Cor 12:25)? Above, I summarized the framework that I proposed in chapters 4 and 5: in sum, a framework informed by a kenotic liturgical theology of availability.

Of course, the fact that the liturgy did not change in the churches I mentioned does not mean that a community who wants to be intentional about welcoming and valuing autistic people does not need to do anything. Attention to sensory input and particular ways of social interacting are key. It may be helpful to use worship bulletins with icons in them and to be clear about the structure of the service before the service starts, to name just a few practicalities.[8] However, it all starts by being present to each other—presence understood as availability, rooted in an identity that finds itself in union with Christ and participating in the divine life, which categorically redraws and shifts the focus away from the boundaries.

In this book, I have tried to make the stories of autistic people central. I did so partly by writing about the experience of worship based on careful listening to stories and experiences of autistic people, especially in chapter 1 and through the examples and discussion in other chapters. That does not mean that the stories of autistic people surfaced at length in every chapter, but I have tried to honor their stories by trying to get at the root cause of the problem of absence and ignoring and by offering a liturgical-theological response. Nevertheless, the last words are for two of my interviewees.

I started this book with words from Rachel; it is fitting to end with her words as well. At one point in the interview, commenting on the unwillingness of the church to make changes to the PowerPoint slides, she said, "I'm not telling you that I don't like the background; I'm telling you I can't read the words because of the background!" The church's audiovisual team had embellished the PowerPoint slides that contained song lyrics with beautiful pictures. As a dyslexic, she could not read the slides. However, the audiovisual team was unwilling (in terms of our discussion, unavailable) to change them. Rachel continued by saying, "And that's an important distinction for people to understand, is that when autistic people are saying I can't access this because, I can't do this because, that they mean that they can't do it, not that they don't like it." The specific example that she gave has more to do with dyslexia than autism (although it should be noted that autism often co-occurs with other particularities such as dyslexia), but the example nonetheless illustrates the point that she was trying to get across in our interview. When autistic Christians are absent from the worship service or church activities, it is not because they are not interested but because it takes too much effort, and they are often met by misunderstanding and even unwillingness—they are met by the absence (indisponibilité) of non-autistic people. Rachel's story is one of many illustrations of this indisponibilité. I suggest that a liturgical-theological response can be found in a kenotic liturgical theology of availability. Hopefully, this is an appropriate response to the plea from another interviewee, Alex. I quoted him already in the epigraph to this chapter as well as in chapter 1:

> I'd like to think there's maybe one or two things that you [as the researcher] will find, and you, it could maybe be mainstreamed into church as an improvement out of this [research], and even if it looks like we're reaching out a little bit to people on the autistic spectrum and saying, you know, we get you. Would be nice.

I hope that this book contributes both to the academic discourse and the liturgical theology of churches, having found "maybe one or two things," so that Alex and his autistic peers will feel understood and often hear the words "We get you." Indeed, I agree with you, Alex, it "would be nice."

Notes

FOREWORD

1 Savantism is actually very rare, and most of the phenomena probably reflect sensory differences, differences in modes of environmental attention, or the cumulative systematic knowledge acquired through special interests (monotropic interest). It remains a popular element in the representation of autism, however, partly through the legacy of the movie *Rain Man*.

INTRODUCTION

1 Interview with Rachel, September 3, 2020. All names of interviewees are fictitious.
2 Brian Brock, *Wondrously Wounded: Theology, Disability, and the Body of Christ* (Waco: Baylor University Press, 2019), 208; see also 219–24.
3 Olivia Bustion, "Autism and Christianity: An Ethnographic Intervention," *Journal of the American Academy of Religion* 85, no. 3 (2017): 672–76. Whether intimacy with God is more special for autistic people than others is not the point—I am only reporting what Bustion found in her study. The point here is that autistic people have something to offer to the church, as any member of the body of Christ has, and therefore the church misses out if that is not recognized and valued.
4 For this last point, see further in chapter 5.
5 See section "Autism Theology: An Emerging Field" below.
6 K. Hess and C. Brown, "Leitourgeō," in *New International Dictionary of New Testament Theology* (Carlisle, UK: Paternoster Press, 1992).
7 Frank C. Senn, *Embodied Liturgy: Lessons in Christian Ritual* (Minneapolis: Fortress, 2016), 18.
8 Hess and Brown, "Leitourgeō," 552.
9 Don E. Saliers, "Toward a Spirituality of Inclusiveness," in *Human Disability and the Service of God: Reassessing Religious Practice*, ed. Nancy L. Eiesland and Don E. Saliers (Nashville: Abingdon, 1998), 21–24.
10 Note that "liturgy" is often translated in this way in liturgical studies, usually to emphasize that liturgy is not done just by the priest or liturgical ministers but by the entire congregation, whereas the original meaning is closer to the work *on behalf of* or *for* the people than the work *of* the people. I will discuss this further in chapter 5.

11 Saliers, "Toward a Spirituality of Inclusiveness," 22.
12 Saliers, "Toward a Spirituality of Inclusiveness," 22.
13 Saliers, "Toward a Spirituality of Inclusiveness," 23.
14 Senn, *Embodied Liturgy*, 19.
15 This does not only pertain to churches with a formal liturgy; churches with an informal style of worship usually also have an underlying structure that is followed in their regular corporate worship.
16 Jill Boucher, *Autism Spectrum Disorder: Characteristics, Causes and Practical Issues*, 2nd ed. (Los Angeles: Sage, 2017), 4–30.
17 *ICD-11* is published by the World Health Organization. Whereas in North America and Australia *DSM-5* is primarily used, *ICD-11* is more widely used in some other parts of the world including Europe. *DSM* includes only mental conditions ("disorders," in *DSM* terminology), whereas *ICD-11* also includes other forms of diseases (*ICD* terminology). See Boucher, *Autism Spectrum Disorder*, 8.
18 John Swinton, "Time, Hospitality, and Belonging: Towards a Practical Theology of Mental Health," *Word & World* 35, no. 2 (2015): 172; emphasis original.
19 Swinton, "Time, Hospitality, and Belonging," 172.
20 Stewart Rapley points out how medical and diagnostic descriptions of autism work through in some of the guides for churches. Stewart Rapley, *Autistic Thinking in the Life of the Church* (London: SCM Press, 2021), 18–19.
21 One of the problems of the medical discourse is that it provides "thin" descriptions of human beings—people are reduced to statistics, which can never tell the richness of experience. Building on the work of Clifford Geertz, Swinton argues, therefore, that we need "thick" descriptions of people, that do justice to the richness and detail of lived experience. John Swinton, *Finding Jesus in the Storm: The Spiritual Lives of Christians with Mental Health Challenges* (Grand Rapids: Eerdmans, 2020), 11–14, 38–39.
22 Swinton, *Finding Jesus in the Storm*, 13.
23 For example, Grant Macaskill, *Autism and the Church: Bible, Theology, and Community* (Waco: Baylor University Press, 2019); Rapley, *Autistic Thinking in the Life of the Church*.
24 This discussion is primarily based on chapter 1 of Macaskill's book *Autism and the Church*. I will not refer to individual page numbers for each aspect of the following discussion; unless stated explicitly, all these points can be found in Macaskill's first chapter (pp. 11–41).
25 Macaskill does not identify as autistic in the book itself, but he has done so in later publications and deliberately positions himself in this way.
26 Macaskill, *Autism and the Church*, 11. This definition has slightly changed and at the time of writing this book reads, "Autism is a lifelong developmental disability which affects how people communicate and interact with the world." https://www.autism.org.uk/advice-and-guidance/what-is-autism, accessed March 19, 2022.
27 See chapter 2 in this book. There is a remarkable correlation between, on the one hand, the availability of support for autistic children and the idea that autism is a childhood condition (although few would still argue that it is) and, on the other hand, the change of (availability of) support for autistic adults. I cannot demonstrate a causal relationship, and we should be careful with drawing conclusions on the basis of such an observation. However, academic research, public awareness, and social policy are interwoven (as impressively demonstrated by Bonnie Evans), and therefore, it is necessary to be alert to such correlations. Bonnie Evans, *The Metamorphosis of Autism: A History of Child Development in Britain* (Manchester: Manchester University Press, 2017).
28 In this regard, see Damian Milton's work on the "double empathy problem," which states that it is not just that autistic people have difficulties understanding aspects

of communication of non-autistic people, but it is just the other way around as well (which then counters the pathologizing of autistic communication). Damian E. M. Milton, "On the Ontological Status of Autism: The 'Double Empathy Problem,'" *Disability & Society* 27, no. 6 (October 2012): 883–87, https://doi.org/10.1080/09687599.2012.710008; Damian Milton, "The Double Empathy Problem," 2018, https://www.autism.org.uk/advice-and-guidance/professional-practice/double-empathy.
29. Macaskill, *Autism and the Church*, 20.
30. For an elaborate illustration of this point, see Camilla Pang's description of how she copes with her morning commute from home to work in London. She prefers or needs to stand at a certain place on the platform, to be farthest away from smelly people as possible, and to sit in a particular seat. She describes how she makes contingency plans for when any of these preferred options is not available. Camilla Pang, *Explaining Humans: What Science Can Teach Us about Life, Love and Relationships* (London: Penguin, 2021), 14–15.
31. Macaskill, *Autism and the Church*, 21.
32. Macaskill explains the subtleties and nuances involved in this cluster of characteristics in his first chapter and devotes an entire chapter to sensory experience later in his book. For another analysis of the sensory experience of worship, see Armand Léon van Ommen and Katy Unwin, "The Sensory Aspects of Worship and Liturgy as Experienced by Autistic People," *Questions liturgiques/Studies in Liturgy* 102 (2022): 267–88.
33. Macaskill, *Autism and the Church*, 25. Macaskill's discussion is rather nuanced. He chooses to speak about autism as a condition, not a disability, although he is not entirely dismissive of using "disability" in certain contexts (see pp. 24–26).
34. Li-Ching Lee et al., "Children with Autism: Quality of Life and Parental Concerns," *Journal of Autism and Developmental Disorders* 38, no. 6 (July 2008): 1147–60, https://doi.org/10.1007/s10803-007-0491-0. It is important to note that this study is based on parental views. The study does not include statistics on parents' frequency of attending religious services, and therefore, the figures could reflect that the parents themselves are less likely to attend church. This is important because the children in at least some of the age groups could not attend church on their own even if they wanted to. Nevertheless, the authors suggest that lesser involvement of autistic children in various activities, including attending worship services, may well be due to the "challenges that accompany separating a child with autism from the home environment" (1158). The statistics in this article do not explain *why*, but they demonstrate *that* autistic children attend religious services less frequently than others in their age group, for whatever reason.
35. Andrew L. Whitehead, "Religion and Disability: Variation in Religious Service Attendance Rates for Children with Chronic Health Conditions," *Journal for the Scientific Study of Religion* 57, no. 2 (June 2018): 379, https://doi.org/10.1111/jssr.12521.
36. Other studies show a similar pattern. For an overview, see Erik W. Carter, *Including People with Disabilities in Faith Communities: A Guide for Service Providers, Families, & Congregations* (Baltimore: Brookes, 2007), 6–8; Erik W. Carter, "Research on Disability and Congregational Inclusion: What We Know and Where We Might Go," *Journal of Disability & Religion*, 8 February 2022, 1–31, https://doi.org/10.1080/23312521.2022.2035297. Susan Crawford Sullivan and Victoria Aramini provide a brief but helpful overview of relevant studies of involvement in faith communities by families with autistic children in "Religion and Positive Youth Development: Challenges for Children and Youth with Autism Spectrum Disorder," *Religions* 10, no. 10 (2019): 4–5, https://doi.org/10.3390/rel10100540.
37. Equating the terms "autism" and "disability," and particularly "autism" and "intellectual disability," is problematic. This makes it difficult to report findings of other studies, which group autism in the category of intellectual (and/or developmental) disabilities, in

a way that is not compatible with more recent thought and terminology. In the study by Ault et al., autism is grouped as such and, in this particular result, compared to children with "mild intellectual disabilities" and "moderate to severe intellectual disabilities." It should be kept in mind that this study was published in 2013, the year in which *DSM-5* was published, which grouped "autistic disorder, Asperger disorder, pervasive developmental disorder not otherwise specified (PDD-NOS), childhood disintegrative disorder, and Rett syndrome" into the one catch-all label "Autism." (See the helpful overview in Boucher, *Autism Spectrum Disorder*, 4–11; quotation on 9.) It is unlikely, therefore, that the results include the views of parents of those with Asperger's syndrome. This is still not to say that all autistic children in this study are correctly thought of as having an intellectual disability, but it helps to understand better which group is included. Melinda Jones Ault, Belva C. Collins, and Erik W. Carter, "Congregational Participation and Supports for Children and Adults with Disabilities: Parent Perceptions," *Intellectual and Developmental Disabilities* 51, no. 1 (2013): 48–61.

38 The results of the study with pastors were 81 percent strongly agreed and 18 percent somewhat agreed with the statement, "A person with a disability (including physical, sensory, cognitive, and intellectual impairments) would feel welcomed and included when coming to our church." For churchgoers, these figures were, respectively, 81 percent and 15 percent. "Pastors' Views on Caring for People with Disabilities: Survey of American Protestant Pastors," LifeWay Research, 2019, http://research.lifeway.com/wp-content/uploads/2020/03/Report-Pastors-Disabilities-Sept-2019.pdf; "Protestant Churchgoer Views on Attendees with a Disability: Survey of American Protestant Churchgoers," LifeWay Research, 2019, http://research.lifeway.com/wp-content/uploads/2020/03/Churchgoers-Disabilities-Sept-2019.pdf.

39 I am not aware of a similar study in Roman Catholic or Eastern Churches.

40 Carter, "Research on Disability and Congregational Inclusion," 2, 8–9; quotation on 2.

41 Stewart Rapley speaks of "cognitive dissonance" in this regard and sees that as something that is key for churches to be aware of in relation to their autistic members. Rapley says that cognitive dissonance not only happens in sermons but can also take place with prayers, hymns, and within the Bible. Cognitive dissonance can be positive when it leads to action—for example, motivating someone to find out more and to solve the dissonance. When this is not possible, however, "then the dissonance can escalate to very uncomfortable, or even painful and distressing, levels." Rapley, *Autistic Thinking in the Life of the Church*, 8.

42 For example, Christopher Barber, "On Connectedness: Spirituality on the Autistic Spectrum," *Practical Theology* 4, no. 2 (August 2011): 201–11, https://doi.org/10.1558/prth.v4i2.201; Daniel Bowman Jr., *On the Spectrum: Autism, Faith, & the Gifts of Neurodiversity* (Grand Rapids: Brazos Press, 2021); Rapley, *Autistic Thinking in the Life of the Church*; Cynthia Tam, *Kinship in the Household of God: Towards a Practical Theology of Belonging and Spiritual Care of People with Profound Autism* (Eugene: Pickwick Publications, 2021).

43 Armand Léon Van Ommen and Topher Endress, "Reframing Liturgical Theology through the Lens of Autism: A Qualitative Study of Autistic Experiences of Worship," *Studia Liturgica* 52, no. 2 (2022), https://doi.org/10.1177/00393207221111573.

44 For an excellent and insightful discussion of "context," see Courtney Goto, *Taking on Practical Theology: The Idolization of Context and the Hope of Community* (Leiden: Brill, 2018).

45 Another research project included participant observation and interviews in L'Arche Kenya. I interviewed some people who were likely autistic, but that was at the time not the concern of my research project, nor was the focus of that project on autism and worship. (The focus was on joy and disability. See Armand Léon van Ommen and

Julie Marie Land, "A Practical-Theological Phenomenology of Joy: Learning from L'Arche," *Journal of Disability & Religion* 24, no. 3 [July 2, 2020]: 281–99, https://doi.org/10.1080/23312521.2019.1698388.)

46 Stacy Clifford Simplican, *The Capacity Contract: Intellectual Disability and the Question of Citizenship* (Minneapolis: University of Minnesota Press, 2015), 15. She worries that the pull to disclose one's identity as disabled or not disabled undermines the disability studies field's own desire to go beyond this exact binary and, ironically, perpetuates unhelpful "us" versus "them" thinking (16).

47 Deborah Beth Creamer, *Disability and Christian Theology: Embodied Limits and Constructive Possibilities* (Oxford: Oxford University Press, 2009), 4–5. In the following pages, I make extensive use of Creamer's work. A most insightful discussion can also be found in Brock, *Wondrously Wounded*, xi–xvii.

48 See, for example, the criticism on the role of parents in Jim Sinclair's famous speech, "Don't Mourn for Us," in *Loud Hands: Autistic People, Speaking*, ed. Julia Bascom (Washington, DC: Autistic Press, 2012), 15–21.

49 This sentiment is obvious in, for example, Julia Bascom, ed., *Loud Hands: Autistic People, Speaking* (Washington, DC: Autistic Press, 2012); Bowman, *On the Spectrum*, 35–37.

50 Creamer, *Disability and Christian Theology*, 5.

51 Creamer, *Disability and Christian Theology*, 5.

52 Creamer, *Disability and Christian Theology*, 5.

53 I will demonstrate this point at length in relation to autism in chapter 2.

54 See also Damian Milton, "Embodied Sociality and the Conditioned Relativism of Dispositional Diversity," *Autonomy* 1, no. 3 (2014): 1–7.

55 Creamer, *Disability and Christian Theology*, 8; emphasis mine.

56 Macaskill, *Autism and the Church*, 155.

57 Macaskill, *Autism and the Church*, 155. He adds, "This is why autism awareness is so important within the church: we need to learn to accommodate the sensory and social needs of those within the church, and to be aware that the effects of failing to accommodate them can be really terrible."

58 Macaskill, *Autism and the Church*, 71–101, see for a discussion of sin esp. 86–87.

59 Leah E. Robinson, *Embodied Peacebuilding: Reconciliation as Practical Theology* (Bern: Peter Lang, 2015), 29–53. The following exploration of reconciliation is by no means intended to exhaustively discuss all key concepts, let alone the full process of reconciliation, which includes many nuances and (pastoral) sensitivities. For elaborate discussions of reconciliation, see, for example, Robinson's book just mentioned; Robert J. Schreiter, *Reconciliation: Mission and Ministry in a Changing Social Order* (Maryknoll, NY: Orbis Books, 1992); Robert J. Schreiter, *The Ministry of Reconciliation: Spirituality & Strategies* (Maryknoll, NY: Orbis Books, 1998); Desmond Tutu, *No Future without Forgiveness* (London: Rider, 1999); Miroslav Volf, *Exclusion and Embrace: A Theological Exploration of Identity, Otherness, and Reconciliation* (Nashville: Abingdon, 1996).

60 Desmond Tutu, reflecting on the work of reconciliation in South Africa after apartheid, writes poignantly, "Unless houses replace the hovels and shacks in which most blacks live; unless blacks gain access to clean water, electricity, affordable health care, decent education, good jobs and a safe environment—all things which the vast majority of whites have taken for granted for so long—we can kiss goodbye to reconciliation." Tutu, *No Future without Forgiveness*, 221. Obviously, the context of apartheid based on race is different from our discussion, but Tutu makes very clear what is at stake and what is lost when the process of reconciliation does not include reparation.

61 On the topic of leadership and disability, it is worth mentioning the special issue in *Theology Today*, edited by Erin Raffety, even though it is not focusing on autism

specifically. Erin Raffety, "From Depression and Decline to Repentance and Transformation: Receiving Disabled Leadership and Its Gifts for the Church," *Theology Today* 77, no. 2 (July 2020): 117–23, https://doi.org/10.1177/0040573620924558.

62 To mention only one example, applied behavioral analysis (ABA), as invented by Erik Lovaas, has used horrific methods, such as electroshocks, in order to change autistic behavior. ABA is still practiced widely, although the sharp edges have fortunately been taken off. However, many in the autistic community advocate strongly against the use of ABA; see, for example, the work of the South African–based Autistic Strategies Network, which calls for a ban on ABA. https://autisticstrategies.net/, accessed March 12, 2022. For a historical account of ABA, see Steve Silberman, *NeuroTribes: The Legacy of Autism and the Future of Neurodiversity* (New York: Avery, 2015), esp. 308–10.

63 Simplican, *Capacity Contract*, 15.

1 SETTING THE SCENE

1 Swinton, *Finding Jesus in the Storm*, 3–4.
2 Brett Webb-Mitchell, *Dancing with Disabilities: Opening the Church to All God's Children* (Cleveland: United Church Press, 1996), xv.
3 A significant number of autistic people do embrace a disability identity, in which case, they often interpret disability from a social model of disability or the neurodiversity paradigm. I will come to these shortly and will also briefly discuss them in chapters 2 and 3.
4 Kristen Bottema-Beutel et al., "Avoiding Ableist Language: Suggestions for Autism Researchers," *Autism in Adulthood* 3, no. 1 (March 2021): 3, https://doi.org/10.1089/aut.2020.0014.
5 It should be noted that this might differ across cultures. For example, Dunn and Andrews note that identity-first language is used more in the United Kingdom than in the United States. Dana S. Dunn and Erin E. Andrews, "Person-First and Identity-First Language: Developing Psychologists' Cultural Competence Using Disability Language," *American Psychologist* 70, no. 3 (2015): 261, https://doi.org/10.1037/a0038636.
6 Michael Wehmeyer, Hank Bersani, and Ray Gagne, "Riding the Third Wave: Self-Determination and Self-Advocacy in the 21st Century," *Focus on Autism and Other Developmental Disabilities* 15, no. 2 (May 2000): 106–15, https://doi.org/10.1177/108835760001500206.
7 H. H. Goddard, *The Kallikak Family: A Study in the Heredity of Feeble-Mindedness* (New York: Macmillan, 1912), 116, cited in Wehmeyer, Bersani, and Gagne, "Riding the Third Wave," 106.
8 Silberman, *NeuroTribes*, 177–200.
9 More on the development of these organizations and historical developments in autism—which runs parallel to the disability movement—in chapter 2.
10 Giacomo Vivanti, "Ask the Editor: What Is the Most Appropriate Way to Talk about Individuals with a Diagnosis of Autism?" *Journal of Autism and Developmental Disorders* 50, no. 2 (February 2020): 691, https://doi.org/10.1007/s10803-019-04280-x; cf. People First of West Virginia, accessed June 6, 2023, http://peoplefirstwv.org/old-front/history-of-people-first/.
11 People First of Washington, https://www.peoplefirstofwashington.org/aboutus.html, accessed May 4, 2021.
12 Vivanti, "Ask the Editor," 691.

13 Monique Botha, Jacqueline Hanlon, and Gemma Louise Williams, "Does Language Matter? Identity-First versus Person-First Language Use in Autism Research: A Response to Vivanti," *Journal of Autism and Developmental Disorders* (2021), https://doi.org/10.1007/s10803-020-04858-w; cf. Dunn and Andrews, "Person-First and Identity-First Language," 257.
14 For example, Nick Walker, *Neuroqueer Heresies: Notes on the Neurodiversity Paradigm, Autistic Empowerment, and Postnormal Possibilities* (Fort Worth: Autonomous Press, 2021). I will say more about the origins of the neurodiversity movement in chapter 2.
15 Creamer, *Disability and Christian Theology*, 22.
16 Creamer, *Disability and Christian Theology*, 23.
17 Botha, Hanlon, and Williams, "Does Language Matter?"
18 Bottema-Beutel et al., "Avoiding Ableist Language," 4.
19 Lorcan Kenny et al., "Which Terms Should Be Used to Describe Autism? Perspectives from the UK Autism Community," *Autism* 20, no. 4 (May 2016): 446, https://doi.org/10.1177/1362361315588200.
20 Kenny et al., "Which Terms Should Be Used?" 446. The total sample size was 3,470 participants, who were divided into four groups, for analysis: "autistic adults (n = 502); parents of people with autism (n = 2270); professionals, including researchers, students and volunteers (n = 1109); and family members and friends (n = 380)" (444).
21 Botha, Hanlon, and Williams, "Does Language Matter?"
22 Bottema-Beutel et al., "Avoiding Ableist Language," 6.
23 Bottema-Beutel et al., "Avoiding Ableist Language," 6.
24 The St. Andrew's Autism Centre itself takes a clear position on their website: "[We] relate to people with autism as unique individuals—person first; autism second." https://www.saac.org.sg/about-us/, accessed March 19, 2022. However, I spoke to a Singaporean autism advocate, who preferred identity-first language.
25 One participant had not thought about the question until recently, when he had heard someone comment that person-first language is better because people should not be reduced to a label. However, earlier he had said it did not matter to him, and as a matter of fact, for most of the interview he used identity-first language himself. Only at the end he corrected himself, at which point I asked him why he did so, and he gave the said explanation.
26 John Swinton, "Reflections on Autistic Love: What Does Love Look Like?" *Practical Theology* 5, no. 3 (December 2012): 265, https://doi.org/10.1558/prth.v5i3.259. The "triad of impairments" explains autism as an impairment in three areas: social communication, social interaction, and social imagination. As we will see in chapter 2, the triad was proposed by Lorna Wing and Judith Gould in 1979 and changed the autism discourse greatly.
27 Bottema-Beutel et al., "Avoiding Ableist Language," 3. See their table with more suggestions to move from (potentially) ableist language to more acceptable alternatives.
28 In this overview, I include only monographs, although I will mention a few articles that mark significant points in the development of the field. In terms of number of publications, theological journal articles show a similar trend to the number of published monographs. That means that before 2018, at most a handful of articles were published each year. I start this overview with publications from 2008. These were preceded by a few other publications on autism and religion and spirituality more broadly, but these would not necessarily be considered as theological works in the Christian tradition. See Abe Isanon, *Spirituality and the Autism Spectrum: Of Falling Sparrows* (London: Jessica Kingsley, 2001); William Stillman, *Autism and the God Connection: Redefining the Autistic Experience through Extraordinary Accounts*

of Spiritual Giftedness (Naperville, Ill.: Sourcebooks, 2006). Of further note in this regard is the work by Olga Bogdashina, who also participated in the research group on autism led by John Swinton and Christine Trevett. See especially Olga Bogdashina, *Autism and Spirituality: Psyche, Self and Spirit in People on the Autism Spectrum* (London: Jessica Kingsley, 2013).

29 Thomas E. Reynolds, *Vulnerable Communion: A Theology of Disability and Hospitality* (Grand Rapids: Brazos Press, 2008).
30 The term "normalcy" can be traced back to disability advocate and scholar Lennard Davis. Lennard J. Davis, *Enforcing Normalcy: Disability, Deafness and the Body* (London: Verso, 1995).
31 John Swinton and Christine Trevett, "Religion and Autism: Initiating an Interdisciplinary Conversation," *Journal of Religion, Disability & Health* 13, no. 1 (February 2009): 2–6, https://doi.org/10.1080/15228960802606193.
32 John Gillibrand, *Disabled Church—Disabled Society: The Implications of Autism for Philosophy, Theology and Politics* (London: Jessica Kingsley, 2010).
33 Gillibrand, *Disabled Church—Disabled Society*.
34 Gillibrand, *Disabled Church—Disabled Society*, 154.
35 Gillibrand, *Disabled Church—Disabled Society*, 155.
36 Barbara J. Newman, *Autism and Your Church*, rev. and updated ed. (Grand Rapids: Faith Alive, 2011).
37 Stephen J. Bedard, *How to Make Your Church Autism-Friendly*, 2nd ed. (St. Catharines, Ont.: Hope's Reason, 2017).
38 Ann Memmott, "Welcoming and Including Autistic People in Our Churches and Communities" (Diocese of Oxford, 2021), https://www.oxford.anglican.org/autism.
39 Monica Spoor, *Spirituality on the Spectrum: Having Autism in the Orthodox Church* (N.p.: Brave New Books, 2017).
40 Mark Arnold, *How to Include Autistic Children and Young People in Church: Creating a Place of Belonging and Spiritual Development for All* (Cambridge: Grove Books, 2022).
41 Memmott, "Welcoming Autistic People," 4.
42 Another resource that may be mentioned here is "Opening the Doors: Ministry with People with Learning Disabilities and People on the Autistic Spectrum" (Church of England, 2009). The resource was produced by a joint working party of the Ministry and the Mission and Public Affairs Divisions of the Church of England. Despite having autism in the title, the resource is focused on learning disabilities and only one brief chapter discusses autism.
43 Jennifer Anne Cox, *Autism, Humanity and Personhood: A Christ-Centred Theological Anthropology* (Newcastle upon Tyne: Cambridge Scholars Publishing, 2017), 2.
44 Grant Macaskill, "Autism Spectrum Disorders and the New Testament: Preliminary Reflections," *Journal of Disability & Religion* 22, no. 1 (January 2018): 15–41, https://doi.org/10.1080/23312521.2017.1373613; Macaskill, *Autism and the Church*.
45 Grant Macaskill, *Autism and the Bible: Beginning a Conversation*, Christ's College Lectures, 2017, https://www.youtube.com/watch?v=qvd_pUvFB-0. On March 11, 2022, the lecture had 10,838 views. On that same day, his 2018 article had 3,214 views on the publisher's website, which again is a high number in the field and made it the fifth most read article in the journal. The fourth most read article on that day is also by Macaskill: Grant Macaskill, "The Bible, Autism and Other Profound Developmental Conditions: Regulating Hermeneutics," *Journal of Disability & Religion*, February 8, 2021, 1–25, https://doi.org/10.1080/23312521.2021.1881024.
46 Brock, *Wondrously Wounded*.

47 Although Brock is certainly not the only one who uses this image in his theology, he has written extensively about it, not only in *Wondrously Wounded* but see also Brock's "Theologizing Inclusion: 1 Corinthians 12 and the Politics of the Body of Christ," *Journal of Religion, Disability & Health* 15, no. 4 (October 2011): 351–76, https://doi.org/10.1080/15228967.2011.620389; Brian Brock and Bernd Wannenwetsch, *A Theological Exposition of Paul's First Letter to the Corinthians. Volume 2: Therapy of the Christian Body* (Eugene: Cascade Books, 2018).

48 Bowman, *On the Spectrum*.

49 Lamar Hardwick's *Disability and the Church* was also published and is relevant to note. Even though the book looks at disabilities more broadly, it is written against the background of his own experiences of being an autistic pastor. In 2017, he published *I Am Strong*, the story of his journey of finding out that he was autistic and of moving from a position of being a youth pastor to senior pastor, roughly at the same time. Lamar Hardwick, *Disability and the Church: A Vision for Diversity and Inclusion* (Downers Grove, Ill.: InterVarsity Press, 2021); Lamar Hardwick, *I Am Strong: The Life and Journey of an Autistic Pastor* (Little Elm, Tex.: eLectio Publishing, 2017).

50 Eilidh Campbell, *Motherhood and Autism: An Embodied Theology of Motherhood and Disability* (London: SCM Press, 2021).

51 Ruth M. Dunster, *The Autism of Gxd: An Atheological Love Story* (Eugene: Pickwick Publications, 2022).

52 Dunster, *Autism of Gxd*, 365. Dunster says that the terms "*a-theology, (a)theology, atheist theology, a/theology* . . . are used to describe a theology of the death of Gxd, not cynical or hostile, but offering a path for a real and deep faith" (48).

53 At the time when the present book was already at the production stage, another book was published that could not be included in this overview but should certainly be mentioned, as it will no doubt prove to be an important book for the emerging discourse on autism and theology: Claire Williams, *Peculiar Discipleship: An Autistic Liberation Theology* (London: SCM Press, 2023).

54 www.abdn.ac.uk/sdhp/cat.

55 Videos of this three-day online conference are on YouTube. Another international academic conference on autism and faith that should be mentioned here was organized by the Centre for Autism in Rijeka, Croatia. Some of the contributions to that conference are published in Tanja Horvat and Saša Horvat, *Autism and Religious Experience: Theory and Practice—Workshop Proceedings* (Rijeka, Croatia: Centre for Autism Rijeka, 2022).

56 Creamer, *Disability and Christian Theology*, 23–24. Creamer does not write about autism specifically, but she offers an insightful explanation of the dynamics of the medical model.

57 In chapter 2, I discuss the rise of the neurodiversity movement.

58 The "medical model" and "social model" are broad terms under which various versions of those models are proposed. The social model has been critiqued by some for ignoring the impairments a person actually has; the impairment itself is a factor that can impact one's well-being, apart from how society deals with it (e.g., if someone is in chronic pain). For a critique of the social model, see, for example, Tom Shakespeare, "The Social Model of Disability," in *The Disability Studies Reader*, ed. Lennard J. Davis (New York: Routledge, 2013), 217–18.

59 Deborah Creamer evaluates the "medical or functional-limitation" and the "social or minority group" models and concludes that both are inadequate, although both offer valuable perspectives. She proposes a third model, the limits model, which "start[s] with

the human variations of ability as the norm, and . . . build[s] theory and theology from that starting place." Creamer, *Disability and Christian Theology*, 22–33; quotation on 32.

60 But see the counterargument to this hesitation by Nick Walker, who argues that the brain is part of the embodied way of being, and therefore to speak of neurodiversity does not need to be reductionistic. Walker, *Neuroqueer Heresies*, 53–55.

61 An additional difficulty with using "neurodiversity" in this book is that the term often includes other conditions, in particular ADHD, dyslexia, dyspraxia, dyscalculia, dysgraphia, and Tourette's syndrome. These other conditions are not the subject of this book, although I should note that autism often co-occurs with one or more of these conditions. One may argue that even "autistic" and "non-autistic" are imprecise categories and point to the wide spectrum (another contested term) of autism. However, in the research that underpins this book, I have tried to include many different people "on the spectrum" and therefore "autistic" and "non-autistic" seem currently the best term to use.

62 Inevitably, the findings from my research are filtered through my (non-autistic) perception. However, the research articles in which I first presented these findings were all read by autistic people to make sure the findings resonated with them. See a detailed discussion of my findings in the following articles: Van Ommen and Endress, "Reframing Liturgical Theology through the Lens of Autism"; Van Ommen and Unwin, "The Sensory Aspects of Worship and Liturgy as Experienced by Autistic People"; Armand Léon van Ommen, "Re-imagining Church through Autism: A Singaporean Case Study," *Practical Theology* 15, no. 6 (2022): 508–19, https://doi.org/10.1080/1756073X.2022.2080630.

63 Katherine Bale, "17 Ways to Make Your Church Autism-Friendly," *Premier Christianity* (blog), April 28, 2017, https://www.premierchristianity.com/Blog/17-ways-to-make-your-church-autism-friendly.

64 Macaskill, *Autism and the Church*, 126. Macaskill talks about both the social and the sensory aspect of worship here.

65 Spoor, *Spirituality on the Spectrum*, 2.

66 The example of honesty is frequently used. See, for example, Bowman, *On the Spectrum*, 109–10; Bustion, "Autism and Christianity," 673; Macaskill, *Autism and the Church*, 104.

67 Spoor, *Spirituality on the Spectrum*, 30. In a personal correspondence, Ian Lasch, an Episcopal priest and PhD student, pushed this point, arguing that the autistic and non-autistic perspectives on this part of our social interaction are not of equal moral value. Similar to Spoor, he wrote, "In daily life there are a million little lies, half-truths, or deceptions that are not just expected but required of people to be deemed polite and/or socially appropriate, and no one will ever actually come out and tell you what they are (or perhaps even be able to articulate the guiding rules or principles behind them)."

68 Bowman, *On the Spectrum*, 112; Spoor, *Spirituality on the Spectrum*, 24.

69 Spoor, *Spirituality on the Spectrum*, 37–38; Rapley, *Autistic Thinking in the Life of the Church*, 8.

70 Spoor, *Spirituality on the Spectrum*, 24.

71 The mutual lack of understanding is sometimes referred to as the "double empathy problem." The idea behind this is that whereas traditionally, autistic people were said not to understand communication, that statement can be turned around by saying that non-autistic people do not understand autistic communication. Milton, "On the Ontological Status of Autism."

72 Elaine Graham, "Words Made Flesh: Women, Embodiment and Practical Theology," *Feminist Theology* 7, no. 21 (May 1999): 118, https://doi.org/10.1177/0966 73509900002108.

2 HOW AUTISM CAME TO BE

1 Stuart Murray, *Representing Autism: Culture, Narrative, Fascination* (Liverpool: Liverpool University Press, 2008).
2 Interestingly, as Steve Silberman demonstrates, Leo Kanner (and others) have painstakingly defined the diagnostic criteria so strictly that many who today would be diagnosed with autism did not receive the diagnosis. Silberman argues that the reasons for such limiting criteria had at times more to do with personal career ambitions and their place in the scientific community than with the condition itself. Silberman, *NeuroTribes*, 207–12.
3 For a detailed and compelling argument of this claim, see Evans, *Metamorphosis of Autism*.
4 Murray, *Representing Autism*, xviii; emphasis original.
5 Ian Hacking, "Kinds of People: Moving Targets," *Proceedings of the British Academy* 151 (2007): 285–318; Ian Hacking, "Making Up People," in *Reconstructing Individualism: Autonomy, Individuality, and the Self in Western Thought*, ed. Thomas C. Heller, Morton Sosna, and David E. Wellbery (Stanford: Stanford University Press, 1986), 222–36. Olga Solomon and Mary C. Lawlor include a brief but insightful discussion, with reference to Hacking, of the conceptual difficulty of researching autism (in their case, the phenomenon of "eloping" and "wandering," which they deliberately write with inverted commas) in their article "'And I Look down and He Is Gone': Narrating Autism, Elopement and Wandering in Los Angeles," *Social Science & Medicine* 94 (October 2013): 108, https://doi.org/10.1016/j.socscimed.2013.06.034. See for a theological discussion of "thin" and "thick" descriptions Swinton, *Finding Jesus in the Storm*, 11–39, esp. 38–39.
6 In chapter 6, this will become clear in the context of the Chapel of Christ Our Hope in Singapore. Elsewhere, I have interpreted this as people being on a journey of accepting their child's autism. Van Ommen, "Re-imagining Church through Autism."
7 Sue Fletcher-Watson and Francesca Happé, *Autism: A New Introduction to Psychological Theory and Current Debate* (London: Routledge, 2019), 20.
8 Penni Winter, "Loud Hands & Loud Voices," in *Loud Hands: Autistic People, Speaking*, ed. Julia Bascom (Washington, DC: Autistic Press, 2012), 115.
9 Winter, "Loud Hands & Loud Voices," 116.
10 Winter, "Loud Hands & Loud Voices," 116.
11 It is worth repeating John Swinton's comment on the influential "triad of impairments" that frames autism as difficulties with social communication, social interaction, and social imagination: "It is, perhaps, worth noting that any attempt to explain human experience that begins by focusing on three difficulties or deficits should be treated with some suspicion." Swinton, "Reflections on Autistic Love," 265. For more on Lorna Wing and her proposal and influence of the "triad of impairments," see Evans, *Metamorphosis of Autism*, 289–301, 348, 376.
12 Krysia Emily Waldock and Rachel Forrester-Jones, "An Exploratory Study of Attitudes toward Autism amongst Church-going Christians in the South East of England, United Kingdom," *Journal of Disability & Religion*, June 11, 2020, 1–22, https://doi.org/10.1080/23312521.2020.1776667.

13 Some excellent histories of autism have been written, notably Silberman, *NeuroTribes*; John Donvan and Caren Zucker, *In a Different Key: The Story of Autism* (London: Allen Lane, 2016); Evans, *Metamorphosis of Autism*; Chloe Silverman, *Understanding Autism: Parents, Doctors, and the History of a Disorder* (Princeton: Princeton University Press, 2011).
14 Evans, *Metamorphosis of Autism*, 10, 41–45.
15 Evans, *Metamorphosis of Autism*, 42.
16 Evans, *Metamorphosis of Autism*, 45.
17 Evans, *Metamorphosis of Autism*, 4–5.
18 Evans, *Metamorphosis of Autism*, 45.
19 Evans, *Metamorphosis of Autism*, 34–39, 45–46. For a theological exploration of the contemporary eugenics debate, see John Swinton and Brian Brock, eds., *Theology, Disability and the New Genetics: Why Science Needs the Church* (London: Continuum, 2007).
20 Evans, *Metamorphosis of Autism*, 80.
21 Evans, *Metamorphosis of Autism*, 75–84.
22 Evans, *Metamorphosis of Autism*, 81, 83.
23 Evans, *Metamorphosis of Autism*, 112–14.
24 Silberman, *NeuroTribes*, 208–14.
25 Hans Asperger, "Die 'autistischen Psychopathen' im Kindesalter," *Archiv für Psychiatrie und Nervenkrankheiten* 117, no. 1 (June 1944): 76–136, https://doi.org/10.1007/BF01837709. Note that Lorna Wing argues that the term "psychopath" was a technical term, meaning "abnormality of personality" and therefore used differently from the modern connotation with sociopathic behavior. See Lorna Wing, "Asperger's Syndrome: A Clinical Account," *Psychological Medicine* 11, no. 1 (February 1981): 115, https://doi.org/10.1017/S0033291700053332. However, while the term did not have the twenty-first-century popular notions of psychopath, Edith Sheffer claims that the term was not as neutral as Wing says. "Asperger had not used a neutral term. Psychopathy in German psychiatry had long connoted social deviance and recalcitrance—which were embedded in his Nazi-era diagnosis." Edith Sheffer, *Asperger's Children: The Origins of Autism in Nazi Vienna* (New York: Norton, 2018), 242; see also 84–85. We turn to Sheffer's work when discussing Asperger's contribution to the history of autism below.
26 Asperger, "Die 'autistischen Psychopathen' im Kindesalter," 84–85.
27 Especially through Wing, "Asperger's Syndrome"; cf. Nick Chown and Liz Hughes, "History and First Descriptions of Autism: Asperger versus Kanner Revisited," *Journal of Autism and Developmental Disorders* 46, no. 6 (June 2016): 2271, https://doi.org/10.1007/s10803-016-2746-0.
28 Chown and Hughes, "History and First Descriptions of Autism," 2271.
29 Evans, *Metamorphosis of Autism*, 302.
30 Berend Verhoeff, "Autism in Flux: A History of the Concept from Leo Kanner to DSM-5," *History of Psychiatry* 24, no. 4 (December 2013): n2, https://doi.org/10.1177/0957154X13500584.
31 Silberman, *NeuroTribes*, chap. 5, esp. 212–14.
32 Chown and Hughes, "History and First Descriptions of Autism," 2271–72.
33 Wing, "Asperger's Syndrome," 115.
34 Chown and Hughes, "History and First Descriptions of Autism."
35 Herwig Czech, "Hans Asperger, National Socialism, and 'Race Hygiene' in Nazi-Era Vienna," *Molecular Autism* 9, no. 1 (December 2018): 29, https://doi.org/10.1186/s13229-018-0208-6.

36 Sheffer, *Asperger's Children*, 69.
37 Cf. Sheffer, *Asperger's Children*, 236, who identifies these positions with Silberman, Donvan and Zucker, and Czech, respectively.
38 This is compellingly argued by Sheffer, but see the discussion between Herwig Czech and Dean Falk; Dean Falk, "More on Asperger's Career: A Reply to Czech," *Journal of Autism and Developmental Disorders* 49, no. 9 (September 2019): 3877–82, https://doi.org/10.1007/s10803-019-04099-6.
39 Sheffer, *Asperger's Children*, 236.
40 Simon Baron-Cohen, "The Truth about Hans Asperger's Nazi Collusion," *Nature* 557, no. 7705 (May 2018): 305–6, https://doi.org/10.1038/d41586-018-05112-1.
41 Verhoeff, "Autism in Flux," 449–50.
42 Michael Rutter, "Concepts of Autism: A Review of Research," *Journal of Child Psychology and Psychiatry* 9, no. 1 (October 1968): 21, https://doi.org/10.1111/j.1469-7610.1968.tb02204.x.
43 Derek M. Ricks and Lorna Wing, "Language, Communication, and the Use of Symbols in Normal and Autistic Children," *Journal of Autism and Childhood Schizophrenia* 5, no. 3 (1975): 191–221.
44 Rutter, "Concepts of Autism," 21; quoted in Verhoeff, "Autism in Flux," 450; emphases original.
45 Verhoeff points to another development in the 1960s—that is, under the influence of the rapid development of cognitive and computer sciences, a new discourse emerged. This discourse was marked by language such as "codes, processing, stimuli and sensory modalities [which] became dominant in investigating, recognizing and thinking about autism." Verhoeff, "Autism in Flux," 450. Such language is still used today. That is not necessarily a bad thing, but it is important that language is reflective of a particular culture, time, or disciplinary perspective. Words like "code" and "process" are not literal descriptions but metaphors. Once we realize this fact, it creates opportunities to see things differently, to start using other terminology and metaphors.
46 Evans, *Metamorphosis of Autism*, 189–90; emphases original.
47 Evans, *Metamorphosis of Autism*, 190ff.
48 Winter, "Loud Hands & Loud Voices," 123–24; emphases original.
49 Lorna Wing and Judith Gould, "Severe Impairments of Social Interaction and Associated Abnormalities in Children: Epidemiology and Classification," *Journal of Autism and Developmental Disorders* 9, no. 1 (March 1979): 11–29, https://doi.org/10.1007/BF01531288.
50 Lorna Wing, "Language, Social, and Cognitive Impairments in Autism and Severe Mental Retardation," *Journal of Autism and Developmental Disorders* 11, no. 1 (March 1981): 37, https://doi.org/10.1007/BF01531339; cited in Verhoeff, "Autism in Flux," 451.
51 Evans, *Metamorphosis of Autism*, 296–97.
52 Evans, *Metamorphosis of Autism*, 289ff, esp. 297–301; Verhoeff, "Autism in Flux," 450–51.
53 Wing, "Asperger's Syndrome."
54 Uta Frith, ed., *Autism and Asperger Syndrome* (Cambridge: Cambridge University Press, 1991).
55 Silverman, *Understanding Autism*, 37. Silverman quotes Hans Asperger, "'Autistic Psychopathy' in Childhood," in *Autism and Asperger Syndrome*, ed. Uta Frith (Cambridge: Cambridge University Press, 1944), 88.

56 Lorna Wing, "Reflections on Opening Pandora's Box," *Journal of Autism and Developmental Disorders* 35, no. 2 (April 2005): 197–203, https://doi.org/10.1007/s10803-004-1998-2.
57 Verhoeff, "Autism in Flux," 452.
58 David C. Giles, "'DSM-V Is Taking Away Our Identity': The Reaction of the Online Community to the Proposed Changes in the Diagnosis of Asperger's Disorder," *Health* 18, no. 2 (2014): 187.
59 Kristen Faye Linton et al., "Opinions of People Who Self-Identify with Autism and Asperger's on *DSM-5* Criteria," *Research on Social Work Practice* 24, no. 1 (January 2014): 75, https://doi.org/10.1177/1049731513495457.
60 Linton et al., "Opinions of People Who Self-Identify with Autism and Asperger's," 75–76.
61 Silverman, *Understanding Autism*.
62 Giles, "'DSM-V Is Taking Away Our Identity,'" 192.
63 Evans, *Metamorphosis of Autism*, 115. Evans points out, however, that this was part of a wider societal and political movement and that therefore "Bowlbyism" is "a far more complex story about the development of children's rights, than is often acknowledged by those who characterise it as merely a dark period in the history of autism."
64 Leo Kanner, "Problems of Nosology and Psychodynamics of Early Infantile Autism," *American Journal of Orthopsychiatry* 19, no. 3 (July 1949): 423, https://doi.org/10.1111/j.1939-0025.1949.tb05441.x.
65 Kanner, "Problems of Nosology and Psychodynamics," 425. Donvan and Zucker trace the origins of the metaphor back to an article in *Time* magazine on April 26, 1948 titled, "Medicine: Frosted Children," in which Kanner is quoted to use exactly the same phrase, saying of autistic children that they were "kept neatly in a refrigerator which didn't defrost." Donvan and Zucker, *In a Different Key*, 79–80, 88; quote on 80.
66 Donvan and Zucker, *In a Different Key*, 88.
67 Bruno Bettelheim, *The Empty Fortress: Infantile Autism and the Birth of the Self* (New York: Free Press/Macmillan, 1967); cf. Murray, *Representing Autism*, 174.
68 Murray, *Representing Autism*, 175. Murray lists the role of mothers in, among others, Joseph Conrad's "The Idiots" and Cammie McGovern's *Eye Contact* and the role of fathers in Mark Haddon's *The Curious Incident of the Dog in the Night-Time* and Simon Armitage's *Little Green Man*. Furthermore, sibling roles are prominent in the movies *Rain Man* and *Silent Fall*, for example.
69 Interestingly, even though theological reflection on autism is only recent, two books in the field reflect explicitly on the role of mothers: Campbell, *Motherhood and Autism*; Williams, *Peculiar Discipleship*.
70 At the first conference of the parent organization the National Society for Autistic Children in 1969, Kanner was the keynote speaker. Silberman recounts Kanner discarding Bettelheim's book as an "empty book" and then reassuring (or perhaps better, absolving) the parents: "And herewith I especially acquit you people as parents." Silberman, *NeuroTribes*, 326. Another point of evidence that Kanner had come to another position regarding parents comes from an article in which he advocated the participation of parents in therapy, "not as etiological culprits." Cited in Silverman, *Understanding Autism*, 95. However, blaming Bettelheim was too easy. Silberman points out that "Bettelheim would go down in history as the primary source of the theory, though he had been virtually parroting Kanner and Eisenberg while adding his own misogynist flourishes" (293). Indeed, Silberman further notes that in 1973, Kanner "reprinted a collection of his essays describing his patients' parents as 'cold, humorless perfectionists' lacking 'genuine warmth,' with no editorial caveats" (326).

Thus, Kanner's legacy in relation to the "refrigerator parent" theory is dubious to say the least. His attempts to appease parents of autistic children seems to have been a strategic move rather than based on scientific evidence or progressing understanding.

71 Silberman, *NeuroTribes*, 373–74; Chloe Phillips, "Elgar, Sybil Lillian," in *Oxford Dictionary of National Biography*, ed. Lawrence Goldman (Oxford: Oxford University Press, 2013), 344. Note that the society was for autistic children. At the time, and to some extent still today, autism was thought of as a childhood condition, and therefore much less thought went into support for autistic adults.
72 Evans, *Metamorphosis of Autism*, 201–2.
73 Evans, *Metamorphosis of Autism*, 252.
74 https://www.autism.org.uk/.
75 Silberman, *NeuroTribes*, 374.
76 Silverman, *Understanding Autism*, 145; cf. 22. See also https://www.autism-society.org/about-the-autism-society/history/.
77 These words became the title of the speech when he published it online; it is reprinted as the opening essay in the *Loud Hands* volume. Sinclair, "Don't Mourn for Us."
78 Sinclair, "Don't Mourn for Us," 16.
79 Sinclair, "Don't Mourn for Us," 20.
80 Sinclair, "Don't Mourn for Us," 19–20; emphasis original.
81 Silberman, *NeuroTribes*, 476–95.
82 Silberman, *NeuroTribes*, 491–93; quotation on 492–93; Donvan and Zucker, *In a Different Key*, 516–17; Harvey Blume, "Neurodiversity: On the Neurological Underpinnings of Geekdom," *The Atlantic*, September 1998, https://www.theatlantic.com/magazine/archive/1998/09/neurodiversity/305909/.
83 Cited in Donvan and Zucker, *In a Different Key*, 513.
84 Cited in Silberman, *NeuroTribes*, 495. See also Joseph F. Kras, "The 'Ransom Notes' Affair: When the Neurodiversity Movement Came of Age," *Disability Studies Quarterly* 30, no. 10 (2010), https://dsq-sds.org/article/%C2%A0view/1065/1254#top. Images of the notes can be found in many places on the internet, for example, Joanne Kaufman, "Campaign on Childhood Mental Illness Succeeds at Being Provocative," *New York Times*, December 14, 2007, https://www.nytimes.com/2007/12/14/business/media/14adco.html (accessed June 6, 2023).
85 Quoted in Donvan and Zucker, *In a Different Key*, 523.
86 Silberman, *NeuroTribes*, 496.
87 Silberman, *NeuroTribes*, 503.
88 Temple Grandin, *Emergence: Labeled Autistic* (Novato: Arena Press, 1986).
89 Donvan and Zucker, *In a Different Key*, 417.
90 Temple Grandin, *Thinking in Pictures: And Other Reports from My Life with Autism* (New York: Doubleday Books, 1995).
91 Oliver Sacks, *An Anthropologist on Mars* (London: Picador, 1995).
92 Donvan and Zucker, *In a Different Key*, 415–17, 435.
93 Giles, "'DSM-V Is Taking Away Our Identity,'" 192.
94 See, for example, Botha, Hanlon, and Williams, "Does Language Matter?" who argue for inclusion in research of people "across the spectrum of communication difficulties" and warn against the assumption that nonspeaking people cannot advocate for themselves (quote on 5).
95 See also Williams, *Peculiar Discipleship* (esp. chap. 4).
96 Silverman, *Understanding Autism*, 22.
97 Silverman, *Understanding Autism*, 12.
98 Verhoeff, "Autism in Flux," 445; emphasis original.

99 Evans, *Metamorphosis of Autism*, 14.
100 Verhoeff, "Autism in Flux," 446. The term "tenacious search for autism's essence" is used by Verhoeff in another article to which he refers here: Berend Verhoeff, "What Is This Thing Called Autism? A Critical Analysis of the Tenacious Search for Autism's Essence," *Biosocieties* 7, no. 4 (2012): 410–32.
101 Macaskill, *Autism and the Church*, 46–47; emphasis original.
102 Punishment was part and parcel of Lovaas' method, including the use of excruciating sound blasts and electroshocks. Silberman, *NeuroTribes*, 330–37.
103 For example, the highly controversial Spectrum 10K study in the United Kingdom, led by Simon Baron-Cohen. https://spectrum10k.org/.
104 For a (nonexhaustive) overview of research approaches, see Boucher, *Autism Spectrum Disorder*; for an analysis of autism research funding in 2016 in the United Kingdom, see Georgina Warner, Heather Cooper, and James Cusack, *A Review of the Autism Research Funding Landscape in the United Kingdom* (London: Autistica, n.d.), https://www.autistica.org.uk/downloads/files/Autistica-Scoping-Report.pdf. The various strands of research fall broadly within either the "medical model" and "social model" which we discussed in chapter 1. For an overview and critique, see further, for example, Tam, *Kinship in the Household of God*, 11–27; Creamer, *Disability and Christian Theology*, 22–31.

3 THE TYRANNY OF THE NORMAL

1 Davis, *Enforcing Normalcy*, 23–24. The analogy with race makes it clear at once how strenuous efforts are needed to move the discussion along. In a recent special issue of the journal *Practical Theology* devoted to whiteness, Anthony Reddie writes in his response that in his almost twenty-five years of writing on racial justice, "I can count on one hand the number of White colleagues whose work has been as concerned with racial justice and wrestling with White privilege as my own. It has often felt that racism was a Black problem and not a White one." This illustrates that even if some scholars are attuned to the issues raised, whether on race, disability, or autism, the "problem" often remains to be seen as one of those on the receiving end of discrimination and oppression—those outside the boundaries of normalcy. Anthony G. Reddie, "Dismantling Whiteness—a Response," *Practical Theology* 15, no. 1–2 (January 2022): 168–73, https://doi.org/10.1080/1756073X.2022.2040728; citation on 168.
2 Reynolds, *Vulnerable Communion*, 112.
3 Reynolds, *Vulnerable Communion*, 112.
4 Reynolds, *Vulnerable Communion*, 113.
5 Whitehead, "Religion and Disability." For some examples of families with autistic members who felt excluded from churches, and testimonies of autistic people themselves, see Van Ommen, "Re-imagining Church through Autism"; Van Ommen and Unwin, "The Sensory Aspects of Worship and Liturgy as Experienced by Autistic People."
6 Stewart Rapley explains at some length the difficulty autistic people may have with situations that are not being explained and in which one is supposed to infer meaning. Rapley, *Autistic Thinking in the Life of the Church*, 21–23.
7 Reynolds, *Vulnerable Communion*, 56.
8 Reynolds, *Vulnerable Communion*, 57. Note that the theme of presence (see next chapter) is hinted at here.
9 Reynolds, *Vulnerable Communion*, 53.

10 Goto, *Taking on Practical Theology*, 45.
11 Goto, *Taking on Practical Theology*, 45.
12 Reynolds, *Vulnerable Communion*, 55.
13 Reynolds, *Vulnerable Communion*, 57.
14 Wendy Lawson, *Concepts of Normality: The Autistic and Typical Spectrum* (London: Jessica Kingsley, 2008), 26.
15 For example, Abraham P. Buunk, Gert Stulp, and Wilmar B. Schaufeli, "Effect of Self-Reported Height on Occupational Rank among Police Officers: Especially for Women It Pays to Be Tall," *Evolutionary Psychological Science* 7, no. 4 (December 2021): 411–18, https://doi.org/10.1007/s40806-021-00281-1. The authors note, "In present Western cultures, height is consistently related to income, the attainment of leadership positions, and other measures of professional success" (411).
16 Graham, "Words Made Flesh," 117.
17 Graham, "Words Made Flesh," 118.
18 Research into camouflaging in autistic people is not unequivocal in terms of methods and validity of the outcomes, as noted in the systematic overview by Julia Cook et al., "Camouflaging in Autism: A Systematic Review," *Clinical Psychology Review* 89 (November 2021): 102080, https://doi.org/10.1016/j.cpr.2021.102080. This is also true for the definition of the term itself, but Cook et al. offer the following definition, which for the purposes of this chapter suffices: "Although definitions of camouflaging are still evolving, here we define camouflaging (also variously referred to in the literature as compensation, masking and adaptive morphing) as the employment of specific behavioural and cognitive strategies by autistic people to adapt to or cope within the predominately non-autistic social world" (1).
19 Here, it is relevant to note that autism is often invisible, which makes autism different from some forms of disability and from race or gender. This adds to the complexity of normalcy and autism and the possibility of camouflaging.
20 Graham, "Words Made Flesh," 118.
21 Especially relevant for Davis' development of the concept is the second chapter in his book *Enforcing Normalcy*, which I already referred to above.
22 Davis, *Enforcing Normalcy*, 24–25.
23 Davis, *Enforcing Normalcy*, 26.
24 Davis, *Enforcing Normalcy*, 26.
25 Davis, *Enforcing Normalcy*, 30.
26 Davis, *Enforcing Normalcy*, 30.
27 Davis, *Enforcing Normalcy*, 32.
28 Davis, *Enforcing Normalcy*, 35.
29 Simplican, *The Capacity Contract*, 7–11.
30 One might argue for distinguishing between normal and typical and say that diagnoses are based on deviation from the typical, which is the average or the mean. As such, "typical" could be said to be a more neutral term than "normal." When it comes to *belonging*, however, the concept of normalcy shows that generally, the typical is valued in society and therefore thought of as the norm.
31 Stanley Hauerwas, "Chapter 2. Community and Diversity: The Tyranny of Normality," *Journal of Religion, Disability & Health* 8, no. 3–4 (February 24, 2005): 40, https://doi.org/10.1300/J095v08n03_05. Originally published as Stanley Hauerwas, "Community and Diversity: The Tyranny of Normality," *National Apostolate for the Mentally Retarded* 8, no. 1–2 (1977): 20–23.

32 Davis, *Enforcing Normalcy*; Damian Milton, "'Filling in the Gaps': A Microsociological Analysis of Autism," *Autonomy, the Critical Journal of Interdisciplinary Autism Studies* 1, no. 2 (2013), http://kar.kent.ac.uk/62634/.
33 Hauerwas, "Community and Diversity," 40.
34 Hauerwas, "Community and Diversity," 40.
35 Hauerwas, "Community and Diversity," 42.
36 There is a striking parallel between the designation of normalcy as a cult by Reynolds and the way Goto talks about a paradigm's symbols. Goto's concept of paradigm is very similar to the concept of normalcy even though she does not use the term and does not refer to Reynolds or Davis. She speaks about the group's "idolization" or "sacralization" of its symbols—symbols being core practices of a group that implicitly express the group's norms and values and are core to the paradigm. Goto, *Taking on Practical Theology*, 8.
37 Note that the prophets in the Hebrew Bible did not necessarily accuse God's people of not worshipping God anymore but of worshipping other gods or idols alongside the one true God.
38 Charles Taylor, *Sources of the Self: The Making of the Modern Identity* (Cambridge, Mass.: Harvard University Press, 1989), 27. The term "qualitative discriminations" is more or less synonymous to "frameworks" in Taylor's argument, which both have a strong moral character—they are used to find meaning, and they are the background to what is good and bad (see also 26).
39 Taylor, *Sources of the Self*, 27.
40 Taylor, *Sources of the Self*, 27–28.
41 Gillibrand, *Disabled Church—Disabled Society*, 154.
42 Gillibrand, *Disabled Church—Disabled Society*, 155.
43 Graham, "Words Made Flesh," 118.
44 Lawson, *Concepts of Normality*, 18, 22.
45 Walker, *Neuroqueer Heresies*, 36; see also 19.
46 Estée Klar-Wolfond and Wendy Lawson, "The Mismeasure of Autism: The Basis for Current 'Autism Advocacy,'" in *Concepts of Normality: The Autistic and Typical Spectrum* (London: Jessica Kingsley, 2008), 105.
47 Klar-Wolfond and Lawson, "Mismeasure of Autism," 106; emphasis original. The reference to Gould is S. J. Gould, *The Mismeasure of Man* (New York: Norton, 1996).
48 Acknowledging the embodied and learned nature of our social interactions and the different ways of social interaction between neurotypical and neurodivergent people, Alan Jurgens argues that "in order to improve the interactions between neurotypical individuals and autistic individuals in shared social institutions, there needs to be a shift in the focus of interventions away from autistic individuals towards the intersubjective realm of neurotypical social practices and institutions." Alan Jurgens, "Neurodiversity in a Neurotypical World: An Enactive Framework for Investigating Autism and Social Institutions," in *Neurodiversity Studies: A New Critical Paradigm*, ed. Hanna Bertilsdotter Rosqvist, Nick Chown, and Anna Stenning (London: Routledge, 2020), 85.
49 Klar-Wolfond and Lawson, "Mismeasure of Autism," 114.
50 Klar-Wolfond and Lawson, "Mismeasure of Autism," 115–16; emphases original.
51 Klar-Wolfond and Lawson, "Mismeasure of Autism," 123.
52 Walker, *Neuroqueer Heresies*, 22–24, 56.
53 Brock, *Wondrously Wounded*, 218; emphases original.
54 For example, Nick Walker claims that these two paradigms are incompatible. Walker, *Neuroqueer Heresies*.

55 See Van Ommen and Endress, "Reframing Liturgical Theology."
56 Reynolds, *Vulnerable Communion*, 51.
57 There is a deliberate association in this sentence with the word "navigate" in relation to Taylor's concept of frameworks, which he says help to orient our lives. It is worth noting that Taylor connects this to a narrative understanding of life, which in turn relates to my own narrative understanding of liturgy. Taylor, *Sources of the Self*, 41–52.

4 PRESENCE AND PARTICIPATION

1 Milton, "On the Ontological Status of Autism."
2 As discussed in the previous chapter, the frameworks in societies are usually not conducive for autistic people to pass the threshold for belonging. This almost inevitably results in the need for masking or camouflaging, which is exhausting. In the words of an autistic Christian, "Leaving church on the verge of tears most of the time from sheer frustration and exhaustion is not how it should be. I'm pleased to report that I now only leave church on the verge of tears less than half of the time, so that's a major improvement." Spoor, *Spirituality on the Spectrum*, 19.
3 Brendan Sweetman, ed., *A Gabriel Marcel Reader* (South Bend, Ind.: St. Augustine's Press, 2011), 2.
4 See Marcel's interview with Paul Ricoeur, excerpt in Sweetman, *A Gabriel Marcel Reader*, 149–55; Neil Pembroke, *The Art of Listening: Dialogue, Shame, and Pastoral Care* (London: T & T Clark, 2002), 2–3.
5 Note that Tom Reynolds works with some of Marcel's reflections; see Reynolds, *Vulnerable Communion*; Neil Pembroke works out the implications of Marcel and Martin Buber's philosophies for pastoral care in *Art of Listening*.
6 Gabriel Marcel, *Creative Fidelity*, trans. R. Rosthal (New York: Noonday Press, 1964), 23; Sweetman, *A Gabriel Marcel Reader*, 3; Brian Treanor, *Aspects of Alterity: Levinas, Marcel, and the Contemporary Debate* (New York: Fordham University Press, 2006), 55.
7 Marcel, *Creative Fidelity*, 61.
8 Treanor, *Aspects of Alterity*, 54.
9 Marcel, *Creative Fidelity*, 23.
10 Gabriel Marcel, *The Mystery of Being: Reflection and Mystery*, trans. G. S. Fraser (Chicago: Henry Regnery, 1950), 1:205; emphases original. Also quoted in Pembroke, *Art of Listening*, 19.
11 Marcel, *Creative Fidelity*, 33.
12 Marcel, *Creative Fidelity*, 33. Marcel expands on this idea on the following pages, esp. 35–36.
13 Marcel is using Buber's well-known distinction between "Thou" and "It" here. Martin Buber, *I and Thou*, trans. Ronald Gregor Smith (Edinburgh: T & T Clark, n.d.).
14 Marcel does not dismiss the "It" entirely. A problem in relationships emerges when we relate to each other only as "Its"—that is, an instrumental way of relating, without moving to relating to each other as "Thous." Sweetman, *Gabriel Marcel Reader*, 7.
15 Sweetman, *Gabriel Marcel Reader*, 82–83.
16 Gabriel Marcel, "On the Ontological Mystery," in *The Philosophy of Existence*, trans. Manya Harari (Providence: Cluny, 2018), 39.
17 Sweetman, *Gabriel Marcel Reader*, 84; emphasis original.
18 Marcel, "On the Ontological Mystery," 38.
19 Marcel, *Creative Fidelity*, 12.

20 In fact, often when Marcel talks about disponibilité he does so by talking about indisponibilité.
21 Marcel, *Mystery of Being*, 1:163; see also Gabriel Marcel, *Being and Having*, trans. Katharine Farrer (London: Dacre Press, 1949), 69–74. I am aware that Marcel's language here sounds similar to what is often thought of autistic people, as "being in their own world" and unable to empathize; see, for example, the discussion of Bettelheim's views in chapter 2. However, that is clearly not what Marcel is talking about here, and the discussion in this section should not be read in light of that association.
22 Marcel, *Mystery of Being*, 1:164.
23 Marcel, *Being and Having*, 69.
24 Marcel, *Being and Having*, 69.
25 Marcel, *Creative Fidelity*, 40.
26 Historically, this argument has been used in oppressive ways, not least toward women. Arguably, a subtle version of such oppressive expectation to give oneself to the other can be seen in autistic people's felt need to mask their autistic traits or behavior in order to belong. Clearly, this is more than a felt need, as the discussion of normalcy in the previous chapter has made clear. This is not the way in which Marcel outlines his argument, and it should be clear that my intention is not to perpetuate such a detrimental use of the argument. I want to thank Kimberly Belcher for pointing me to this historical effect that this argument has had and still can have for autistic and other people.
27 Marcel, *Creative Fidelity*, 46.
28 Marcel, *Creative Fidelity*, 97.
29 Marcel, *Creative Fidelity*, 99; emphasis original.
30 Marcel, *Creative Fidelity*, 100.
31 Marcel, *Creative Fidelity*, 100–101.
32 For an elaborate discussion of Bonhoeffer's vision of community in relation to autism, see Tam, *Kinship in the Household of God*, 140–58.
33 Dietrich Bonhoeffer, *Life Together*, trans. John W. Doberstein (London: SCM Press, 1954), 11; also on 13.
34 Bonhoeffer, *Life Together*, 15.
35 Tam, *Kinship in the Household of God*, 144, 152.
36 Marcel, "On the Ontological Mystery," 39; emphasis original.
37 See also the discussion in Pia Matthews, "Complementary Understandings of Availability: Jean Vanier in Conversation with the Philosophers Emmanuel Levinas and Gabriel Marcel," *Journal of Disability & Religion* 24, no. 2 (2020): 174–205, https://doi.org/10.1080/23312521.2020.1718576.
38 Marcel, *Creative Fidelity*, 91.
39 Reynolds, *Vulnerable Communion*, 122.
40 Marcel, "On the Ontological Mystery," 39.
41 Marcel, "On the Ontological Mystery," 40.
42 Reynolds, *Vulnerable Communion*, 127.
43 To be sure, the framework we live in gives us a sense of safety, but there is a difference between the need for safety and an unwillingness to step out of our comfort zone.
44 Reynolds, *Vulnerable Communion*, 128.
45 Reynolds, *Vulnerable Communion*, 127; emphasis mine.
46 Reynolds, *Vulnerable Communion*, 128.
47 "Our" here includes autistic and non-autistic people and is not meant as "us/our" versus "them/their." Waldock and Forrester-Jones demonstrate how subtle yet troublesome these words can be if used when speaking about "our church." Waldock

and Forrester-Jones, "An Exploratory Study of Attitudes toward Autism amongst Church-going Christians," 9.
48 Reynolds, *Vulnerable Communion*, 128.
49 Relating disponibilité to kenosis also helps to push back further on any oppressive use of the argument (see note 26). Sarah Johnson explains that kenosis involves "power giving itself into weakness" but immediately continues to say that "kenosis is *not* an expectation for the weak to submit to the powerful." Kenosis does involve the risk of loss; "however, each moment also contains the possibility of revelation." That possibility resonates strongly with the deep connection that Marcel argues is the result of being available to each other. Sarah Kathleen Johnson, "Poured Out: A Kenotic Approach to Initiating Children at a Distance from the Church," *Studia Liturgica* 49, no. 2 (September 2019): 187, https://doi.org/10.1177/0039320719866302; emphasis mine.
50 John M. G. Barclay, "Kenosis and the Drama of Salvation in Philippians 2," in *Kenosis: The Self-Emptying of Christ in Scripture and Theology*, ed. Paul T. Nimmo and Keith L. Johnson (Grand Rapids: Eerdmans, 2022), 7–23; Susan Grove Eastman, *Paul and the Person: Reframing Paul's Anthropology* (Grand Rapids: Eerdmans, 2017), 126–50.
51 Barclay, "Kenosis and the Drama of Salvation in Philippians 2," 8. Barclay points out that there is discussion as to whether these verses are in fact a hymn.
52 For recent and detailed discussions of various (theological) readings of this passage, see the collection of essays in Paul T. Nimmo and Keith L. Johnson, eds., *Kenosis: The Self-Emptying of Christ in Scripture and Theology* (Grand Rapids: Eerdmans, 2022). See also the elaborate and critical historical overview of the question of kenotic Christologies in Bruce Lindley McCormack, *The Humility of the Eternal Son: Reformed Kenoticism and the Repair of Chalcedon* (Cambridge: Cambridge University Press, 2021), 27–195.
53 The origins of the passage are uncertain. Some scholars have argued that it was a hymn, others some other kind of text. I am not arguing here for either and use "Christ hymn" for ease of reference to this passage. See Barclay, "Kenosis and the Drama of Salvation in Philippians 2," 8.
54 I put quotation marks around "mindset" because of the potential overcognitive associations that this word might have for contemporary readers. The meaning of the Greek here should be interpreted in a more holistic way, as a "quite particular 'way of thinking, acting, and feeling.'" Hanna Reichel, "The End of Humanity and the Beginning of Kenosis," in *Kenosis: The Self-Emptying of Christ in Scripture and Theology*, ed. Paul T. Nimmo and Keith L. Johnson (Grand Rapids: Eerdmans, 2022), 305; Reichel quotes Michael Gorman.
55 Barclay, "Kenosis and the Drama of Salvation in Philippians 2," 19; emphases original.
56 Barclay, "Kenosis and the Drama of Salvation in Philippians 2," 20; emphases original.
57 Barclay, "Kenosis and the Drama of Salvation in Philippians 2," 20–21.
58 Barclay, "Kenosis and the Drama of Salvation in Philippians 2," 22.
59 Barclay, "Kenosis and the Drama of Salvation in Philippians 2," 22; emphases original.
60 For recent overviews of the debates in the twentieth century, see Constantine R. Campbell, *Paul and Union with Christ: An Exegetical and Theological Study* (Grand Rapids: Zondervan, 2012); Grant Macaskill, *Union with Christ in the New Testament* (Oxford: Oxford University Press, 2013); Teresa Morgan, *Being "in Christ" in the Letters of Paul: Saved through Christ and in His Hands* (Tübingen: Mohr Siebeck, 2020); Kevin J. Vanhoozer, "From 'Blessed in Christ' to 'Being in Christ,'" in *"In Christ" in Paul: Explorations in Paul's Theology of Union and Participation*, ed.

Michael J. Thate, Kevin J. Vanhoozer, and Constantine R. Campbell (Tübingen: Mohr Siebeck, 2014), 3–33.

61 Eastman applies in her work what she calls a "second-person perspective hermeneutics." The second-person approach has gained influence in theological anthropology in recent years. However, some theologians use autism in highly problematic and dehumanizing ways as a "test case" for answering the question of what it means to be human, as Joanna Leidenhag has demonstrated. Eastman avoids that trap. Eastman, *Paul and the Person*, 15; Joanna Leidenhag, "The Challenge of Autism for Relational Approaches to Theological Anthropology," *International Journal of Systematic Theology* 23, no. 1 (January 2021): 109–34, https://doi.org/10.1111/ijst.12453.

62 In the hymn itself, the term "in Christ" is not being used, but it is in the preceding verse (5). At this point in the discussion, I should mention Teresa Morgan's criticism of reading a participatory theology in the "in Christ" references in the seven undisputed Pauline letters. Morgan argues that the phrase "in Christ" is better understood encheiristically—that is, as "being in the hands/power/responsibility/care of" Christ. Morgan, *Being "in Christ" in the Letters of Paul*. However, that does not mean that theological concept of participation in Christ is absent from Paul's thought altogether and even less so that the concept is not present in the New Testament; see especially Macaskill, *Union with Christ in the New Testament*.

63 A keyword in the passage that is used in this way of the blurred lines between actor and the role is *homoiōma* ("likeness"). "The meaning of *homoiōma* moves along a spectrum between equivalence and difference, but primarily it has the sense of a 'copy' or 'what is made similar.' In Plato it is closely related to the idea of imitation, because 'people become like' those they imitate through action. To imitate is to become a copy (*homoiōma*) of a model and to move toward assimilation (*homoiotēs*) with that model." Eastman, *Paul and the Person*, 132–33.

64 Eastman, *Paul and the Person*, 131–34.

65 Eastman, *Paul and the Person*, 134.

66 Eastman, *Paul and the Person*, 135–40. A careful study of the language of "participation with Christ" or "union with Christ" in the New Testament will show the biblical understanding of the ontology of Christ, as both human and divine, which is kept distinct from the ontology of the believers, who participate in the divine life but never turn into the divine ontologically. For this argument, see throughout Macaskill, *Union with Christ in the New Testament*.

67 Eastman, *Paul and the Person*, 138.

68 Macaskill carefully distinguishes between Christ who *is* the image of God and Adam who is made *according to* that image. Similarly, the believers are remade (conformed) *according to* that image but not the image itself. Throughout, the distinction between God (and Christ) and human beings is maintained. Macaskill, *Union with Christ in the New Testament*, 230–31, 241–42.

69 Eastman, *Paul and the Person*, 141.

70 Eastman, *Paul and the Person*, 148.

71 Eastman, *Paul and the Person*, 148.

72 Andrew Root, *Christopraxis: A Practical Theology of the Cross* (Minneapolis: Fortress, 2014), 72–75.

73 I am using the term "double participation" to denote Christ's participation in humanity on the one hand and human participation in Christ on the other hand. This is a different use of the term than Eastman, who uses it to denote the human participation in the realm of the "present evil age" (Gal 1:4) and "the system of body-environment intersubjectivity in relationship to Christ and to other believers."

Eastman, *Paul and the Person*, 147; she uses this in the same way in Susan Eastman, "Double Participation and the Responsible Self in Romans 5–8," in *Apocalyptic Paul: Cosmos and Anthropos in Romans 5–8*, ed. Beverly Roberts Gaventa (Waco: Baylor University Press, 2013), 93–110.

74 Douglas A. Campbell, "Participation and Faith in Paul," in *"In Christ" in Paul: Explorations in Paul's Theology of Union and Participation*, ed. Michael J. Thate, Kevin J. Vanhoozer, and Constantine R. Campbell (Tübingen: Mohr Siebeck, 2014), 50; emphasis original. Campbell associates the "mindset" of Christ directly with a "way of thinking." As said before, "mindset" should be interpreted more broadly to avoid dualistic connotations of mind versus body and feeling that contemporary readers might have and can be interpreted as a disposition or attitude or a way of being.

75 For a discussion of the Galatians passage in relation to participation from a practical theological perspective, see Root, *Christopraxis*, 71–73.

76 Eastman, *Paul and the Person*, 162.

77 In another essay, writing about the role of the Spirit in relation to being "in Christ" and commenting on Romans 8, Eastman explains, "To be 'in Christ' is to be in relationship with people in the midst of whom Christ dwells through his Spirit, and thereby to share experiences not only with Christ but also with one another. It is to have an identity that is always shaped and constituted in relation to others within the bond generated and sustained by the Spirit. It is to be constituted as interpersonal beings at the very foundation of our identity, always to be oneself-in-another, never oneself in isolation or autonomy." Susan G. Eastman, "Oneself in Another," in *"In Christ" in Paul: Explorations in Paul's Theology of Union and Participation*, ed. Michael J. Thate, Kevin J. Vanhoozer, and Constantine R. Campbell (Tübingen: Mohr Siebeck, 2014), 113.

78 Eastman, *Paul and the Person*, 147. In this discussion, it is important to note that participation should not lead to conflating divine and human identities. Constantine Campbell reminds his readers of the marriage metaphor that Paul uses, which "preserves the distinctive identities of Christ and church as husband and wife, avoiding unhelpful theories of union in which identities are blurred." Constantine R. Campbell, "Metaphor, Reality, and Union with Christ," in *"In Christ" in Paul: Explorations in Paul's Theology of Union and Participation*, ed. Michael J. Thate, Kevin J. Vanhoozer, and Constantine R. Campbell (Tübingen: Mohr Siebeck, 2014), 67. See also Campbell, *Paul and Union with Christ*.

79 Eastman, *Paul and the Person*, 155.

80 Eastman, *Paul and the Person*, 157.

81 Eastman, *Paul and the Person*, 158.

82 Eastman, *Paul and the Person*, 167.

83 Eastman, *Paul and the Person*, 159.

84 Eastman, *Paul and the Person*, 160. Elsewhere, Eastman makes a similar argument, commenting on Romans 8:17: "Those whom the Spirit joins together find themselves in a new network of saving relations that surpasses and cuts through the web of deception and destructive relationships woven by sin and its use of the law to deceive and kill (7:9)." Eastman, "Oneself in Another," 116.

85 Eastman, *Paul and the Person*, 160.

86 Eastman, *Paul and the Person*, 169.

87 Grant Macaskill, *Living in Union with Christ: Paul's Gospel and Christian Moral Identity* (Grand Rapids: Baker Academic, 2019), 87.

88 Eastman, *Paul and the Person*, 171–72; emphasis original.

89 Eastman, *Paul and the Person*, 172.

90. Eastman translates verse 6 as, "The mindset of the flesh is death, but the mindset of the Spirit is life and peace." Her translation highlights the "mindset." Eastman, "Oneself in Another," 120.
91. Eastman, "Oneself in Another," 120.
92. Eastman, "Oneself in Another," 112–13.
93. See Brock, *Wondrously Wounded*, 220–21.
94. Unity in Christ does not mean uniformity; diversity is still there and is to be celebrated as God-given. See Vanhoozer, "From 'Blessed in Christ' to 'Being in Christ,'" 20. On this point, Vanhoozer refers to Campbell, *Paul and Union with Christ*, 268–89; and Macaskill, *Union with Christ in the New Testament*, 147–59.
95. See, for example, Erin Raffety, "From Inclusion to Leadership: Disabled 'Misfitting' in Congregational Ministry," *Theology Today* 77, no. 2 (July 2020): 198–209, https://doi.org/10.1177/0040573620920698; John Swinton, *Becoming Friends of Time: Disability, Timefullness, and Gentle Discipleship* (Waco: Baylor University Press, 2016).

5 A TEMPLE COMMUNITY

1. Don E. Saliers, *Worship as Theology: Foretaste of Glory Divine* (Nashville: Abingdon, 1994), 27; emphasis original.
2. Saliers continues by saying, "Worship that focuses primarily on self-expression fails to be worship in Spirit and in truth." Saliers, *Worship as Theology*, 27.
3. Bowman, *On the Spectrum*, 109–10.
4. Bowman, *On the Spectrum*, 110.
5. Bowman, *On the Spectrum*, 111.
6. This often-cited phrase is from *Lumen Gentium*, 11 and refers particularly to the Eucharist.
7. Campbell, *Paul and Union with Christ*, 289–98; Macaskill, *Union with Christ in the New Testament*, 147–91. This section is largely based on Macaskill's work.
8. An exception is the theology of worship of the praise and worship movement in a particular branch of Pentecostalism. Based on the premise of Ps 22:3, that "Thou art holy, O thou that inhabitest the praises of Israel" (KJV), this movement developed an elaborate theology of praise and worship modeled after the Mosaic and Davidic tabernacles and the temple. The movement saw Ps 22:3 as God's promise that God would be present in the praise of the people. Lester Ruth and Swee-Hong Lim, *A History of Contemporary Praise & Worship: Understanding the Ideas That Reshaped the Protestant Church* (Grand Rapids: Baker Academic, 2021), 43–73. I will come back to the close association between divine presence and the temple below. Despite the fact that my take on this is different from the praise and worship movement, pointing out the emphasis on the temple/tabernacles in this branch of Christianity may invite further ecumenical dialogue on this imagery and theology.
9. Macaskill, *Union with Christ in the New Testament*, 147–91. Macaskill adds a fourth use of temple, which is more complex—that is, the church as the New Jerusalem in the book of Revelations, which is related to the heavenly sanctuary.
10. Macaskill, *Union with Christ in the New Testament*, 302–4.
11. Macaskill, *Union with Christ in the New Testament*, 191.
12. Macaskill, *Union with Christ in the New Testament*, 149–59.
13. Macaskill argues that this verse underlies the close connection between body and temple imagery in the New Testament. Macaskill, *Union with Christ in the New Testament*, 147–71.

14 It is beyond the scope of this book and my expertise to deal in any detail with these backgrounds. Grant Macaskill discusses these throughout his book.
15 Macaskill, *Union with Christ in the New Testament*, 161.
16 Saliers, *Worship as Theology*, 60–61.
17 Aidan Kavanagh, *On Liturgical Theology* (New York: Pueblo Publishing, 1984), 74–75. For further discussion, see, for example, Gordon W. Lathrop, *Holy Things: A Liturgical Theology* (Minneapolis: Fortress, 1993), 4–8; note that Lathrop adds "pastoral liturgical theology" as a third term. Bryan Cones, *This Assembly of Believers: The Gifts of Difference in the Church at Prayer* (London: SCM Press, 2020), 10–16.
18 Saliers, *Worship as Theology*, 86. See the adage by Evagrius of Pontus in his sixtieth chapter on prayer: "If you are a theologian, you will pray truly; and if you pray truly, you will be a theologian." Evagrius, *Evagrius of Pontus: The Greek Ascetic Corpus*, trans. Robert E. Sinkewicz (Oxford: Oxford University Press, 2003), 199. See also Louis Weil, who describes the assembled church in worship as engaged in a "theological act." Louis Weil, *A Theology of Worship* (Lanham, Md.: Cowley Publications, 2002), 25.
19 Weil, *Theology of Worship*, 35; see also 40.
20 Weil, *Theology of Worship*, 27.
21 Saliers, *Worship as Theology*, 86. At this point it is useful to refer to the liturgical theologian David Power, who has reflected extensively on kenosis. In the first chapter of his book, he briefly reviews how the "Christ hymn" (Phil 2:6–11) has surfaced explicitly and implicitly in historical liturgical texts and rituals. David Noel Power, *Love without Calculation: A Reflection on Divine Kenosis* (New York: Crossroad Publishing, 2005).
22 Saliers, *Worship as Theology*, 182.
23 See also Saliers, *Worship as Theology*, 182.
24 Saliers, *Worship as Theology*, 86.
25 During medieval times, the celebration of the mass had become defined by the actions of the priest. In combination with the mass being said in Latin, the laity was limited in their participation. Martin Luther's emphasis on the Word in the liturgy, including replacing daily masses with a service of the Word in the morning and evening, may have been a necessary correction to the liturgical celebrations of his time. However, in the contemporary liturgical landscape, a renewed emphasis on nonverbal, sensory participation may be a necessary corrective to modern hypercognitive liturgies. Approaching liturgy from the perspective of autism can be helpful in this regard. Bard Thompson, *Liturgies of the Western Church* (Cleveland: World Publishing, 1961), 98; Van Ommen and Unwin, "The Sensory Aspects of Worship and Liturgy as Experienced by Autistic People." I borrow the term "hypercognitive" from John Swinton, who refers to Stephen Post in turn: Swinton, *Becoming Friends of Time*, 12–13.
26 Gordon W. Lathrop, *The Assembly: A Spirituality* (Minneapolis: Fortress, 2022), 9.
27 Lathrop, *Assembly*, 9.
28 Note that leitourgia is often translated as "the work of the people." The translation "the work on behalf of the people" is closer to the original meaning of the term. For a discussion of the term as well as some other terms to describe what happens when Christians gather, see, for example, Benjamin Gordon-Taylor, "Liturgy," in *The Study of Liturgy and Worship: An Alcuin Guide*, ed. Juliette Day and Benjamin Gordon-Taylor (London: SPCK, 2013), 12–20; Gordon W. Lathrop, *Saving Images: The Presence of the Bible in Christian Liturgy* (Minneapolis: Fortress, 2017), 119–15; Lathrop, *Assembly*, 10–11; Saliers, *Worship as Theology*, 27–31; Saliers, "Toward a Spirituality of Inclusiveness"; Senn, *Embodied Liturgy*, 18–20.

29 Saliers, *Worship as Theology*, 87, quoting Geoffrey Wainwright.
30 By foregrounding gratitude, praise, and thanksgiving, Saliers by no means denies the place of lament and intercession in liturgy. On the contrary, he is one of the (few) liturgical theologians whose attention to the "human pathos," as he calls it, pervades his liturgical theology explicitly.
31 See also 1 John 4:19–20: "We love because he first loved us. Whoever claims to love God yet hates a brother or sister is a liar."
32 Saliers, *Worship as Theology*, 104.
33 Saliers, *Worship as Theology*, 111.
34 Saliers, *Worship as Theology*, 88; see also 174, 190.
35 Saliers, *Worship as Theology*, 116. As modes of prayer, Saliers identifies praise and thanksgiving, invoking and beseeching, lamenting, confessing, and interceding.
36 Walter M. Abbott, ed., "Constitution on the Sacred Liturgy—Sacrosanctum Concilium," in *The Documents of Vatican II* (London: Geoffrey Chapman, 1967), para. 14.
37 I have elaborated on this narrative approach to liturgy at length in A. L. van Ommen, *Suffering in Worship: Anglican Liturgy in Relation to Stories of Suffering People* (London: Routledge, 2017).
38 Saliers, *Worship as Theology*, 48.
39 The relationship between liturgy and ethics pervades the work of many liturgical theologians. Some more explicit examples are Stanley Hauerwas and Samuel Wells, eds., *The Blackwell Companion to Christian Ethics* (Malden, Mass.: Blackwell, 2004); Bruce T. Morrill, *Practical Sacramental Theology: At the Intersection of Liturgy and Ethics* (Eugene: Cascade Books, 2021); Pieter Vos, ed., *Liturgy and Ethics: New Contributions from Reformed Perspectives* (Leiden: Brill, 2018).
40 For example, Saliers, *Worship as Theology*, 171–90; see also E. Byron Anderson and Bruce T. Morrill, eds., *Liturgy and the Moral Self: Humanity at Full Stretch before God* (Collegeville, Minn.: Liturgical Press, 2002), which is a collection of essays in honor of Saliers and includes some of his own essays.
41 Charles Taylor, *A Secular Age* (Cambridge, Mass.: Belknap Press, 2007), 171–76. Taylor draws on his earlier discussion of this term in his *Modern Social Imagination* (Durham, N.C.: Duke University Press, 2004).
42 Taylor, *Secular Age*, 171.
43 Taylor, *Secular Age*, 175–76.
44 A point for further reflection but is beyond the scope of this book is, to what extent this part of Taylor's argument works for autistic people, who often say that they do not intuit (social) situations. Taylor gives exactly the same example of a social situation that is given as an example in autism studies of presenting a difficulty for autistic people. "At any given time, we can speak of the 'repertory' of collective actions at the disposal of a given group of society. These are the common actions which they know how to undertake, all the way from the general election, involving the whole society, to knowing how to strike up a polite but uninvolved conversation with a casual group in the reception hall. The discriminations we have to make to carry these off, knowing whom to speak to and when and how, carry an implicit 'map' of social space, of what kinds of people we can associate with in what ways in what circumstances. Perhaps I don't initiate the conversation at all, if the group are all socially superior to me, or outrank me in the bureaucracy, or consist entirely of women." Taylor, *Secular Age*, 173. One of my interviewees said that she struggled with social time after church exactly because she did not know how to start a conversation. Likewise, the social script of answering the "uninvolved" question of how you are doing eludes some autistic people, as Dan Bowman testifies in his memoir. Bowman, *On the Spectrum*, 109–10.

Again, it is beyond the scope of this book to analyze Taylor's argument along these lines. The point here is that societies are structured in this way, or at least the frameworks or majority paradigms that dominate society, as we saw in chapter 3. This is precisely what autistic people often run into and what can lead to the ignoring of their presence or even to their exclusion. However, more positively, it is important to be aware that frameworks or social imaginaries are formed in these implicit, embodied, and storied ways because liturgy can shape social imaginaries, as argued extensively by James K. A. Smith, *Desiring the Kingdom: Worship, Worldview, and Cultural Formation* (Grand Rapids: Baker Academic, 2009).

45 This example is adapted from an example Taylor gives, when he says that social imaginary compares to theory as growing up in a neighborhood (and therefore "understanding in practice" the neighborhood) to a map of that area. Taylor, *Secular Age*, 173; James Smith elaborates on this example in Smith, *Desiring the Kingdom*, 67.

46 Smith, *Desiring the Kingdom*, 65; emphases original.

47 Sarah Jean Barton, *Becoming the Baptized Body: Disability and the Practice of Christian Community* (Waco: Baylor University Press, 2022), 122.

48 Kimberly Hope Belcher, *Efficacious Engagement: Sacramental Participation in the Trinitarian Mystery* (Collegeville, Minn.: Liturgical Press, 2011), 27.

49 Belcher, *Efficacious Engagement*, 27. Interestingly, Belcher refers to exactly the passage that is central in the kenotic theology of availability that I started to outline in the previous chapter, Phil 2:12–13.

50 Belcher, *Efficacious Engagement*, 115.

51 Simon Chan, a Singaporean liturgical theologian, also describes liturgy in a spatial way, but instead of using the west-east symbolism, he speaks of ascending and descending. In the Eucharist, "we ascend the Mount of Transfiguration so that we may descend to face the painful reality of this world," and "the church feeds on Christ in order that it might be the extension of Christ to the world." Simon Chan, *Liturgical Theology: The Church as Worshiping Community* (Downers Grove, Ill.: IVP Academic, 2006), 146, 143, respectively; see also 145. Elsewhere in his book, Chan does comment on the baptismal symbolism of the candidates first turning to the west and then to the east. Chan connects this with the eschatological orientation of the liturgy (118, 188n69).

52 Macaskill, *Union with Christ in the New Testament*, 204, 207. For a discussion of sacraments specifically in relation to the debate of the "participation in Christ" language in the New Testament, see Mary Patton Baker, "Participation in the Body and Blood of Christ: Christian 'Koinonia' and the Lord's Supper," in *"In Christ" in Paul: Explorations in Paul's Theology of Union and Participation*, ed. Michael J. Thate, Kevin J. Vanhoozer, and Constantine R. Campbell (Tübingen: Mohr Siebeck, 2014), 503–28; Macaskill, *Union with Christ in the New Testament*, 192–218; Isaac Augustine Morales, "Baptism and Union with Christ," in *"In Christ" in Paul: Explorations in Paul's Theology of Union and Participation*, ed. Michael J. Thate, Kevin J. Vanhoozer, and Constantine R. Campbell (Tübingen: Mohr Siebeck, 2014), 157–79; see also Macaskill, *Living in Union with Christ*, 59–96.

53 Macaskill, *Union with Christ in the New Testament*, 197.

54 Macaskill, *Union with Christ in the New Testament*, 216–17.

55 Barton, *Becoming the Baptized Body*, 108.

56 Belcher, *Efficacious Engagement*, 1.

57 Belcher, *Efficacious Engagement*, 3.

58 We should add that Macaskill is adamant that the "sonship" of Jesus is ontologically different from that of the believers. Only Jesus is son of God (and fully human). As

adopted children of God, our identity is derivative of that of Jesus, and while we participate in the divine life, we do not become God. Macaskill, *Union with Christ in the New Testament*, 196–97. Throughout his study, Macaskill vocalizes this point strongly; Macaskill, *Living in Union with Christ*, 98–105.

59 Belcher, *Efficacious Engagement*, 129.
60 Belcher, *Efficacious Engagement*, 129.
61 This is reminiscent of Gabriel Marcel's statement that only Christ can rightfully say, "You belong to me." See previous chapter.
62 Belcher, *Efficacious Engagement*, 137.
63 Lathrop, *Assembly*, 61.
64 Because Belcher's arguments apply equally to both baptismal traditions, I will not explore further the differences between infant and adult/believers' baptism as that is outside of the scope of this book, although further discussions may be had.
65 Weil, *Theology of Worship*, 13.
66 Barton, *Becoming the Baptized Body*, 1; emphases original.
67 I add "presumed" here because some autistic people were believed to have profound learning disabilities, but when they learned to communicate (in this case, with augmentative or alternative communication [AAC] technology such as a spelling board), it turned out that they had no learning disabilities, but their inability to speak was related to different causes. See also, for example, Douglas Biklen et al., *Autism and the Myth of the Person Alone* (New York: New York University Press, 2005); Ido Kedar, *Ido in Autismland: Climbing out of Autism's Silent Prison* (N.p.: n.p., 2012).
68 Rebecca F. Spurrier, *The Disabled Church: Human Difference and the Art of Communal Worship* (New York: Fordham University Press, 2019), 16.
69 Spurrier aptly notes that "descriptions of Christian worship often assume an ideal worshiper, who is also an able-bodied, able-minded congregant capable of demonstrating that he is being shaped by God through the sacraments and Christian practices in a particular way." She continues by pointing out the danger of such an assumption: "If, as a liturgical theologian, I focus only on ideal individual capacities to perform and grasp Christian practices of prayer, interpretation of Scripture, and participation in communion, then I imply that certain people with disabilities lack the ability to be in relationship with God. Graver still, I imply that they lack the preferred abilities to participate in Christian worship in a way that reflects the depth of liturgy's symbolic meaning." This warning pertains to not only liturgical theologians but also worshipping communities at large, as it lays bare assumptions that pastors and congregations may unwittingly hold. Spurrier, *Disabled Church*, 16.
70 This is one of the reasons why Belcher's discussion of infant baptism has much to offer to disability theology. Throughout her book, she discusses at length the ways in which even infants of only a couple of weeks or months old engage with the ritual of baptism. By doing so, she offers a profound baptismal theology that does not depend on cognitive capacities.
71 Sarah Johnson discusses the problematic theological and pastoral implications of what she calls a covenantal approach to infant baptism and contrasts this with a kenotic approach. In a covenantal approach, access to baptism is gained through the faith of the parents or guardians, and clergy become gatekeepers. The context of Johnson's discussion is different to the one in this book in that she researches the problem that clergy face when someone who is at best loosely attached to the church asks for their child to be baptized. She argues that a kenotic approach is more appropriate. The "kenotic flow" of the Christian story is that God gives Godself in Christ, Christ gives himself in the church, the church gives itself in its liturgy, and liturgy pours itself out

in self-giving lives. The characteristic features of kenosis are "kenosis is a gift of self, into the other, without expectation of reward, and with the risk of loss." While in a covenantal approach, a "reward" or "return gift" is expected—for example, more participation in church life—a kenotic approach emphasizes the self-giving nature of God in the sacraments. Johnson rejects the notion of a return gift in the sense that Louis-Marie Chauvet speaks about it in his linguistically grounded model but says that a symbolic return gift is possible, which Johnson sees in the "interpretant" of the gift ("interpretant" seems to be a semiotic term of "interpretation" here; Johnson follows Graham Hughes' semiotic approach to worship at this point). The upshot of Johnson's article for our discussion here is, first, that clergy are not gatekeepers of the sacraments, which is an additional argument for not denying people the sacrament of baptism based on cognitive abilities (an argument that in some cases applies to autistic people). Second, Johnson strengthens and broadens our discussion of kenosis in relation to baptism by showing how the kenotic logic works in and through the sacraments. Johnson, "Poured Out," quotation on 186; the "kenotic flow" on 187; discussion of return gift and "interpretant" on 189–92.

72 For example, Rom 6:1–14, Rom 8:15, Gal 3:27, and 2 Cor 5:17. Macaskill, *Union with Christ in the New Testament*, 192–201; Saliers, *Worship as Theology*, 56–60; see also Lathrop, *Assembly*, 60–61.

73 Barton, *Becoming the Baptized Body*, 113. In a discussion that is very similar to ours in terms of normalcy, Amy Jacober redefines perfect in a way that echoes Barton's comments. Whereas Jacober's old definition of perfect requires people to "look like me, sound like me, think like me," in the new definition, not only those with disabilities know "in the depths of their being that they are valued but . . . the community that surrounds them knows this, too, and acts accordingly. *That* is perfect." Amy Jacober, *Redefining Perfect: The Interplay between Theology & Disability* (Eugene: Cascade Books, 2017), 103; emphasis original.

74 Barton, *Becoming the Baptized Body*, 114.

75 Barton, *Becoming the Baptized Body*, 114, quoting Rowan Williams.

76 Barton, *Becoming the Baptized Body*, 115.

77 Saliers, "Toward a Spirituality of Inclusiveness," 28; Saliers' phrase "humanity at full stretch" is often quoted in liturgical studies.

78 Barton, *Becoming the Baptized Body*, 108.

79 Macaskill, *Union with Christ in the New Testament*, 307.

80 I am grateful to Kim Belcher and Marie-Claire Klassen for pointing out the problematic use of "purity" and for helping me to think through not only the objections but also the ways in which we may reclaim this term.

81 Katie Cross, "'I Have the Power in My Body to Make People Sin': The Trauma of Purity Culture and the Concept of 'Body Theodicy,'" in *Feminist Trauma Theologies: Body, Scripture & Church in Critical Perspective*, ed. Karen O'Donnell and Katie Cross (London: SCM Press, 2020), 21–39.

82 See also Lathrop, *Assembly*, 112–13. "The ecclesiology of the Lord's Prayer is this: This assembly stands with the world, praying for the needy, knowing itself to be needy. It does not distinguish itself from the world. Rather, identifies with the world and does so especially in its longing and urgent prayer."

83 Barton, *Becoming the Baptized Body*, 116–17.

84 Barton, *Becoming the Baptized Body*, 164.

85 Swinton, *Becoming Friends of Time*, 208; quoted in Barton, *Becoming the Baptized Body*, 169.

86 Morrill, *Practical Sacramental Theology*, 107; the reference is to Irénée Henri Dalmais, Pierre Marie Gy, and Pierre Jounel, *The Church at Prayer: An Introduction to the Liturgy*, vol. 1, *Principles of the Liturgy*, new ed., ed. Aimé Georges Martimort (Collegeville, Minn.: Liturgical Press, 1987), 266.
87 Morrill, *Practical Sacramental Theology*, 108.
88 Martha L Moore-Keish, "Eucharist: The Table That Unites and Divides the Church," in *What Does It Mean to "Do This"? Supper, Mass, Eucharist*, ed. Michael Root and James J. Buckley (Eugene: Cascade Books, 2014), 89, 98. For the term "ec-centric," Moore-Keish refers to the work of David Kelsey.
89 Weil, *Theology of Worship*, 9.
90 Weil, *Theology of Worship*, 19–20; emphases original.
91 The phrase "process of socialization" is from Weil, *A Theology of Worship*, 9.
92 Morrill, *Practical Sacramental Theology*, 110.
93 As noted in the previous chapter, this is not to say that availability should be at the expense of self-care and self-protection.
94 Macaskill, *Union with Christ in the New Testament*, 208–9.
95 Macaskill, *Living in Union with Christ*, 87.
96 Moore-Keish, "Eucharist," 92.
97 Moore-Keish, "Eucharist," 92.
98 Morrill, *Practical Sacramental Theology*, 114.
99 Morrill, *Practical Sacramental Theology*, 116.
100 Note the powerful argument along these lines, although not specifically focusing on autism, in Erin Raffety, *From Inclusion to Justice: Disability, Ministry, and Congregational Leadership* (Waco: Baylor University Press, 2022). See also the discussion on reconciliation in the introduction to the present book.
101 See, for example, Williams, *Peculiar Discipleship*.
102 Morrill, *Practical Sacramental Theology*, 116.
103 See Raffety's comments on the fact that many disabled people find themselves at the outskirts of the temple but also the possible need for separate communities as testified by disabled people themselves. Raffety, *From Inclusion to Justice*, 125–28.

6 AVAILABILITY IN PRACTICE

1 For a much briefer description but in the words of two of the leading founders of the chapel, see David Teo and Keng Hong Leong, "Chapel of Christ Our Hope," in *Enabling Hearts: A Primer for Disability-Inclusive Churches*, ed. Wen Pin Leow (Singapore: Koinonia Inclusion Network, 2021), 158–63; see also my reflections on church in "Re-imagining Church through Autism."
2 Melanie Yergeau rightly protests that autistic people are often defined by what they cannot do, in contrast to what society values. I am aware that this description can be read as perpetuating that negative way of framing autism. That is why I add "whose way of being in the world would not be much valued" to help us think more positively about autism. The description here is meant to highlight why, in the Singaporean culture, it is not self-evident that the president and bishop would have such a conversation and concern for autistic people. Yergeau reminds us that we need to protest the fact that this is remarkable. One may say that the conversation of these two people, which led to the founding of St. Andrew's Autism Centre, is a positive move in itself and perhaps, in a way, part of the protest. Melanie Yergeau, *Authoring Autism: On Rhetoric and Neurological Queerness* (Durham, N.C.: Duke University Press, 2018), 2.

3 St. Andrew's Autism Centre includes two schools (at the time of my visit, only one) and, for adults, day centers and a residential facility. https://www.saac.org.sg/.
4 To some, it may sound "un-Anglican" to use the word "pastor." However, this is the preferred terminology used in the chapel.
5 At that point, there were no parents of autistic people in the group. When the group started to meet once a week for preparation and training, two parents came along a few times to give input.
6 Interview with Pastor David, June 16, 2019.
7 Ronald L. Grimes, *The Craft of Ritual Studies* (Oxford: Oxford University Press, 2014), 235. Grimes spends a long chapter on explaining these elements and suggesting numerous questions to ask with each element. I have replaced his "rituals" in the center of the figure with "worship service."
8 I do not claim to offer a neutral or objective description, as descriptions are always influenced by the one describing. Moreover, any description comes from a particular angle and interest. Here, that angle is autism and my interest is in seeing what it means for a worship service to be thought through from a desire for autistic people to truly belong as valued participants in the liturgy.
9 Van Ommen, *Suffering in Worship*, chap. 2.
10 Sarah H. Baum, Ryan A. Stevenson, and Mark T. Wallace, "Behavioral, Perceptual, and Neural Alterations in Sensory and Multisensory Function in Autism Spectrum Disorder," *Progress in Neurobiology* 134 (November 2015): 140–60, https://doi.org/10.1016/j.pneurobio.2015.09.007. For an exploration of autistic sensory perception in worship, see also Van Ommen and Unwin, "Sensory Aspects of Worship and Liturgy as Experienced by Autistic People."
11 The importance of the sensory aspect of liturgy is recognized by liturgical theologians; see, for example, Belcher, *Efficacious Engagement*; Saliers, *Worship as Theology*, 154–70; Senn, *Embodied Liturgy*.
12 We encountered olfaction as a significant sense at several points in the previous chapter. One more vivid description might be helpful: "For the person who finds smells difficult . . . the sanctuary becomes a torture chamber: perfume, cologne, deodorant, hand soap, hair product. It is not simply that these things smell strongly: they smell *painfully*. The smell like a screwdriver being stabbed into the eyes, or the brain being pulled apart." Macaskill, *Autism and the Church*, 28; emphasis original.
13 Grimes, *Craft of Ritual Studies*, 249.
14 For a more elaborate reflection on this point, see Van Ommen, "Re-imagining Church through Autism," 512–14.
15 An exception is the fifth Sunday in a month, when Rainbow of Hope is more actively involved throughout the service and does not leave for their own gathering. From the interviews, it became clear that this is a recent development for which the structure and way of doing it is not yet firmly developed. As such, it is not possible to say much about those Sundays in terms of describing the services. A difference between the chapel pre– and post–COVID-19 is that post–COVID-19, the Eucharist is celebrated every week, whereas before, that happened only once a month. The description in this chapter is based on a service without the Eucharist. It is worth noting that in my interviews with the five autistic people, in May 2022, several of these interviewees had taken pictures of and commented on the celebration of Holy Communion (the term used in the chapel most often).
16 Morning prayer is one of the liturgies in Anglican churches for which the structure and words are printed in a liturgical book and which is authorized by the bishops and is used throughout the diocese.

17 For some, this may have to do with other conditions, such as ADHD.
18 For a similar discussion about having separate worship services for disabled people, see Raffety, *From Inclusion to Justice*, 125–28.
19 In addition, some of these interviewees had taken pictures of lunch in the canteen. Also, lunch was clearly appreciated by some (although here, we cannot infer anything about the value of having separate times from their families).
20 On liturgical language, see Juliette J. Day, *Reading the Liturgy: An Exploration of Texts in Christian Worship* (London: Bloomsbury, 2014), esp. chap. 6.
21 We may make a critical comment here, respectfully, which is that autistic people themselves were not involved in these early stages of the chapel. This remains a point that the chapel may need to be more intentional about. I offered this point of reflection during a workshop with some of the leaders during which I presented my research findings, and at least one leader confirmed this point. See also Van Ommen, "Reimagining Church through Autism."
22 That does not mean that John sees no room for improvement and the need to continually learn—one of his desires is to involve all members in different roles even more.
23 Weil, *Theology of Worship*, 13.
24 Saliers, *Worship as Theology*, 86.
25 Saliers, *Worship as Theology*, 86.
26 For the distinction between inclusion and belonging and the necessity to go beyond inclusion, see John Swinton, "From Inclusion to Belonging: A Practical Theology of Community, Disability and Humanness," *Journal of Religion, Disability & Health* 16, no. 2 (2012): 172–90.

CONCLUSION

1 This is not to deny that parents, caregivers, and physicians often have had the best intentions for autistic people. I refer here to some of the earliest history of autism research, with its uncomfortable ties to the eugenics movement and the Nazi regime, as described in chapter 2.
2 Communities need to walk the fine line between guarding the necessary safety of their members and fearfully remaining in the comfort zone of the framework.
3 As a non-autistic person, I am not pretending to perceive exactly the same as autistic people. However, if non-autistic people listen carefully, as I have tried to do in this study, they can try and change their perspective, which enables them to see dynamics that they would not see otherwise.
4 Saliers, *Worship as Theology*, 27; emphasis original.
5 Saliers, *Worship as Theology*, 86.
6 See chapter 5; Bowman, *On the Spectrum*, 111.
7 See chapter 1, section "Autistic Experiences of Worship"; Bale, "17 Ways to Make Your Church Autism-Friendly"; Bowman, *On the Spectrum*; Spoor, *Spirituality on the Spectrum*.
8 In the literature overview in chapter 1, I have mentioned a few practical guides for churches. These include Arnold, *How to Include Autistic Children and Young People in Church*; Bedard, *How to Make Your Church Autism-Friendly*; Memmott, "Welcoming Autistic People"; Newman, *Autism and Your Church*; Spoor, *Spirituality on the Spectrum*.

Bibliography

Abbott, Walter M., ed. "Constitution on the Sacred Liturgy—Sacrosanctum Concilium." In *The Documents of Vatican II*, 137–78. London: Geoffrey Chapman, 1967.
Anderson, E. Byron, and Bruce T. Morrill, eds. *Liturgy and the Moral Self: Humanity at Full Stretch before God*. Collegeville, Minn.: Liturgical Press, 2002.
Arnold, Mark. *How to Include Autistic Children and Young People in Church: Creating a Place of Belonging and Spiritual Development for All*. Cambridge: Grove Books, 2022.
Asperger, Hans. "'Autistic Psychopathy' in Childhood." In *Autism and Asperger Syndrome*, edited by Uta Frith, 37–92. Cambridge: Cambridge University Press, 1944.
———. "Die 'autistischen Psychopathen' im Kindesalter." *Archiv für Psychiatrie und Nervenkrankheiten* 117, no. 1 (June 1944): 76–136. https://doi.org/10.1007/BF01837709.
Ault, Melinda Jones, Belva C. Collins, and Erik W. Carter. "Congregational Participation and Supports for Children and Adults with Disabilities: Parent Perceptions." *Intellectual and Developmental Disabilities* 51, no. 1 (2013): 48–61.
Baker, Mary Patton. "Participation in the Body and Blood of Christ: Christian 'Koinonia' and the Lord's Supper." In *"In Christ" in Paul: Explorations in Paul's Theology of Union and Participation*, edited by Michael J. Thate, Kevin J. Vanhoozer, and Constantine R. Campbell, 503–28. Tübingen: Mohr Siebeck, 2014.
Bale, Katherine. "17 Ways to Make Your Church Autism-Friendly." *Premier Christianity* (blog), April 28, 2017. https://www.premierchristianity.com/Blog/17-ways-to-make-your-church-autism-friendly.
Barber, Christopher. "On Connectedness: Spirituality on the Autistic Spectrum." *Practical Theology* 4, no. 2 (August 2011): 201–11. https://doi.org/10.1558/prth.v4i2.201.
Barclay, John M. G. "Kenosis and the Drama of Salvation in Philippians 2." In *Kenosis: The Self-Emptying of Christ in Scripture and Theology*, edited by Paul T. Nimmo and Keith L. Johnson, 7–23. Grand Rapids: Eerdmans, 2022.
Baron-Cohen, Simon. "The Truth about Hans Asperger's Nazi Collusion." *Nature* 557, no. 7705 (May 2018): 305–6. https://doi.org/10.1038/d41586-018-05112-1.
Barton, Sarah Jean. *Becoming the Baptized Body: Disability and the Practice of Christian Community*. Waco: Baylor University Press, 2022.

Bascom, Julia, ed. *Loud Hands: Autistic People, Speaking*. Washington, DC: Autistic Press, 2012.

Baum, Sarah H., Ryan A. Stevenson, and Mark T. Wallace. "Behavioral, Perceptual, and Neural Alterations in Sensory and Multisensory Function in Autism Spectrum Disorder." *Progress in Neurobiology* 134 (November 2015): 140–60. https://doi.org/10.1016/j.pneurobio.2015.09.007.

Bedard, Stephen J. *How to Make Your Church Autism-Friendly*. 2nd ed. St. Catharines, Ont.: Hope's Reason, 2017.

Belcher, Kimberly Hope. *Efficacious Engagement: Sacramental Participation in the Trinitarian Mystery*. Collegeville, Minn.: Liturgical Press, 2011.

Bettelheim, Bruno. *The Empty Fortress: Infantile Autism and the Birth of the Self*. New York: Free Press/Macmillan, 1967.

Biklen, Douglas, Richard Attfield, Larry Bissonnette, Lucy Blackman, Jamie Burke, Alberto Frugone, Tito Rajarshi Mukhopadhyay, and Sue Rubin. *Autism and the Myth of the Person Alone*. New York: New York University Press, 2005.

Blume, Harvey. "Neurodiversity: On the Neurological Underpinnings of Geekdom." *The Atlantic*, September 1998. https://www.theatlantic.com/magazine/archive/1998/09/neurodiversity/305909/.

Bogdashina, Olga. *Autism and Spirituality: Psyche, Self and Spirit in People on the Autism Spectrum*. London: Jessica Kingsley, 2013.

Bonhoeffer, Dietrich. *Life Together*. Translated by John W. Doberstein. London: SCM Press, 1954.

Botha, Monique, Jacqueline Hanlon, and Gemma Louise Williams. "Does Language Matter? Identity-First versus Person-First Language Use in Autism Research: A Response to Vivanti." *Journal of Autism and Developmental Disorders* (2021). https://doi.org/10.1007/s10803-020-04858-w.

Bottema-Beutel, Kristen, Steven K. Kapp, Jessica Nina Lester, Noah J. Sasson, and Brittany N. Hand. "Avoiding Ableist Language: Suggestions for Autism Researchers." *Autism in Adulthood* 3, no. 1 (March 2021): 18–29. https://doi.org/10.1089/aut.2020.0014.

Boucher, Jill. *Autism Spectrum Disorder: Characteristics, Causes and Practical Issues*. 2nd ed. Los Angeles: Sage, 2017.

Bowman, Daniel, Jr. *On the Spectrum: Autism, Faith, & the Gifts of Neurodiversity*. Grand Rapids: Brazos Press, 2021.

Brock, Brian. "Theologizing Inclusion: 1 Corinthians 12 and the Politics of the Body of Christ." *Journal of Religion, Disability & Health* 15, no. 4 (October 2011): 351–76. https://doi.org/10.1080/15228967.2011.620389.

———. *Wondrously Wounded: Theology, Disability, and the Body of Christ*. Waco: Baylor University Press, 2019.

Brock, Brian, and Bernd Wannenwetsch. *A Theological Exposition of Paul's First Letter to the Corinthians. Volume 2: Therapy of the Christian Body*. Eugene: Cascade Books, 2018.

Buber, Martin. *I and Thou*. Translated by Ronald Gregor Smith. Edinburgh: T & T Clark, n.d.

Bustion, Olivia. "Autism and Christianity: An Ethnographic Intervention." *Journal of the American Academy of Religion* 85, no. 3 (2017): 653–81.

Buunk, Abraham P., Gert Stulp, and Wilmar B. Schaufeli. "Effect of Self-Reported Height on Occupational Rank among Police Officers: Especially for Women It Pays to Be Tall." *Evolutionary Psychological Science* 7, no. 4 (December 2021): 411–18. https://doi.org/10.1007/s40806-021-00281-1.

Campbell, Constantine R. "Metaphor, Reality, and Union with Christ." In *"In Christ" in Paul: Explorations in Paul's Theology of Union and Participation*, edited by Michael J.

Thate, Kevin J. Vanhoozer, and Constantine R. Campbell, 61–86. Tübingen: Mohr Siebeck, 2014.

———. *Paul and Union with Christ: An Exegetical and Theological Study*. Grand Rapids: Zondervan, 2012.

Campbell, Douglas A. "Participation and Faith in Paul." In *"In Christ" in Paul: Explorations in Paul's Theology of Union and Participation*, edited by Michael J. Thate, Kevin J. Vanhoozer, and Constantine R. Campbell, 37–60. Tübingen: Mohr Siebeck, 2014.

Campbell, Eilidh. *Motherhood and Autism: An Embodied Theology of Motherhood and Disability*. London: SCM Press, 2021.

Carter, Erik W. *Including People with Disabilities in Faith Communities: A Guide for Service Providers, Families, & Congregations*. Baltimore: Brookes, 2007.

———. "Research on Disability and Congregational Inclusion: What We Know and Where We Might Go." *Journal of Disability & Religion*, February 8, 2022, 1–31. https://doi.org/10.1080/23312521.2022.2035297.

Chan, Simon. *Liturgical Theology: The Church as Worshiping Community*. Downers Grove, Ill.: IVP Academic, 2006.

Chown, Nick, and Liz Hughes. "History and First Descriptions of Autism: Asperger versus Kanner Revisited." *Journal of Autism and Developmental Disorders* 46, no. 6 (June 2016): 2270–72. https://doi.org/10.1007/s10803-016-2746-0.

Cones, Bryan. *This Assembly of Believers: The Gifts of Difference in the Church at Prayer*. London: SCM Press, 2020.

Cook, Julia, Laura Hull, Laura Crane, and William Mandy. "Camouflaging in Autism: A Systematic Review." *Clinical Psychology Review* 89 (November 2021): 102080. https://doi.org/10.1016/j.cpr.2021.102080.

Cox, Jennifer Anne. *Autism, Humanity and Personhood: A Christ-Centred Theological Anthropology*. Newcastle upon Tyne: Cambridge Scholars Publishing, 2017.

Crawford Sullivan, Susan, and Victoria Aramini. "Religion and Positive Youth Development: Challenges for Children and Youth with Autism Spectrum Disorder." *Religions* 10, no. 10 (2019): 540. https://doi.org/10.3390/rel10100540.

Creamer, Deborah Beth. *Disability and Christian Theology: Embodied Limits and Constructive Possibilities*. Oxford: Oxford University Press, 2009.

Cross, Katie. "'I Have the Power in My Body to Make People Sin': The Trauma of Purity Culture and the Concept of 'Body Theodicy.'" In *Feminist Trauma Theologies: Body, Scripture & Church in Critical Perspective*, edited by Karen O'Donnell and Katie Cross, 21–39. London: SCM Press, 2020.

Czech, Herwig. "Hans Asperger, National Socialism, and 'Race Hygiene' in Nazi-Era Vienna." *Molecular Autism* 9, no. 1 (December 2018): 29. https://doi.org/10.1186/s13229-018-0208-6.

Dalmais, Irénée Henri, Pierre Marie Gy, and Pierre Jounel. *The Church at Prayer: An Introduction to the Liturgy*. Vol. 1 *Principles of the Liturgy*. New ed. Edited by Aimé Georges Martimort. Collegeville, Minn.: Liturgical Press, 1987.

Davis, Lennard J. *Enforcing Normalcy: Disability, Deafness and the Body*. London: Verso, 1995.

Day, Juliette J. *Reading the Liturgy: An Exploration of Texts in Christian Worship*. London: Bloomsbury, 2014.

Donvan, John, and Caren Zucker. *In a Different Key: The Story of Autism*. London: Allen Lane, 2016.

Dunn, Dana S., and Erin E. Andrews. "Person-First and Identity-First Language: Developing Psychologists' Cultural Competence Using Disability Language." *American Psychologist* 70, no. 3 (2015): 255–64. https://doi.org/10.1037/a0038636.

Dunster, Ruth M. *The Autism of Gxd: An Atheological Love Story*. Eugene: Pickwick Publications, 2022.

Eastman, Susan. "Double Participation and the Responsible Self in Romans 5–8." In *Apocalyptic Paul: Cosmos and Anthropos in Romans 5–8*, edited by Beverly Roberts Gaventa, 93–110. Waco: Baylor University Press, 2013.

Eastman, Susan G. "Oneself in Another." In *"In Christ" in Paul: Explorations in Paul's Theology of Union and Participation*, edited by Michael J. Thate, Kevin J. Vanhoozer, and Constantine R. Campbell, 103–25. Tübingen: Mohr Siebeck, 2014.

Eastman, Susan Grove. *Paul and the Person: Reframing Paul's Anthropology*. Grand Rapids: Eerdmans, 2017.

Evagrius. *Evagrius of Pontus: The Greek Ascetic Corpus*. Translated by Robert E. Sinkewicz. Oxford: Oxford University Press, 2003.

Evans, Bonnie. *The Metamorphosis of Autism: A History of Child Development in Britain*. Manchester: Manchester University Press, 2017.

Falk, Dean. "More on Asperger's Career: A Reply to Czech." *Journal of Autism and Developmental Disorders* 49, no. 9 (September 2019): 3877–82. https://doi.org/10.1007/s10803-019-04099-6.

Fletcher-Watson, Sue, and Francesca Happé. *Autism: A New Introduction to Psychological Theory and Current Debate*. London: Routledge, 2019.

Frith, Uta, ed. *Autism and Asperger Syndrome*. Cambridge: Cambridge University Press, 1991.

Giles, David C. "'DSM-V Is Taking Away Our Identity': The Reaction of the Online Community to the Proposed Changes in the Diagnosis of Asperger's Disorder." *Health* 18, no. 2 (2014): 179–95.

Gillibrand, John. *Disabled Church—Disabled Society: The Implications of Autism for Philosophy, Theology and Politics*. London: Jessica Kingsley, 2010.

Goddard, H. H. *The Kallikak Family: A Study in the Heredity of Feeble-Mindedness*. New York: Macmillan, 1912.

Gordon-Taylor, Benjamin. "Liturgy." In *The Study of Liturgy and Worship: An Alcuin Guide*, edited by Juliette Day and Benjamin Gordon-Taylor, 12–20. London: SPCK, 2013.

Goto, Courtney. *Taking on Practical Theology: The Idolization of Context and the Hope of Community*. Leiden: Brill, 2018.

Gould, S. J. *The Mismeasure of Man*. New York: Norton, 1996.

Graham, Elaine. "Words Made Flesh: Women, Embodiment and Practical Theology." *Feminist Theology* 7, no. 21 (May 1999): 109–21. https://doi.org/10.1177/096673509900002108.

Grandin, Temple. *Emergence: Labeled Autistic*. Novato: Arena Press, 1986.

———. *Thinking in Pictures: And Other Reports from My Life with Autism*. New York: Doubleday Books, 1995.

Grimes, Ronald L. *The Craft of Ritual Studies*. Oxford: Oxford University Press, 2014.

Hacking, Ian. "Kinds of People: Moving Targets," *Proceedings of the British Academy* 151 (2007): 285–318.

———. "Making Up People." In *Reconstructing Individualism: Autonomy, Individuality, and the Self in Western Thought*, edited by Thomas C. Heller, Morton Sosna, and David E. Wellbery, 222–36. Stanford: Stanford University Press, 1986.

Hardwick, Lamar. *Disability and the Church: A Vision for Diversity and Inclusion*. Downers Grove, Ill.: InterVarsity Press, 2021.

———. *I Am Strong: The Life and Journey of an Autistic Pastor*. Little Elm, Tex.: eLectio Publishing, 2017.
Hauerwas, Stanley. "Chapter 2. Community and Diversity: The Tyranny of Normality." *Journal of Religion, Disability & Health* 8, no. 3–4 (February 24, 2005): 37–43. https://doi.org/10.1300/J095v08n03_05.
———. "Community and Diversity: The Tyranny of Normality." *National Apostolate for the Mentally Retarded* 8, no. 1–2 (1977): 20–23.
Hauerwas, Stanley, and Samuel Wells, eds. *The Blackwell Companion to Christian Ethics*. Malden, Mass.: Blackwell, 2004.
Hess, K., and C. Brown. "Leitourgeō." In *New International Dictionary of New Testament Theology*, 3:551–53. Carlisle, UK: Paternoster Press, 1992.
Horvat, Tanja, and Saša Horvat. *Autism and Religious Experience: Theory and Practice—Workshop Proceedings*. Rijeka, Croatia: Centre for Autism Rijeka, 2022.
Isanon, Abe. *Spirituality and the Autism Spectrum: Of Falling Sparrows*. London: Jessica Kingsley, 2001.
Jacober, Amy. *Redefining Perfect: The Interplay between Theology & Disability*. Eugene: Cascade Books, 2017.
Johnson, Sarah Kathleen. "Poured Out: A Kenotic Approach to Initiating Children at a Distance from the Church." *Studia Liturgica* 49, no. 2 (September 2019): 175–94. https://doi.org/10.1177/0039320719866302.
Jurgens, Alan. "Neurodiversity in a Neurotypical World: An Enactive Framework for Investigating Autism and Social Institutions." In *Neurodiversity Studies: A New Critical Paradigm*, edited by Hanna Bertilsdotter Rosqvist, Nick Chown, and Anna Stenning, 73–88. London: Routledge, 2020.
Kanner, Leo. "Problems of Nosology and Psychodynamics of Early Infantile Autism." *American Journal of Orthopsychiatry* 19, no. 3 (July 1949): 416–26. https://doi.org/10.1111/j.1939-0025.1949.tb05441.x.
Kaufman, Joanne. "Campaign on Childhood Mental Illness Succeeds at Being Provocative." *New York Times*, December 14, 2007. https://www.nytimes.com/2007/12/14/business/media/14adco.html. Accessed June 6, 2023.
Kavanagh, Aidan. *On Liturgical Theology*. New York: Pueblo Publishing, 1984.
Kedar, Ido. *Ido in Autismland: Climbing out of Autism's Silent Prison*. N.p.: n.p., 2012.
Kenny, Lorcan, Caroline Hattersley, Bonnie Molins, Carole Buckley, Carol Povey, and Elizabeth Pellicano. "Which Terms Should Be Used to Describe Autism? Perspectives from the UK Autism Community." *Autism* 20, no. 4 (May 2016): 442–62. https://doi.org/10.1177/1362361315588200.
Kinard, Summer. *Of Such Is the Kingdom: A Practical Theology of Disability*. Chesterton: Ancient Faith Publishing, 2019.
Klar-Wolfond, Estée, and Wendy Lawson. "The Mismeasure of Autism: The Basis for Current 'Autism Advocacy.'" In *Concepts of Normality: The Autistic and Typical Spectrum*, 104–29. London: Jessica Kingsley, 2008.
Kras, Joseph F. "The 'Ransom Notes' Affair: When the Neurodiversity Movement Came of Age." *Disability Studies Quarterly* 30, no. 10 (2010). https://dsq-sds.org/article/%C2%A0view/1065/1254#top.
Lathrop, Gordon W. *The Assembly: A Spirituality*. Minneapolis: Fortress, 2022.
———. *Holy Things: A Liturgical Theology*. Minneapolis: Fortress, 1993.
———. *Saving Images: The Presence of the Bible in Christian Liturgy*. Minneapolis: Fortress, 2017.

Lawson, Wendy. *Concepts of Normality: The Autistic and Typical Spectrum*. London: Jessica Kingsley, 2008.
Lee, Li-Ching, Rebecca A. Harrington, Brian B. Louie, and Craig J. Newschaffer. "Children with Autism: Quality of Life and Parental Concerns." *Journal of Autism and Developmental Disorders* 38, no. 6 (July 2008): 1147–60. https://doi.org/10.1007/s10803-007-0491-0.
Leidenhag, Joanna. "The Challenge of Autism for Relational Approaches to Theological Anthropology." *International Journal of Systematic Theology* 23, no. 1 (January 2021): 109–34. https://doi.org/10.1111/ijst.12453.
Linton, Kristen Faye, Taylor E. Krcek, Leonard M. Sensui, and Jessica L. H. Spillers. "Opinions of People Who Self-Identify with Autism and Asperger's on *DSM-5* Criteria." *Research on Social Work Practice* 24, no. 1 (January 2014): 67–77. https://doi.org/10.1177/1049731513495457.
Macaskill, Grant. *Autism and the Bible: Beginning a Conversation*. Christ's College Lectures, 2017. https://www.youtube.com/watch?v=qvd_pUvFB-0.
———. *Autism and the Church: Bible, Theology, and Community*. Waco: Baylor University Press, 2019.
———. "Autism Spectrum Disorders and the New Testament: Preliminary Reflections." *Journal of Disability & Religion* 22, no. 1 (January 2, 2018): 15–41. https://doi.org/10.1080/23312521.2017.1373613.
———. "The Bible, Autism and Other Profound Developmental Conditions: Regulating Hermeneutics." *Journal of Disability & Religion*, February 8, 2021, 1–25. https://doi.org/10.1080/23312521.2021.1881024.
———. *Living in Union with Christ: Paul's Gospel and Christian Moral Identity*. Grand Rapids: Baker Academic, 2019.
———. *Union with Christ in the New Testament*. Oxford: Oxford University Press, 2013.
Marcel, Gabriel. *Being and Having*. Translated by Katharine Farrer. London: Dacre Press, 1949.
———. *Creative Fidelity*. Translated by R. Rosthal. New York: Noonday Press, 1964.
———. *The Mystery of Being: Reflection and Mystery*. Vol. 1. Translated by G. S. Fraser. Chicago: Henry Regnery, 1950.
———. "On the Ontological Mystery." In *The Philosophy of Existence*, translated by Manya Harari, 5–46. Providence: Cluny, 2018.
Matthews, Pia. "Complementary Understandings of Availability: Jean Vanier in Conversation with the Philosophers Emmanuel Levinas and Gabriel Marcel." *Journal of Disability & Religion* 24, no. 2 (2020): 174–205. https://doi.org/10.1080/23312521.2020.1718576.
McCormack, Bruce Lindley. *The Humility of the Eternal Son: Reformed Kenoticism and the Repair of Chalcedon*. Cambridge: Cambridge University Press, 2021.
Memmott, Ann. "Welcoming and Including Autistic People in Our Churches and Communities." Diocese of Oxford, 2021. https://www.oxford.anglican.org/autism.
Milton, Damian. "The Double Empathy Problem." 2018. https://www.autism.org.uk/advice-and-guidance/professional-practice/double-empathy.
———. "Embodied Sociality and the Conditioned Relativism of Dispositional Diversity." *Autonomy* 1, no. 3 (2014): 1–7.
———. "'Filling in the Gaps': A Micro-sociological Analysis of Autism." *Autonomy, the Critical Journal of Interdisciplinary Autism Studies* 1, no. 2 (2013). http://kar.kent.ac.uk/62634/.
Milton, Damian E. M. "On the Ontological Status of Autism: The 'Double Empathy Problem.'" *Disability & Society* 27, no. 6 (October 2012): 883–87. https://doi.org/10.1080/09687599.2012.710008.

Moore-Keish, Martha L. "Eucharist: The Table That Unites and Divides the Church." In *What Does It Mean to "Do This"? Supper, Mass, Eucharist*, edited by Michael Root and James J. Buckley, 88–103. Eugene: Cascade Books, 2014.

Morales, Isaac Augustine. "Baptism and Union with Christ." In *"In Christ" in Paul: Explorations in Paul's Theology of Union and Participation*, edited by Michael J. Thate, Kevin J. Vanhoozer, and Constantine R. Campbell, 157–79. Tübingen: Mohr Siebeck, 2014.

Morgan, Teresa. *Being "in Christ" in the Letters of Paul: Saved through Christ and in His Hands*. Tübingen: Mohr Siebeck, 2020.

Morrill, Bruce T. *Practical Sacramental Theology: At the Intersection of Liturgy and Ethics*. Eugene: Cascade Books, 2021.

Murray, Stuart. *Representing Autism: Culture, Narrative, Fascination*. Liverpool: Liverpool University Press, 2008.

Newman, Barbara J. *Autism and Your Church*. Rev., upd. ed. Grand Rapids: Faith Alive, 2011.

Nimmo, Paul T., and Keith L. Johnson, eds. *Kenosis: The Self-Emptying of Christ in Scripture and Theology*. Grand Rapids: Eerdmans, 2022.

"Opening the Doors: Ministry with People with Learning Disabilities and People on the Autistic Spectrum." Church of England, 2009.

Pang, Camilla. *Explaining Humans: What Science Can Teach Us about Life, Love and Relationships*. London: Penguin, 2021.

"Pastors' Views on Caring for People with Disabilities: Survey of American Protestant Pastors." LifeWay Research, 2019. http://research.lifeway.com/wp-content/uploads/2020/03/Report-Pastors-Disabilities-Sept-2019.pdf.

Pembroke, Neil. *The Art of Listening: Dialogue, Shame, and Pastoral Care*. London: T & T Clark, 2002.

People First of West Virginia. Accessed June 6, 2023. http://peoplefirstwv.org/old-front/history-of-people-first/.

Phillips, Chloe. "Elgar, Sybil Lillian." In *Oxford Dictionary of National Biography*, edited by Lawrence Goldman, 343–45. Oxford: Oxford University Press, 2013.

Power, David Noel. *Love without Calculation: A Reflection on Divine Kenosis*. New York: Crossroad Publishing, 2005.

"Protestant Churchgoer Views on Attendees with a Disability: Survey of American Protestant Churchgoers." LifeWay Research, 2019. http://research.lifeway.com/wp-content/uploads/2020/03/Churchgoers-Disabilities-Sept-2019.pdf.

Raffety, Erin. "From Depression and Decline to Repentance and Transformation: Receiving Disabled Leadership and Its Gifts for the Church." *Theology Today* 77, no. 2 (July 2020): 117–23. https://doi.org/10.1177/0040573620924558.

———. *From Inclusion to Justice: Disability, Ministry, and Congregational Leadership*. Waco: Baylor University Press, 2022.

———. "From Inclusion to Leadership: Disabled 'Misfitting' in Congregational Ministry." *Theology Today* 77, no. 2 (July 2020): 198–209. https://doi.org/10.1177/0040573620920698.

Rapley, Stewart. *Autistic Thinking in the Life of the Church*. London: SCM Press, 2021.

Reddie, Anthony G. "Dismantling Whiteness—a Response." *Practical Theology* 15, no. 1–2 (January 2, 2022): 168–73. https://doi.org/10.1080/1756073X.2022.2040728.

Reichel, Hanna. "The End of Humanity and the Beginning of Kenosis." In *Kenosis: The Self-Emptying of Christ in Scripture and Theology*, edited by Paul T. Nimmo and Keith L. Johnson, 289–308. Grand Rapids: Eerdmans, 2022.

Reynolds, Thomas E. *Vulnerable Communion. A Theology of Disability and Hospitality*. Grand Rapids: Brazos Press, 2008.

Ricks, Derek M., and Lorna Wing. "Language, Communication, and the Use of Symbols in Normal and Autistic Children." *Journal of Autism and Childhood Schizophrenia* 5, no. 3 (1975): 191–221.

Robinson, Leah E. *Embodied Peacebuilding: Reconciliation as Practical Theology*. Bern: Peter Lang, 2015.

Root, Andrew. *Christopraxis: A Practical Theology of the Cross*. Minneapolis: Fortress, 2014.

Ruth, Lester, and Swee-Hong Lim. *A History of Contemporary Praise & Worship: Understanding the Ideas That Reshaped the Protestant Church*. Grand Rapids: Baker Academic, 2021.

Rutter, Michael. "Concepts of Autism: A Review of Research." *Journal of Child Psychology and Psychiatry* 9, no. 1 (October 1968): 1–25. https://doi.org/10.1111/j.1469-7610.1968.tb02204.x.

Sacks, Oliver. *An Anthropologist on Mars*. London: Picador, 1995.

Saliers, Don E. "Toward a Spirituality of Inclusiveness." In *Human Disability and the Service of God: Reassessing Religious Practice*, edited by Nancy L. Eiesland and Don E. Saliers, 19–31. Nashville: Abingdon, 1998.

———. *Worship as Theology: Foretaste of Glory Divine*. Nashville: Abingdon, 1994.

Schreiter, Robert J. *The Ministry of Reconciliation: Spirituality & Strategies*. Maryknoll, N.Y.: Orbis Books, 1998.

———. *Reconciliation: Mission and Ministry in a Changing Social Order*. Maryknoll, N.Y.: Orbis Books, 1992.

Senn, Frank C. *Embodied Liturgy: Lessons in Christian Ritual*. Minneapolis: Fortress, 2016.

Shakespeare, Tom. "The Social Model of Disability." In *The Disability Studies Reader*, edited by Lennard J. Davis, 214–21. New York: Routledge, 2013.

Sheffer, Edith. *Asperger's Children: The Origins of Autism in Nazi Vienna*. New York: Norton, 2018.

Silberman, Steve. *NeuroTribes: The Legacy of Autism and the Future of Neurodiversity*. New York: Avery, 2015.

Silverman, Chloe. *Understanding Autism: Parents, Doctors, and the History of a Disorder*. Princeton: Princeton University Press, 2011.

Simplican, Stacy Clifford. *The Capacity Contract: Intellectual Disability and the Question of Citizenship*. Minneapolis: University of Minnesota Press, 2015.

Sinclair, Jim. "Don't Mourn for Us." In *Loud Hands: Autistic People, Speaking*, edited by Julia Bascom, 15–21. Washington, DC: Autistic Press, 2012.

Smith, James K. A. *Desiring the Kingdom: Worship, Worldview, and Cultural Formation*. Grand Rapids: Baker Academic, 2009.

Solomon, Olga, and Mary C. Lawlor. "'And I Look down and He Is Gone': Narrating Autism, Elopement and Wandering in Los Angeles." *Social Science & Medicine* 94 (October 2013): 106–14. https://doi.org/10.1016/j.socscimed.2013.06.034.

Spoor, Monica. *Spirituality on the Spectrum: Having Autism in the Orthodox Church*. N.p.: Brave New Books, 2017.

Spurrier, Rebecca F. *The Disabled Church: Human Difference and the Art of Communal Worship*. New York: Fordham University Press, 2019.

Stillman, William. *Autism and the God Connection: Redefining the Autistic Experience through Extraordinary Accounts of Spiritual Giftedness*. Naperville, Ill.: Sourcebooks, 2006.

Sweetman, Brendan, ed. *A Gabriel Marcel Reader*. South Bend, Ind.: St. Augustine's Press, 2011.

Swinton, John. *Becoming Friends of Time: Disability, Timefullness, and Gentle Discipleship*. Waco: Baylor University Press, 2016.

———. *Finding Jesus in the Storm: The Spiritual Lives of Christians with Mental Health Challenges*. Grand Rapids: Eerdmans, 2020.

———. "From Inclusion to Belonging: A Practical Theology of Community, Disability and Humanness." *Journal of Religion, Disability & Health* 16, no. 2 (2012): 172–90.

———. "Reflections on Autistic Love: What Does Love Look Like?" *Practical Theology* 5, no. 3 (December 2012): 259–78. https://doi.org/10.1558/prth.v5i3.259.

———. "Time, Hospitality, and Belonging: Towards a Practical Theology of Mental Health." *Word & World* 35, no. 2 (2015): 171–81.

Swinton, John, and Brian Brock, eds. *Theology, Disability and the New Genetics: Why Science Needs the Church*. London: Continuum, 2007.

Swinton, John, and Christine Trevett. "Religion and Autism: Initiating an Interdisciplinary Conversation." *Journal of Religion, Disability & Health* 13, no. 1 (February 3, 2009): 2–6. https://doi.org/10.1080/15228960802606193.

Tam, Cynthia. *Kinship in the Household of God: Towards a Practical Theology of Belonging and Spiritual Care of People with Profound Autism*. Eugene: Pickwick Publications, 2021.

Taylor, Charles. *Modern Social Imagination*. Durham, N.C.: Duke University Press, 2004.

———. *A Secular Age*. Cambridge, Mass.: Belknap, 2007.

———. *Sources of the Self: The Making of the Modern Identity*. Cambridge, Mass.: Harvard University Press, 1989.

Teo, David, and Keng Hong Leong. "Chapel of Christ Our Hope." In *Enabling Hearts: A Primer for Disability-Inclusive Churches*, edited by Wen Pin Leow, 1:158–63. Singapore: Koinonia Inclusion Network, 2021.

Thompson, Bard. *Liturgies of the Western Church*. Cleveland: World Publishing, 1961.

Treanor, Brian. *Aspects of Alterity: Levinas, Marcel, and the Contemporary Debate*. New York: Fordham University Press, 2006.

Tutu, Desmond. *No Future without Forgiveness*. London: Rider, 1999.

Van Ommen, A. L. *Suffering in Worship: Anglican Liturgy in Relation to Stories of Suffering People*. London: Routledge, 2017.

Van Ommen, Armand Léon. "Re-imagining Church through Autism: A Singaporean Case Study." *Practical Theology* 15, no. 6 (2022): 508–19. https://doi.org/10.1080/1756073X.2022.2080630.

Van Ommen, Armand Léon, and Topher Endress. "Reframing Liturgical Theology through the Lens of Autism: A Qualitative Study of Autistic Experiences of Worship." *Studia Liturgica* 52, no. 2 (2022). https://doi.org/10.1177/00393207221111573.

Van Ommen, Armand Léon, and Julie Marie Land. "A Practical-Theological Phenomenology of Joy: Learning from L'Arche." *Journal of Disability & Religion* 24, no. 3 (July 2, 2020): 281–99. https://doi.org/10.1080/23312521.2019.1698388.

Van Ommen, Armand Léon, and Katy Unwin. "The Sensory Aspects of Worship and Liturgy as Experienced by Autistic People." *Questions liturgiques/Studies in Liturgy* 102 (2022): 267–88.

Vanhoozer, Kevin J. "From 'Blessed in Christ' to 'Being in Christ.'" In *"In Christ" in Paul: Explorations in Paul's Theology of Union and Participation*, edited by Michael J. Thate, Kevin J. Vanhoozer, and Constantine R. Campbell, 3–33. Tübingen: Mohr Siebeck, 2014.

Verhoeff, Berend. "Autism in Flux: A History of the Concept from Leo Kanner to DSM 5." *History of Psychiatry* 24, no. 4 (December 2013): 442–58. https://doi.org/10.1177/0957154X13500584.

———. "What Is This Thing Called Autism? A Critical Analysis of the Tenacious Search for Autism's Essence." *Biosocieties* 7, no. 4 (2012): 410–32.

Vivanti, Giacomo. "Ask the Editor: What Is the Most Appropriate Way to Talk about Individuals with a Diagnosis of Autism?" *Journal of Autism and Developmental Disorders* 50, no. 2 (February 2020): 691–93. https://doi.org/10.1007/s10803-019-04280-x.

Volf, Miroslav. *Exclusion and Embrace: A Theological Exploration of Identity, Otherness, and Reconciliation*. Nashville: Abingdon, 1996.

Vos, Pieter, ed. *Liturgy and Ethics: New Contributions from Reformed Perspectives*. Leiden: Brill, 2018.

Waldock, Krysia Emily, and Rachel Forrester-Jones. "An Exploratory Study of Attitudes toward Autism amongst Church-going Christians in the South East of England, United Kingdom." *Journal of Disability & Religion*, June 11, 2020, 1–22. https://doi.org/10.1080/23312521.2020.1776667.

Walker, Nick. *Neuroqueer Heresies: Notes on the Neurodiversity Paradigm, Autistic Empowerment, and Postnormal Possibilities*. Fort Worth: Autonomous Press, 2021.

Warner, Georgina, Heather Cooper, and James Cusack. *A Review of the Autism Research Funding Landscape in the United Kingdom*. London: Autistica, n.d. https://www.autistica.org.uk/downloads/files/Autistica-Scoping-Report.pdf.

Webb-Mitchell, Brett. *Dancing with Disabilities: Opening the Church to All God's Children*. Cleveland: United Church Press, 1996.

Wehmeyer, Michael, Hank Bersani, and Ray Gagne. "Riding the Third Wave: Self-Determination and Self-Advocacy in the 21st Century." *Focus on Autism and Other Developmental Disabilities* 15, no. 2 (May 2000): 106–15. https://doi.org/10.1177/108835760001500206.

Weil, Louis. *A Theology of Worship*. Lanham, Md.: Cowley Publications, 2002.

Whitehead, Andrew L. "Religion and Disability: Variation in Religious Service Attendance Rates for Children with Chronic Health Conditions." *Journal for the Scientific Study of Religion* 57, no. 2 (June 2018): 377–95. https://doi.org/10.1111/jssr.12521.

Williams, Claire. *Peculiar Discipleship: An Autistic Liberation Theology*. London: SCM Press, 2023.

Wing, Lorna. "Asperger's Syndrome: A Clinical Account." *Psychological Medicine* 11, no. 1 (February 1981): 115–29. https://doi.org/10.1017/S0033291700053332.

———. "Language, Social, and Cognitive Impairments in Autism and Severe Mental Retardation." *Journal of Autism and Developmental Disorders* 11, no. 1 (March 1981): 31–44. https://doi.org/10.1007/BF01531339.

———. "Reflections on Opening Pandora's Box." *Journal of Autism and Developmental Disorders* 35, no. 2 (April 2005): 197–203. https://doi.org/10.1007/s10803-004-1998-2.

Wing, Lorna, and Judith Gould. "Severe Impairments of Social Interaction and Associated Abnormalities in Children: Epidemiology and Classification." *Journal of Autism and Developmental Disorders* 9, no. 1 (March 1979): 11–29. https://doi.org/10.1007/BF01531288.

Winter, Penni. "Loud Hands & Loud Voices." In *Loud Hands: Autistic People, Speaking*, edited by Julia Bascom, 115–28. Washington, DC: Autistic Press, 2012.

Yergeau, Melanie. *Authoring Autism: On Rhetoric and Neurological Queerness*. Durham, N.C.: Duke University Press, 2018.

Index

abnormal, 50, 53–54, 56, 73, 83, 91–92, 94, 96, 126
absence, 33, 53, 103, 110, 112, 123–24, 195, 197, 220n62; of autistic people, 3, 19, 20, 41, 71, 99, 101–3, 111, 124–26, 129, 161, 182, 185–86, 190–92, 194–97
absent: *see* absence
Altizer, Thomas J. J., 32
Andrews, Erin E., 25, 204n5
Ang, John, 163
anthropology, 33; Pauline, 118; theological, 30, 34, 61
Applied Behavioral Analysis (ABA), 204n62
Aramini, Victoria, 201n36
Arnold, Mark, 30
Asperger, Hans, 46, 49–52, 55–56, 58, 68, 210n25
Asperger disorder: *see* Asperger's Syndrome
Asperger's Syndrome, 45, 52, 55–57, 63–64, 202n37
attendance: church/worship services, 1, 9–10, 12, 38, 136, 176, 201n34; Rainbow of Hope, 179; *see also* absence; presence
Ault, Melinda Jones, 10, 202n37
autism: acceptance of, 11–12, 61–62, 97, 169–70, 176–77, 181, 185, 187, 209n6; as disability, 6–9, 22, 24, 50, 63, 94, 201n33, 201n37, 204n3; definition of/defining, 4–9, 48–50, 53–55, 60, 63–64, 68, 94–95, 200n26, 209n2, 228n2; history of, 7, 17, 42–69, 91, 190, 212n63, 212n70, 230n1; medical model, 5–8, 19, 24–25, 27, 30, 33–34, 48, 50, 64, 83–85, 92–93, 96, 163, 200n20, 200n21, 207n56, 207n58, 207n59, 214n104; neurodiversity model/movement, 24–25, 27, 33–34, 55, 62–65, 67, 90, 93, 95–96, 204n3, 208n60, 208n61; social model, 9, 33, 204n3, 207n58, 214n104
available/availability, 20, 38, 58, 88, 99, 101–2, 105–6, 109–18, 124–26, 128–29, 131, 134–35, 137, 140, 143, 148–50, 154, 157–59, 161–62, 182–83, 185–87, 192–97, 200n27, 201n30, 218n37, 219n49, 225n49, 228n93; *see also disponibilité*

Baker, Mary Patton, 225n52
Bale, Katherine, 35–40, 196
baptism, 129, 134–36, 139, 141–55, 157–59, 184, 194, 225n51, 226n64, 226n70, 226–27n71
baptismal ecclesiology: *see* baptism
baptized body: *see* body, of Christ
Barber, Christopher, 202n42
Barclay, John M. G., 112–15, 219n51
Baron-Cohen, Simon, 211n41, 214n103
Barton, Sarah Jean, 141, 144, 146–51
Bascom, Julie, 203n49
Baum, Sarah H., 229n10

241

Index

Bedard, Stephen J., 30
being with, 105, 114–15, 125
Belcher, Kimberly Hope, 134, 141–46, 148–49, 218n26, 225n49, 226n64, 226n70, 227n80, 229n11
bell curve, 82–83, 90
belonging, 3, 12, 17–18, 20, 30, 32, 40, 46, 51, 71, 76, 81, 83–84, 96–97, 106–10, 112–14, 119, 122–24, 126, 129, 132, 135, 138, 140–41, 144–45, 147, 149, 152–54, 156, 162, 169–70, 177, 181, 184, 187, 189, 191–95, 215n30, 217n2, 218n26, 226n61, 229n8, 230n26
Bender, Lauretta, 49
Bettelheim, Bruno, 50, 59, 212n70, 218n21
Bersani, Hank, 23
Biklen, Douglas, 226n67
Binet, Alfred, 48
Bleuler, Eugen, 46–49
Blume, Harvey, 62
body, 1, 14, 25, 41–42, 71, 73, 75, 78–83, 86, 89, 113, 119, 141–42, 145, 148, 155, 175, 185, 220n73, 221n74; of Christ, 2, 4, 11, 16, 18–19, 31, 40, 69, 87, 113, 119–20, 128–30, 132, 134–35, 140–42, 145–46, 148, 151, 154, 158, 183–84, 187, 193, 195, 199n3, 222n13
Bogdashina, Olga, 206n28
Bonhoeffer, Dietrich, 108, 218n32
Botha, Monique, 24–26, 213n94
Bottema-Beutel, Kristen, 26–27
Boucher, Jill, 200n16, 200n17, 202n37, 214n104
boundaries, 71–72, 75, 77, 79–81, 84, 86–88, 92–93, 104, 110, 118, 121–23, 127, 129, 138, 149–59, 168, 183, 185–86, 191–94, 196, 214n1
Bowman, Daniel Jr., 31, 34, 128–29, 139, 148, 157–58, 194, 196, 202n42, 208n66, 224n44
Brock, Brian, 2, 31–32, 34, 93–94, 96, 203n47, 207n47
Brown, C., 199n6, 199n8
Brown, Jane, 43–44
Buber, Martin, 193, 217n5, 217n13
Buckley, Carole, 25–26, 28
Bustion, Olivia, 2, 208n66
Buunk, Abraham P., 215n15

Campbell, Constantine R., 219n60, 221n78, 222n94
Campbell, Douglas A., 118
Campbell, Eilidh, 32, 212n69
Carter, Erik W., 10, 201n36, 202n37
Chan, Simon, 222n51
Chapel of Christ Our Hope, 3, 18, 20, 27, 95, 126, 159, 161–87, 192, 194–95, 209n6
Chew, John, 163
Chown, Nick, 49–50
Christ, 4, 30, 87, 96, 104, 107–8, 111–36, 138, 141–42, 145, 147–48, 154–55, 158, 184, 193–95, 220n68, 220n73, 225n51, 226n71; being/participating in, 99, 102, 107–8, 111, 113, 115–29, 132–37, 139–40, 143–44, 147–49, 151, 153–57, 159, 184–85, 193–96, 220n62, 220n66, 220n73, 221n78, 222n94; one in: *see* union with Christ; prayer of, 4, 135–40, 142, 154, 157, 185, 193, 195; *see also* body, of Christ
Collins, Belva C., 10, 202n37
Cones, Bryan, 223n17
Cook, Julie, 215n18
Cooper, Heather, 214n104
Cox, Jennifer Anne, 30, 34, 206n43
Crane, Laura, 215n18
Crawford Sullivan, Susan, 201n36
Creamer, Deborah Beth, 13–15, 24, 33, 207n59
Cross, Katie, 227n81
cult, 15, 28–29, 72–73, 77, 80–81, 85–90, 93–96, 98–99, 102, 104, 116, 120–24, 129, 132–34, 138–39, 147, 150–51, 154, 157–58, 162, 186–87, 192, 216n36; *see also* normalcy
Cusack, James, 214n104
Czech, Herwig, 51, 211n37, 211n38

Davis, Lennard, 14, 19, 71, 81–83, 85, 91, 93–94, 96, 190, 206n30, 216n36
Day, Juliette J., 230n20
dehumanizing, 44, 91, 103, 220n61
Despert, Louise, 49
Diagnostic and Statistical Manual of Mental Disorders (DSM), 5–6, 25, 52, 55–57, 63–64, 68, 84, 200n17, 202n37
disponibilité/disposability, 99, 101–2, 105–6, 108, 110–11, 114–15, 124, 129,

192–93, 197, 218n20, 219n49; *see also* availability
disposal, 105, 109, 114, 224n44
disposed, 118
disposition, 88, 140, 203n54, 221n74
diversity, 27, 29, 91, 93, 125, 129, 135, 151, 158, 184–85, 190, 222n94; *see also* autism, neurodiversity model/movement
Donvan, John, 59, 64, 210n13, 211n37, 212n65
double empathy problem, 200n28, 208n71
Dunn, Dana S., 25, 204n5
Dunster, Ruth M., 32

Eastman, Susan Grove, 104, 112, 116–23, 125–26
Elgar, Sybil, 59–60
embody/embodiment, 4, 13, 41, 75–76, 79–82, 120, 140–41, 151, 155, 185, 191, 208n60, 216n48, 225n44; *see also* body
economy of exchange, 72–73, 75, 78, 81, 85–86, 89, 96
Eisenberg, Leon, 50, 212n70
Endress, Topher, 202n43, 208n62, 217n55
epistemic break, 29, 89, 95–96
eschatological, 89, 94, 98, 112–13, 153, 225n51
estrange: *see* strange
ethical, 11, 112, 117–18, 122, 126, 140, 155
ethics, 140, 150, 154, 224n39
Eucharist, 129, 135–37, 142–43, 147, 150, 154–56, 158, 174–75, 194, 222n6, 225n51, 229n15
eugenics, 47, 53, 82–83, 85, 230n1
Evagrius of Pontus, 223n18
Evans, Bonnie, 47–48, 52–54, 66, 200n27, 209n3, 209n11, 210n13
exclusion, 11, 15–16, 19–20, 26, 29, 49–50, 72–73, 76–78, 72, 83, 86–87, 93, 96, 98, 103, 113, 115, 123, 125, 132–34, 138, 144, 146–47, 150–54, 156–58, 169, 184, 191–92, 194, 214n5, 225n44; *see also* reject; rejection

Falk, Dean, 211n38
Fletcher-Watson, Sue, 44–45
Forrester-Jones, Rachel, 209n12, 218n47
Foucault, Michel, 29

framework, 72, 75–81, 83, 85, 87–90, 92–98, 115, 119, 121, 123, 127, 129, 134, 140, 148, 152–53, 158, 169, 171, 177, 183–84, 186–87, 189–96, 217n57, 217n2, 218n43, 225n44, 230n2
Freud, Sigmund, 47
Frith, Uta, 55

Gagne, Ray, 23
Galton, Francis, 82–83, 85, 90
Giles, David, 56–58, 64
Gillibrand, John, 29, 31–32, 34, 89
Goddard, H. H., 204n7
Gordon-Taylor, Benjamin, 223n28
Gorman, Michael, 219n54
Goto, Courtney, 76, 78, 92–93, 96, 202n44, 216n36
Gould, S. J., 54, 91, 205n26
Graham, Elaine, 41, 79–81, 89
Grandin, Temple, 64
Grimes, Ronald L., 171–72, 176, 181

Hacking, Ian, 44
Hand, Brittany N., 26–27
Hanlon, Jacqueline, 213n94
Happé, Francesca, 44–45
Hardwick, Lamar, 207n49
Hattersley, Caroline, 25–26, 28
Hauerwas, Stanley, 84, 224n39
Hess, K., 199n6, 199n8
Holy Spirit, 2, 85, 111, 115–17, 119–20, 122–23, 126, 133, 136–38, 140–41, 143, 145–46, 148, 151–52, 155, 158, 193–94, 221n77, 221n84, 222n2
Hong Leong, Keng, 228n1
Horvat, Saša, 207n55
Horvat, Tanja, 207n55
hospitality, 109, 111, 115, 125, 168
Hughes, Graham, 227n71
Hughes, Liz, 49–50
Hull, Laura, 215n18
humble/humbleness, 17, 112–14, 163
humility, 112

ideal, 77–78, 81–84, 104, 152, 163, 226n69
identify, as autistic, 1–2, 5, 13–14, 17–18, 20, 24, 32, 34, 50, 57, 60, 64, 68, 99, 177; as disabled, 13–14, 204n3
identity, 56–57, 88, 121, 129, 135–36, 139–43, 151–52, 154; autistic, 24, 43,

56–57; baptismal, 144–49, 154, 157, 184; in Christ, 111, 116, 118–24, 126, 129, 135, 139, 143–44, 147–48, 151, 153, 155, 157, 159, 184–85, 193–96: *see also* Christ, being in; body, of Christ; identify, as autistic

ignoring, of people, 3, 19–20, 41, 71, 101–3, 108, 110–11, 123–26, 129, 134, 158, 161, 186, 190–96, 225n44

include: *see* inclusion

including: *see* inclusion

inclusion, 11, 15, 29, 33, 46, 147, 151–53, 162, 170, 172, 177, 180–81, 187

indisponibilité/non-disposability: *see disponibilité*; *see also* unavailable

International Classification of Diseases (ICD), 5–6, 52, 84

intersubjective: *see* intersubjectivity

intersubjectivity, 104–5, 111, 115, 122, 216n48, 220n73

Isanon, Abe, 205n28

Johnson, Keith L., 219n52

Johnson, Sarah Kathleen, 219n49, 226–27n71

Jurgens, Alan, 216n48

Kanner, Chaim Leib (Leo), 23, 46, 48–50, 56, 58–59, 66, 68, 209n2, 212–13n70

Kapp, Steven K., 26–27

Kavanagh, Aidan, 223n17

Kedar, Ido, 226n67

Kenny, Lorcan, 25–26, 28

kenosis, 20, 99, 102, 111–12, 114–16, 120–21, 123, 125–27, 129, 131, 135–37, 141, 143, 149–50, 154, 157–59, 161–62, 182, 185–86, 193–97, 225n49, 226–27n71

kenotic: *see* kenosis

Kinard, Summer, 31

Klar-Wolfond, Estée, 90–93

Koplewicz, Harold, 63

Kras, Joseph F., 213n84

Krcek, Taylor E., 57

Land, Julie Marie, 203n45

language: identity-first, 21–27, 41; person-first, 21–27, 41; precise use of, 7

Lathrop, Gordon, 136–37, 145, 223n17, 223n28

Lawlor, Mary C., 209n5

Lawson, Wendy, 78, 90, 92–93

Lee, Li-Ching, 9

Leidenhag, Joanna, 220n61

Lester, Jessica Nina, 26–27

Lim, Swee-Hong, 222n8

Linton, Kristen Faye, 57

liturgical theology, 2–4, 18–20, 29, 34, 41, 67, 124, 126–30, 134, 136–37, 141, 143, 146, 149–50, 152, 157–59, 161–62, 182, 185–86, 190–97

liturgy, 2–5, 18–19, 34–35, 38–41, 46, 69, 81, 85–87, 96–98, 120, 126–30, 133–44, 149, 151–58, 161–62, 171–73, 175–76, 182, 185–87, 191–96, 217n57

Lovaas, Erik, 68, 204n62, 214n102

Macaskill, Grant, 6–8, 15–16, 30, 32, 34, 36, 67, 118, 122, 130–33, 143–44, 149–50, 155–56, 219n60

Mackenzie, Donald A., 82

Mandy, William, 215n18

Marcel, Gabriel, 20, 99, 101–11, 114–15, 117, 124–25, 129, 192, 226n61

Matthews, Pia, 218n37

McCormack, Bruce Lindley, 219n52

Memmott, Ann, 30, 33

Milton, Damian E. M., 200n28, 203n54, 208n71, 216n32, 217n1

Molins, Bonnie, 25–26, 28

Moore-Keish, Martha, 152, 155

Morales, Isaac Augustine, 225n52

Morgan, Teresa, 219n60, 220n62

Morrill, Bruce T., 150, 152–56, 158, 224n39

Murray, Stuart, 43–45, 59, 69, 99, 100–101, 110, 124, 195

mutual: *see* mutuality

mutuality, 7, 39, 77, 107, 109–10, 114–17, 120, 124, 148–49, 152

Natan, R. S., 163

National Autistic Society, 7, 23, 59–60

Ne'eman, Ari, 62–64

neurodivergent: *see* neurodiversity

neurodiverse: *see* neurodiversity

neurodiversity, 24–25, 27, 33–34, 37, 54–55, 62–65, 67, 90, 92–93, 95–96, 170, 204n3; *see also* autism, neurodiversity model

neurotypical: *see* neurodiversity

Newman, Barbara J., 30, 33

Nimmo, Paul T., 219n52
norm, 28, 29, 38, 71–72, 74–76, 78–84, 86, 88, 90–91, 93, 95–97, 115–16, 119–21, 126, 128–30, 141, 144, 151, 153, 158, 169, 177, 189–94, 208n59, 215n30
normal, 1, 18, 24–25, 28, 33, 36, 38, 45–48, 53, 71–72, 77–79, 81–87, 90–96, 102, 110–11, 118, 121–23, 126–27, 140, 157, 191, 215n30; hegemony of the, 83–85, 87; tyranny of the, 71, 81, 84–85, 92; *see also* abnormal
normalcy, 14–16, 19, 27, 29, 37, 40, 71–75, 77–99, 110–11, 114, 121–27, 129, 134, 138, 143, 148–49, 151–56, 161, 183, 185–86, 189–92, 194–95, 218n26, 227n73; cult of: *see* cult
normalizing, 45–46, 91, 190
normative: *see* norm
norming, 95

Obama, Barack, 63

Pang, Camilla, 201n30
paradigm, 25, 48, 76, 78, 90, 92–93, 96, 143, 163, 168–70, 177, 183, 195, 204n3, 216n36, 225n44
paradigmatic: *see* paradigm
parents, 10–11, 17, 23, 26–27, 32, 45–46, 50, 58–61, 64, 73–74, 84, 86, 145, 162–63, 168–70, 176, 179–81, 183, 203n48, 205n20, 226n71, 229n5, 230n1; fathers, 14, 29, 32, 59, 102, 112–13, 131, 155, 184; mothers, 31–32, 50, 58–59, 102, 146, 180
participant, 17, 26–27, 74, 101, 104, 124, 141, 151, 155, 229n8
participate: *see* participation
participation, 2, 10, 12, 17, 20, 26, 36, 39–40, 48, 51–52, 58, 74–75, 96–97, 99–102, 110–12, 115–18, 120–27, 129, 131–49, 152–57, 162, 172, 184–85, 192–96, 212n70, 220n62; in Christ: *see* Christ, being in
Pastor David, 162–64, 168–69, 175, 179, 182, 186, 195; *see also* Teo, David
pathologizing: *see* pathology
pathology, 5, 8, 24–25, 27, 29, 33, 35, 41, 47, 92, 201n28; *see also* autism, medical model
Pellicano, Elizabeth, 25–26, 28
Pembroke, Neil, 217n4, 217n5, 217n10

Phillips, Chloe, 213n71
Post, Stephen, 223n25
Povey, Carol, 25–26, 28
Power, David Noel, 223n21
prayer, 31, 36, 86, 94, 133–35, 138, 177, 179, 182, 202n41; of Jesus/Christ, 4, 127, 132, 135–42, 142, 154, 157, 185, 193–95; of the church, 127, 134, 136–38, 142, 178
presence, 3, 20, 27–28, 44, 49, 69, 73, 75–76, 79, 99–101, 103–6, 108–12, 115, 117–18, 124–26, 133, 144, 152, 158, 163, 176, 182–87, 190, 192–96, 214n8, 225n44; of God, 111, 115, 117, 119–20, 123, 126, 132–36, 138–39, 153, 157–58, 182, 193–94, 222n8; theology of, 20, 28, 88, 98, 102, 115, 117, 124, 148
processing, 80, 211n45; cognitive, 55; of communication, 52, 134; of information, 100; sensory, 8, 194; speed, 194; time, 39–40
purity, 20, 149–58

Quetelet, Adolphe, 82

Raffety, Erin, 203–4n61, 222n95, 228n100, 228n103, 230n18
Ransom Notes, 62–63
Rapley, Stewart, 31, 34, 38, 200n20, 200n23, 202n41, 202n42, 214n6
reconciliation, 12, 16, 18, 132, 228n100
Reddie, Anthony G., 214n1
Reichel, Hanna, 219n54
reject, 71, 77, 86, 130, 132, 134, 146, 177, 183–84; *see also* exclusion
rejection, 80, 86, 102, 146
repent: *see* repentance
repentance, 15–17, 149, 195
representation of autism, 43, 45, 59, 63, 92, 162, 199n1
Reynolds, Thomas E., 15, 19, 29, 31–33, 72–73, 75–80, 84–85, 87–89, 97, 109–10, 125, 216n36, 217n5
Ricks, Derek M., 211n43
Ricoeur, Paul, 217n4
Rimland, Bernard, 60
Robinson, Leah E., 16
Root, Andrew, 117, 221n75
Ruth, Lester, 222n8
Rutter, Michael, 52

Sacks, Oliver, 64
sacrament, 20, 129, 135, 137, 139, 141–47, 150, 152–58, 194, 225n52, 226n69, 227n71
sacramental: *see* sacrament
Sacrosanctum Concilium, 139
safe, 65, 76–77, 79, 95, 104, 203n60
safeguarding, 3, 78
safety, 5, 72, 110, 187, 191, 218n43, 230n2
Saliers, Don, 4–5, 127, 129, 134–38, 140, 149, 153, 185–86, 193
Sartre, Jean-Paul, 102
Sasson, Noah J., 26–27
Schaufeli, Wilmar B., 215n15
Schillebeeckx, Edward, 155–56
Schreiter, Robert J., 203n59
self-emptying, 111–12, 120, 193; *see also* kenosis
self-giving, 114–15, 121, 127, 135–38, 185, 187, 193, 227n71; *see also* kenosis
Senn, Frank C., 5, 199n7, 223n28, 229n11
sensory, 8, 10–11, 15, 36, 38–41, 97, 100, 156, 168, 171, 173–76, 185, 187, 189, 194, 196, 202n38, 211n45, 223n25
Sensui, Leonard M., 57
Sheffer, Edith, 51, 210n25
Silberman, Steve, 48, 63, 209n2, 210n13, 211n37, 212n70
Silverman, Chloe, 55, 58, 65–66, 210n13
Simplican, Stacy Clifford, 13, 17, 83
Sinclair, Jim, 60–63, 65, 203n48
Singapore, 12, 18, 20, 27, 33, 35, 41, 46, 95, 126, 159, 161, 163, 170–71, 174–75, 177, 182–84, 194, 225n51; *see also* Chapel of Christ Our Hope
Singer, Judy, 62
Smith, James K. A., 141, 225n44, 225n45
social, 14–15, 17, 22–23, 33, 36, 37–38, 46, 48, 51–52, 54–59, 63, 66, 72, 74–75, 77, 79–80, 83, 88, 91, 93–94, 96–97, 102, 119–22, 126, 148, 151, 153–56, 163, 178, 180, 182, 184, 190, 194, 200n27, 203n57, 205n26, 208n64, 209n11, 210n25, 216n48, 224n44; acceptance, 38, 62; capital, 74, 80, 83, 89, 95–96, 189; expectations, 2, 7, 38–39, 62, 126; interaction, 7, 36–40, 52, 54, 56, 62–63, 66, 72, 80, 100, 178, 191, 196, 216n48; *see also* autism, social model

social imaginary, 140–43, 147–49, 151, 158, 183, 186, 225n44
socialization, 153
Solomon, Olga, 209n5
soteriological, 112–16, 125, 141–43, 148, 193
Spillers, Jessica L. H., 57
spiritual, 2, 46, 80, 86–87, 106–7, 130–32, 168, 177, 181, 183–84
spirituality, 88, 102, 104, 106–7, 149, 157–58, 205n28
Spoor, Monica, 30, 37–38, 196, 217n2
Spurrier, Rebecca F., 147, 226n69
Stevenson, Ryan A., 229n10
Stillman, William, 205n28
strange, 47, 73, 77, 80, 110, 124, 183
stranger, 80, 103–6, 108, 128, 192
Stulp, Gert, 215n15
Sweetman, Brendan, 102, 217n14
Swinton, John, 5, 22–23, 28–29, 32, 151, 206n28, 209n5, 209n11, 223n25, 230n26

Tam, Cynthia, 31, 34, 202n42
Tannehill, Robert, 116
Tavris, Carol, 90
Taylor, Charles, 76, 84–85, 87–89, 91, 93, 97, 119, 127, 140–42, 149, 151, 153, 183, 190, 217n57, 225n45
temple, 4, 20, 127, 129–40, 145–46, 149–51, 154, 156–58, 183, 185, 193, 195–96
Teo, David, 228n1; *see also* Pastor David
Thompson, Bard, 223n25
Titchkosky, Tanya, 14
Treanor, Brian, 217n6, 217n8
Trevett, Christine, 29, 206n28
triad of impairments, 28, 54, 66, 209n11
Tutu, Desmond, 203n59, 203n60

unavailability: *see* unavailable
unavailable, 106, 110, 196
union with Christ, 111, 113, 115–16, 129, 134, 149, 151, 159, 193–94, 196; *see also* Christ, being in
Unwin, Katy, 201n32, 208n62, 214n5, 223n25, 229n10

van Ommen, Armand Léon, 201n32, 202n43, 202n45, 208n62, 209n6, 214n5, 217n55, 223n25, 224n37, 229n9, 229n10, 229n14, 230n21

Vanhoozer, Kevin J., 219n60, 222n94
Verhoeff, Berend, 56, 65–67, 211n45
Vivanti, Giacomo, 23
Volf, Miroslav, 203n59

Wainwright, Geoffrey, 137
Waldock, Krysia Emily, 209n12, 218n47
Walker, Nick, 90, 92–93, 205n14, 208n60, 216n54
Wallace, Mark T., 229n10
Wannenwetsch, Bernd, 207n47
Warner, Georgina, 214n104
Webb-Mitchell, Brett, 22
Wehmeyer, Michael, 23
Weil, Louis, 134–35, 146, 152–53, 223n18, 228n91
Whitehead, Andrew, 9
Williams, Claire, 207n53, 212n69, 213n95, 228n101
Williams, Gemma Louise, 24–26, 213n94
Wing, John, 60
Wing, Lorna, 46, 49, 52, 54–56, 60, 205n26, 209n11, 210n25, 211n43
Wing, Susie, 60
Winter, Penni, 45, 54
worship, 1, 3–5, 10, 12, 16, 19–21, 29–30, 34–36, 41–42, 44, 69, 74, 80, 85–87, 96–97, 113, 123, 126, 130, 133–38, 140–44, 148–49, 151, 153–56, 159, 161–62, 170–71, 173–74, 176, 182–83, 185–87, 190, 192–96, 222n8; experience of, 3, 18–19, 21–22, 30, 35–42, 67, 173, 196; space, 9, 36, 75, 179, 185; *see also* liturgy
worship, corporate: *see* worship service
worship service, 1, 2, 5, 8, 10–11, 18, 20, 34–36, 38–40, 44, 74–75, 80, 88, 97, 100, 129, 136, 142, 162, 170–82, 186–87, 191, 193, 197
worshipping community, 3, 17, 20, 46, 80–81, 102, 104, 111, 124, 149–50, 152, 156, 159, 177, 182, 194–95

Yergeau, Melanie, 228n2

Zucker, Caren, 59, 64, 210n13, 211n37, 212n65

www.ingramcontent.com/pod-product-compliance
Lightning Source LLC
Chambersburg PA
CBHW021834131125
35289CB00010B/187